SWEATIN' OUT THE MISSION

8TH AIR FORCE GROUND SUPPORT IN WORLD WAR TWO

MALCOLM A. HOLLAND

First published 2010

The History Press
The Mill, Brimscombe Port
Stroud, Gloucestershire, GL5 2QG
www.thehistorypress.co.uk

British Library Cataloguing in Publication Data.
A catalogue record for this book is available from the British Library.

ISBN 978 0 7524 5708 6

Typesetting and origination by The History Press
Printed in Great Britain

Contents

	Acknowledgements	4
	Preface	5
	Introduction	7
1	Preparing for the Mission	11
2	Infrastructure & Support	25
3	The Airfield	41
4	Headquarters Site	60
5	Aircraft Dispersals	74
6	Technical Site	97
7	The Control Tower	122
8	Communal Site	143
9	Domestic Site	168
10	Sick Quarters	184
11	The Final Act	198
	References	214
	Glossary	216
	Veterans	218
	Bibliography	220
	Index	222

Acknowledgements

This work has been long in gestation and like many other publications, owes its existence to a large number of people. First in this long list of individuals and organisations has to be my 'fellow' author and mentor, Bob Clarke, who has suffered years of pestering regarding the finer points of historical writing, not to mention a drain on his aviation knowledge, although whether I thank him for putting me through this is another matter!

I hope that my efforts meet with the approval of those who the book is about. I am especially indebted to those veterans and their families who have willingly dug deep into their memories to provide extra detail and reminiscences. In particular, special thanks go to Art Watson, Whit Hill, Jack Gaffney, the late Joe Harlick, Paul Kovitz, Rod Ryan, Leroy Keeping, Rich Creutz, Lawrence Scholze, Arthur Ferwerda, Rudi Steel, C.J. Leleux, as well as civilians Bernie Fosdike and Robert Gould. In addition I should like to thank Jenny Harlick and the families of Walter Stubbs and John Borchert. I hope this work in some way goes to highlight your efforts and redress the balance a little in favour of the 'ground-pounders'.

Instrumental in assisting me making contact with veterans were the many bomb group associations, in particular, the 91st, 92nd, 95th and 390th organisations; my thanks go to them all for allowing me to post messages on their websites and in their newsletters. Top of the list is Helyn Schufletowski of the 95th Bomb Group Association, who provided links to all the ground veterans from her group's association.

Various archives provided valuable information and services, including the RAF Archive at Hendon, The National Archives at Kew, Manston Fire Museum, The American Red Cross archives in Washington, Lisa Moak of the US Exchange Service, The Science Museum Library, the Swindon and Wiltshire Historical Centre and the Bedford and Luton History Centre.

Special thanks go to Paul Marriott and Clive Stevens for their knowledge of 8th Air Force matters, James Davis for US Army fire-fighting information, James Grey and Peter Kindred, owners of parts of Ridgewell and Framlingham airfields respectively, for allowing access to take photographs. Also to Aldon P. Ferguson, Bonnie and Dean Selje, Kevin Taylor and members of ArmyAirForces.com for advice and additional input and to Clive Pattison and Simon Austwick for reading, appraising and correcting my work.

A very big thank you goes to my wife Tracey and family – Jess, Zoe, James, Emma and Peter and their respective partners – for putting up with the 'grumpy' bloke in the study and accepting my penchant for looking at wartime concrete with good-natured humour!

Finally thanks to Amy Rigg, my commissioning editor, who has stuck with this project through some very trying times and has had to put up with the worry that this finished work may not appear!

To any I have missed my apologies and, as is usual, the final statement, all mistakes are naturally mine.

Preface

The reason this book came about was both as a response to my own search for information on the ground aspect of the US 8th Army Air Force mission during the Second World War and from Bob Clarke, my 'mentor', pushing me to write down such information as I had collected. I have been collecting memorabilia connected with the 8th Air Force for some years; wanting to keep to a theme I have concentrated on the ground operations. As an engineer myself, I felt an affinity towards the personnel that kept the aircraft flying.

Although a vast amount has been written about the 8th, only a very small percentage of that has been about the work of the men and women in a ground support role. I hope I have in some small way been able to illustrate some of their stories. It has been stated that for every bomber with ten crew members, it took at least a further thirty men on the ground to get it into and keep it in the air, and that's just engineering and ground crew. It doesn't include all the other support staff needed to run each airfield. Some figures suggest that as many as 70 per cent of United States Army Air Force (USAAF) personnel who were stationed in Britain in the Second World War were occupied in a non-flying role. The majority of ground personnel were based in Britain for the duration, many for nearly three years. It was they who formed the majority of the links with the British population, which have bound some English communities with America for over sixty years and continue to do so today. Here then is a collection of material from many sources, with the addition of first-hand accounts to bring it to life. This, I believe, is the sort of book I had been looking for!

Why the title? 'Sweatin' it out' or 'Sweatin' out the mission', seems to have been a universally used expression favoured by ground crews to describe the time leading up to the return of aircraft to base after a mission. Those on the ground literally sweated it out waiting to see if their charge would return or had been lost.

This book is not concerned with operational missions or bomber crews, except where their sphere of operation overlaps that of ground personnel. Although limiting the subject matter to one facet of 8th Air Force operations – the bomb groups – much of the day-to-day 'colour' is as much applicable to other USAAF Groups based in Britain, examples from which have been included for illustrative purposes, where more appropriate examples are not available.

Differences in operating procedures existed from station to station, however the space available in this publication only permits for generic illustrations of operational activity. The same also applies to the use of some terminology, such as 8th AF. The air force changed its organisation and structure during the war and although it wasn't always titled thus, for the purposes of brevity and avoidance of confusion, in general the title '8th AF' shall be used. In much the same way, although the terms 'airfield' or 'aerodrome' are used to describe an entity as a whole, the text will be interspersed with the more commonly used American terms of 'station', 'field' or 'camp'. All generally mean the same thing and will be used when referring to an airfield. The USAAF allocated a station number to every site they occupied and so usually referred to their sites as such, but British reference was normally done using the RAF prefix. Podington, for instance, could equally have been referred to as RAF Podington, Podington Aerodrome, AAF Station 109 (Podington), Podington Field or Podington Camp.

As a final note, some airfields such as Ridgewell, Bassingbourn and Framlingham appear within the photo record far more often than others. The main reason for this is that they were among the closest airfields to London, and as such tended to be more often visited by official photographers and members of the press and consequently a greater record exists.

NB – The endnotes shown in the References list the sources (sometimes used in more than one instance) from which particular material is taken for each chapter.

Introduction

Through the summer of 1940 what became known as the 'Battle of Britain' was fought, mainly in the skies over south-east England. The primary defence of the nation was placed in the hands of the RAF and Royal Navy; Fighter Command fended off the German Air Force, while Bomber Command attacked the German naval build-up in the Channel ports. The Royal Navy, while providing additional air support with fighter pilots from its Fleet Air Arm, also positioned warships to prevent any German attempt at a seaborne invasion. When on the night of 7 September the Luftwaffe changed tactics from attacking RAF targets to bombing London's Docklands, there was a twofold effect. Firstly, they caused the demise of any idea of an invasion of Britain as, by not appreciating how close they were to delivering the 'knockout blow', they unwittingly gave the RAF time to recuperate. They also set in motion an aerial war of attrition that was to rain destruction on Europe's towns and cities until war's end in May 1945.

Post-Battle of Britain, thoughts turned to how to take the fight to the enemy and for the time being an air campaign was the only option. The air strategies of the inter-war period had been dominated by the experiences of the First World War. Tacticians were desperate to find ways of waging war without using the traditional methods of massing vast armies against each other and all that that entailed. Aerial bombing was seen to be the way to beat an enemy in a future conflict, although long-range bomber design was very much in its infancy.

The first recorded attempts at aerial bombing go back to 1912, although Russia formed the first bomber force at the advent of the First World War. However, it was Germany in 1915 that started 'long-range' bombing using airships on the British mainland. These early raids were judged to be more a terror tactic than part of a wider bombing strategy however. A far more serious threat came between May 1917 and May 1918. The German Air Force deployed its *Gotha* bombers on a series of raids on the south-east of England and in particular, London. A total of twenty-two raids caused considerable damage and, loss of life. This campaign led to a major rethink in home air defence and ultimately led, in 1918, to the creation of a wholly independent air force: the RAF.

The power of the German operation spread far beyond its physical damage. The image stayed in the public consciousness and had ramifications on political and military thinking right through the inter war period. In 1938, in his analysis on predicting the importance of the bombing of civilian targets in the perceived approaching war in Europe, Air Commodore Lionel Charlton recalled 13 June 1917, the day Germany had carried out its first daylight raid on London, as 'a date marking the beginning of a new epoch in the history of warfare'.

During the 1920s, many countries explored the use of bombing tactics in their colonies as a way of dealing with unrest. Britain, for one, found it a very cost-effective solution to dealing with tribal 'policing' in the Middle East. However, the potential for danger closer to home was realised by some. Britain's Prime Minister, Stanley Baldwin, famously commented in 1932:

I think that it is well for the man in the street to realise that there is no power on earth which can protect him from being bombed. Whatever people may tell him; the bomber will always get through...The only defence is in offence, which means that you have to kill more women and children more quickly than the enemy if you want to save yourselves.

Aerial bombing became a very popular theory in Britain, as its financial merits had not been lost on the holders of military budgets in Whitehall. It was considered by many strategists that a future conflict might swiftly be brought to a conclusion by air power alone. The thought of being able to provide a knock-out blow to any potential enemy with a relatively small force was very appealing to Government thinking of the time.

The late 1920s saw Britain start to establish a ring of defensive and offensive airfields around the south-east. A period of financial cutbacks then followed, reducing military spending and leaving the forces, especially the infant RAF, severely wanting. Initially this was due in part to the global financial situation, but later the situation was more of a response to the increased tensions caused by the rise of the Nazi movement in Germany. The British Government instead followed a policy of appeasement, as it was realised that she neither had, nor could afford, the necessary aircraft equipment or munitions to wage war or a bombing campaign.

It was not until 1935 that Britain moved to expand its air power, when on 4 March the Government announced that it could no longer ignore Germany and consequently planned to rearm. What followed was a huge programme of military construction, in particular the creation of many new airfields and air force expansion. Conversely, through the 1930s, as tension in Europe increased, public opinion generally turned against the idea of re-militarisation and, in particular, bombing. One event more than any other that had a major effect on turning public opinion occurred in April 1937 with the bombing of Guernica, Spain, carried out by the German Condor Legion in support of General Franco during the Spanish Civil War. This event caused widespread death and destruction in the city, and brought home vividly to the people of many nations the awesome potential of aerial warfare. It acted as a portent for what could and unfortunately did happen across the globe during the following few years.

With the outbreak of the Second World War, Britain had temporarily abandoned the idea of bombing. The indiscriminate use of bombing by the Germans during their sweep across Europe, her own inability to strike with weapons at her disposal, and the chance of hitting civilian targets all conspired to take bombing strategies off the agenda. For the latter reason, President Roosevelt appealed at the time to both sides to avoid using the tactic. Such bomber forces that Britain did have were in the main put to work harassing German shipping in the English Channel and dropping propaganda pamphlets on occupied Europe. The latter activity was, in the view of Sir Arthur Harris, Marshall of the RAF, 'a questionable employ ... the only thing achieved was largely to supply the Continent's requirements of toilet paper for the five long years of the war.'[1] It was later acknowledged, however, that these operations did provide Bomber Command pilots with invaluable navigational training across northern Europe.

Regardless of these issues, Britain had her hands full playing catch up with a fighter defence force, having realised that it was possible to stop some of the bombers getting through. When, in late 1940, Germany started hitting civilian targets in Britain, public opinion changed again. By now, rapid developments in technology were starting to enable a more effective retaliatory bombing campaign to take place.

For the foreseeable future, expanding an air front was seen as the only way to take the war to the enemy. It would be some time before the ground forces would be of a significant strength to attempt an invasion of mainland Europe, which would require the close co-ordination of existing and additional Allied nations. It was through these events of the first two years of war that the RAF learned the impact and hard lessons of fighting a modern aerial war. These lessons would have to be learnt all over again by any ally joining the fray.

By the late 1930s the possibilities of aerial bombing had become honed down by some tacticians to the theory of 'strategic' bombing. By moving away from the idea of delivering widespread and largely arbitrary destruction, aircraft, equipment and tactics were being developed that would allow bombing of far greater accuracy. In addition to the European nations, the developing US Army Air Corps had been pursuing a similar line of thinking, although initially only for home defence.

Many strategists, particularly in the US, realised that any military machine relied on a small number of specific industries to support its output at source. Destroy these key targets and any enemy would be unable to sustain war. The argument against widespread area bombing helped in strengthening the case for accurate strategic pinpoint bombing inasmuch as it was seen as a way of helping to minimise innocent casualties. Getting America to actively pursue its military theories, however, would be a wholly different challenge.

British Prime Minister Winston Churchill had long been trying to get President Roosevelt to commit the US fully on side, but the isolationist stance that had arisen in America after the First World War held; memories of the sacrifices made by the country's youth were still fresh. Besides, during the 1930s there were far more pressing home issues to deal with, particularly the effects of the Great Depression: a global economic slump that had profoundly affected the USA. President Roosevelt had come to office in 1933 promising to provide relief for the disastrous effects of the Depression and had implemented a new initiative – the 'New Deal': a sequence of programmes to provide long-term recovery to the people and the economy. One of the first programmes created by the new administration and considered the most popular and effective among the general public was the Civilian Conservation Corps (CCC). As the name implies, tasks undertaken were generally of a conservation nature, working in forestry or the National Park service.

The CCC camps were operated by the US Army, using 3,000 reserve personnel called to active duty. The army thereby gained valuable experience in handling large numbers of young men, but there was no obvious military drill or training in the camps until 1940, and the work projects were primarily civilian in nature. Roosevelt said at the implementation of the scheme:

> First, we are giving opportunity of employment to one-quarter of a million of the unemployed, especially the young men who have dependents, to go into the forestry and flood prevention work. This is a big task because it means feeding, clothing and caring for nearly twice as many men as we have in the regular Army itself. In creating this civilian conservation corps we are killing two birds with one stone. We are clearly enhancing the value of our natural resources and second, we are relieving an appreciable amount of actual distress.[2]

Roosevelt had, however, privately felt for some time that the US would ultimately be drawn into a new global conflict. He had the difficult task of balancing his own feelings while not losing sight of the isolationist stance of the majority who had brought him back to power. At that time, to do otherwise would have been political suicide. The idea of any military mobilisation and war preparation was totally unacceptable to the American people. However, a third unheralded benefit gained from the formation of the CCC was the creation of a quasi-militarised and disciplined youth, fitter and healthier, with many new skills and practical abilities. Many of these young men would later find themselves drafted into military service. Other agencies, such as the American Red Cross and the Army Chaplaincy Corps, also gained a great deal of valuable experience during this period assisting with such projects and enabling them to better carry out their mission in the coming years of conflict.

After 1938, Roosevelt gradually became more public in his views on re-armament and started to lead the nation away from isolationism. He began providing extensive support to the British war effort. Roosevelt felt that it was in the United States' best interests to stop the spread of Nazi Germany because it would ultimately affect them if left unchecked.

By mid-1941 Britain's war supplies were being supplemented by equipment from the United States. From 11 March 1941 the Lend-Lease Act became effective, permitting the president of the United States to:

> ... sell, transfer title to, exchange, lease, lend or otherwise dispose of, to any such government (who's defence the President deems vital to the defense of the United States) any defense article.[3]

At the end of October 1941 the scheme was extended, and President Roosevelt approved $1 billion in Lend-Lease aid to Britain.

Tensions had also been rising in the Pacific for some years, with Japanese attempts to exploit more territory. America was involved in diplomatic wrangles with Japan and it was increasingly feared that the US would be unavoidably drawn into the growing global conflict. The 7 December surprise attack on the US Pacific Fleet base at Pearl Harbor changed everything, galvanising the majority of American public opinion into converting to a war footing.

It is generally accepted that the Japanese plan, although exceedingly bold and well executed, was one of the worst military and political blunders in history. Far from forcing America out of the area, it had the opposite effect, activating the manufacturing might of the biggest industrialised democracy in the world and applying it to military production virtually overnight. On 8 December 1940, the day after the attack, the US declared war on Japan. By 11 December, Italy, followed by Germany, due to their Tripartite Pact with the Japanese, declared war on the United States. Long angered at America's provision of aid to Britain, Hitler also cited lend-lease as another major factor in his declaration of war.

Virtually straight away, Britain's Prime Minister, Winston Churchill, travelled to Washington to meet up with President Roosevelt for talks – under the code name 'ARCADIA' – to plan their combined strategy for total war. Priority was given to the defeat of Germany and Italy and the liberation of Europe prior to a full attack on Japan. The United States of America was now fully committed to the Second World War.

1

Preparing for the Mission

Expanding an Air Force

At the outset of the Second World War, the US Air Force was still an integral part of the Army, hence US Army Air Force (USAAF). Progress had been made steadily since the mid-1930s to turn it into an independent organisation. Just before America's entry into the war it had grown from being the Army Air Corps (AAC) into an air force, but still not fully relinquished by its parent and only finally becoming the US Air Force (USAF) in 1947.

One man considered responsible for having driven this evolution more than any other was Henry 'Hap' Arnold. Arnold's rise to prominence as a leader of the disparate parts of the AAC began after the high-profile court martial and subsequent resignation of his mentor William Mitchell in 1926. Widely considered to be the 'Father of the US Air Force', 'Billy' Mitchell, a First World War air ace and outspoken advocate of US air power, had constantly courted controversy by questioning the US Navy's traditional defence of the nation. The navy was not happy about being pushed into second place by this new technology and did all in its power to prevent the AAC from getting a foothold in military strategic planning.

Even after his resignation, Mitchell continued to campaign for air power but died in 1936 before seeing much of the transformation occur. Arnold, however, carried the baton forward and, with fellow proponents of air power, was finally able to create an organisation, despite many obstacles placed in his way, largely outside the control of its parent. Due to his depth of knowledge and experience across the whole spectrum of air operations, Arnold had the vision to implement the many programmes required to bring the whole organisation to a war footing.

All of his efforts were driven by the need to ultimately enable the air force to exist as a wholly separate branch of service. To this end, as well as the obvious development of aircraft and infrastructure, he also focused on the expansion of support organisations such as aero-medical services, aircraft servicing and maintenance and even its own chaplaincy. He, like many others, believed that if the effectiveness of air combat could be proven then a fully autonomous air force could be the prize.

However, since 1926, the AAC had existed as a two-prong organisation. Although Arnold had become chief of the Air Corps in 1938 he didn't get control of the 'combat' flying side, then under the control of GHQ Air Force (Air Force Combat Command), until the two elements joined to become the USAAF in June 1941. In the 1930s, with the concept of strategic bombing stimulating US military thinking as a means of defending America's borders, the air lobby would once again be drawn into direct conflict with the navy. For the time being, however, there was a more pressing need, that of developing suitable bomber aircraft.

At the forefront of development were companies like Douglas, Boeing and Glenn L. Martin. All had been working on multi-engine designs for some time. These companies all had an interest in the potential of civil aviation in the Americas and also as a way to win lucrative mail and government contracts away from the traditional carriers, the railroads. They saw this being made possible with fast, reliable, long-range aircraft with a good weight-carrying capacity.

Boeing's bomber programme went back to 1928, when the company's chief designer was put to work on a 'flying battleship' idea, after a meeting with navy officials who reiterated their stance that bombers were unnecessary as no aircraft could ever replace the battleship. The design and development programme that ultimately followed eventually led to the construction in 1935 of Boeing's model 299, which it tendered in answer to an AAC specification for a multi-engine bomber.

When rolled out on 17 July 1935, its sleek design was like nothing seen before and was an immediate hit with all who saw it. Apparently, one *Seattle Times* reporter who was present likened it to a 'flying fortress', as its role was to defend American frontiers. Boeing liked the name and made it a trademark.

Arnold had also started to assist men of foresight and experience up through the ranks. During the late 1930s two of these, both exponents of the strategic bombing theory and highly influential in later developments, started to rise to prominence. Both Ira Eaker and Carl Spaatz were supporters of both Mitchell and Arnold. Spaatz was promoted and assigned to the office of the chief of Air Corps, working directly for 'Hap' Arnold. He was working for Arnold when war broke out in Europe and was sent to England as an observer during the Battle of Britain. On his return, in October 1940, he was appointed assistant to chief of Air Corps. After various roles, in 1942 Eaker was assigned to establishing US air operations in Britain.

Meanwhile, aircraft development had been carrying on apace. Unfortunately after the initial euphoria surrounding Boeing's Fortress subsided, the programme received some major setbacks. First, the original airframe was lost in a fatal crash, while being trialled by the Air Corps. Fortunately for the design, blame was apportioned to pilot error, allowing a contract to be placed for thirteen Y1B-17 prototypes. Questions over the aircraft's cost also stalled further contracts, although these were later reinstated.

The programme also suffered a high-profile showdown, again involving the US Navy. On 12 May 1938, three B-17 Flying Fortresses intercepted the previously undetected Italian liner *Rex* while it was still over 700 miles off New York. The opportunity was not lost to publicise the defence potential of the new bomber; after all, that was what it had been procured for. The navy didn't see things the same way; they saw instead a young upstart trying to score political points. They managed to severely clip the new weapon's wings by getting its offshore flights limited to just 100 miles.

The Fortress itself, however, was already starting to implant itself into the public consciousness. The programme started to generate more publicity and endear itself, as a proud product of American defence, in the hearts of the nation with a series of highly publicised tours and record attempts. Through the Flying Fortress programme and other such aircraft developments, it could be argued that the American public were slowly being brought back from isolation into militarisation through these new indicators of national strength and security.

Despite political meddling, the push was still on for more bombers. In 1938 the AAC requested the Consolidated Aircraft Corporation to build B-17s in an early attempt to prepare for increased production and also to drive down the cost. Instead Consolidated produced a four-engine, high-wing design with tricycle landing gear. Arnold approved the plans and gave a contract for a prototype, which was delivered in December 1939. Even before the prototype flew, orders came in from the AAC and the French, most of the latter ultimately ended in service with the RAF, being used for anti-submarine work and gaining the name 'Liberator'. After several iterations, the B-24, beginning at the D model, began production in earnest. The aircraft ultimately became one of the most prolific of any US design, with over 18,000 built.

Many other developments were pursued and championed under Arnold's guidance, including new oxygen systems, cabin pressurisation and engine superchargers as well as the other major piece of the strategic bombing puzzle, the latest development of the Norden bombsight.

The Norden bombsight was designed by émigré Dutchman Carl Norden as early as 1923. Originally intended for use on US Navy aircraft, it was a highly sophisticated instrument, costly to manufacture and complicated to maintain. In theory this device allowed bombing accuracy to be within a 100ft-diameter circle from altitudes of over 20,000ft.

There is still much debate over the worth of the unit in practice, as all trials and training were under 'artificial' conditions in clear skies, good weather and with no enemy retaliation. The Norden bombsight, however, was pushed as the tool to win the war and as such was one of America's most closely guarded military secrets of the Second World War. Considering the difficulties the navy had placed in the way of the developing air force over the past two decades, it was ironic that one of the most important items in ultimately establishing the air force as a totally independent service arm was a piece of equipment 'borrowed' from them in the first place!

Early in January 1942 President Roosevelt announced to the nation the production goals for the coming years, in order to provide the material for war. Among the items he listed were 60,000 aircraft in 1942 and 125,000 in 1943.

Not only was it going to have to build the machinery of war, but the US military also needed to rapidly call to arms thousands of men and women. Congress had last called up its youth in 1917, when it passed the Selective Service Act. After the First World War, the size of US forces had been radically reduced. Although the 1920 National Defence Act had provided the system for voluntary recruitment, it was going to take a far wider range of powers to provide for the manning levels envisaged for this emerging conflict.

In November 1940, US Congress enacted the Selective Training and Service Act, establishing the Selective Service System as an independent agency to oversee all draft issues on behalf of the government. All males between the ages of twenty-one and thirty-five were ordered to register for the draft and the first peacetime conscription occurred, conducted by a lottery-style draw. Draftees started to be shipped to army induction centres around the country.

Following the attack on Pearl Harbor, manpower expansion was increased even more, eventually leading to the US having over 16 million men and women in uniform. Congress gave the President the power to send draftees anywhere in the world. It also removed the distinctions between draftees, regulars, National Guardsmen and Reservists, and created one 'citizens army' made up of all – enlisted and officers. As the war progressed, the draft age was lowered to eighteen and men were called to service not by lottery number but by age, with the oldest going first. Initially, draft service duration was for just twelve months, then by 1941, eighteen months. Once war had been declared, service was required until six months after the end of the war. The rush to volunteer after Pearl Harbor so overwhelmed the recruiting system, however, that many men were temporarily turned away.

Paul Kovitz recalls his induction into the USAAF:

We were working at a factory at the time, my brother and I, in Newburgh, New York. We were looking for another job but no one wanted to hire you because they knew you were going to get drafted. My brother got drafted and some of our buddies got drafted. Then in April 1942 I volunteered because I knew I was going to get drafted and fortunately I got into the Air Corps. We got aptitude tests and my score was good enough to go in the Air Corps. I was glad, I didn't want to get a rifle and go in the trenches!

Many of these volunteers elected to directly apply for service in the Air Corps/Force. The symbol of the new air power had inspired many of the nation's youth. Raised during the

Depression era they were inspired to seek out this new branch of the military and join up to be pilots and engineers and immerse themselves in these new technologies. The attack on Pearl Harbor only fired enthusiasm for this new and 'glamorous' form of fighting. Art Watson was one who was drawn to volunteer:

> I tried to join the services on Dec 8th after the raid on Pearl Harbour, but was turned down because I wore glasses, but I was drafted in April of '42. Prior to being drafted I worked for Black & Decker, a tool manufacturer as a repairer of electric tools. I worked on electric tools of all descriptions and learned the theory of electricity. Because of my knowledge of electricity, I was given the opportunity when drafted, to go to school in electronics.
>
> After much schooling in the Auto Pilot and Bomb Sight, I was placed with the 95th Bomb Group (BG).

High-profile aviation combat in various parts of the world involving American pilots aided the image and helped recruitment. Action such as the RAF's struggle against German forces, aided by US volunteers in the 'Eagle' squadrons, were portrayed favourably by pro-British elements of the US press. The 'Flying Tigers' fighting for China against the Japanese and the daring first strike back against Japan by Doolittle's 'Raiders' in April 1942 only went to enhance the public perception of the image.

Training schools were established or expanded all over America to train pilots and other aircrew, as well as the thousands of engineers and technical specialists to service the aircraft. Although the US Army listed hundreds of skills, or Military Occupational Specialities (MOS), that personnel could be trained for, the air force grouped the majority for their requirements into just five: engineering, ordnance, weather, photographic and communications. Once an individual had successfully passed through one of the AAF schools they were considered 'skilled' and entitled to wear an appropriate patch on their uniform indicating this. Other branches of the army also had specialist training programmes ranging from schools for cookery, typing and fire fighting; all would be required.

Once through basic training, recruits would be sent for further specialised training based on aptitude. Once trained, they would be deployed to centres for forming into units. Air squadrons would be formed and then combined to create groups, where some or all of the supporting structure would be drawn together before being sent to a combat theatre.

Trainee Army Air Force aircraft mechanics class at Randolph Field, Texas. (USAAF)

Paul Kovitz continues his recollection of his induction:

They sent me to Miami Beach for basic training, then to Sheppard Field Texas to airplane mechanics school. I wound up getting a promotion to Staff Sergeant going to train as a top turret gunner – that was ninety-six dollars a month instead of thirty odd dollars a month as a buck private; that was a lot of money in those days. I was waiting to go to Brownsville Texas where they trained you for the top turret. I had a call to go down to headquarters where some captain interviewed me. He said 'well son you're going to Chanute Field, Illinois, to become an engineering officer'. As a 2nd Lt. that's one-hundred & fifty dollars a month, I thought wow that's better yet! In January 1943, I became a 2nd Lt. instead of a Staff Sergeant. That was pretty swift promotion, from volunteering as a buck private and not knowing what you were getting into, to becoming a 2nd Lt. We went to Officers training school, back down in Miami Beach again. You know the army had taken over all the hotels and we were parading up and down Collins Avenue down there. I trained as a recruit there and now we were getting officers training there.

From there we went to Salt Lake City by train and from there I went to Spokane, Washington, where I joined the 390th BG.

We didn't realise at the time where this was all going, all this stuff just came along at you and you went along with it. It was very exciting meeting all these new people making new friends. After all the training everybody went in different directions though, there were only a couple of us that ended up in the 390th.

The 8th Air Force

One decision made by the Allies at the ARCADIA conferences in early 1942 as part of its 'Europe first' strategy, was to move US forces to Britain as soon as possible, with an air force forming part of this deployment. However, at this point it had not been fully decided what form this air force would take.

The USAAF comprised a number of separate air forces allocated to distinct geographical areas, the total number during the Second World War reaching sixteen. The 8th was essentially the next number in the sequence at the time, created but unassigned to any particular theatre. This force, which ultimately became the largest air combat organisation the world has seen, was a far cry from its original structure. Based on its experience at the time, the USAAF tended to see the air forces it sent abroad as smaller and flexible, able to respond to the ebb and flow of battle fronts. This was how the order of battle for this air force was originally envisaged. It only had one heavy bomber group allocated, the rest of the force comprised of medium bomber, fighter and transport groups.

US-based air forces, First to Fourth, were given the task during the war of creating new forces. The 3rd Air Force activated the 8th Headquarters Squadron at Savannah Air Force Base, Georgia, on 28 January 1942; meanwhile the 8th Bomber Command had been raised by the 1st Air Force at Langley Field, Virginia, on 1 February 1942. It wasn't until after August 1942, however, that it became the 8th Air Force; up until that point it was still officially the 8th Bomber Command.

Until the end of March 1942, the 8th remained uncommitted and nobody seemed to know for sure where its new pastures lay. They were soon to find that the pastures were the very ones being ploughed up to make airfields in England! Even though the 'Europe First' decision had been attained, during the first six months of America's involvement in the Second World War there were still a number of calls on US military output, especially aircraft. Industrial production was only just beginning to ramp up and anticipated wartime production targets were still a way off. Britain and now Russia were being supplied with lend-lease support and materiel was being pushed toward the Pacific theatre. The Allies were desperate to stop the Japanese advance from going any further by providing a defensive buffer between the enemy and the Australian mainland.

There was also indecision over where in Europe to go first, with a lot of pressure being applied to attack up through 'the soft underbelly' of southern Europe after establishing a jumping off point in North Africa. Eventually the origins of a plan that would ultimately lead to the invasion of Europe from Britain – operation OVERLORD – started to come into being. However, until sufficient land forces could be established it was decided that the only way to begin opening the new battlefront was by air – from Britain.

On 31 March 1942, General Carl Spaatz, who had been tasked with taking an air force to Britain, suggested that the presently task-less 8th be used. Spaatz saw the opportunity of using the 8th to show the world the true potential of strategic bombing, although it took a significant period of restructuring before this new role was fully defined.

To adapt and equip the 8th for its new mission, much manoeuvring and re-shuffling of staff and units had to be accomplished before it could be ready for the task ahead. More changes and decision-making took place in April and May as more groups and commands were added, which further shaped the embryonic air force as it was honed to suit its new purpose.

A problem that it had in common with all the other services was that of recruitment. The 8th had a particular shortage of experienced staff officers to oversee its rapid expansion. It was therefore deemed necessary to recruit directly from those civilian professionals and businessmen who had volunteered. The new volunteers were placed into specific roles that suited their experience and skills gained in civilian life. Many went overseas without any military training, some of which was only remedied later in

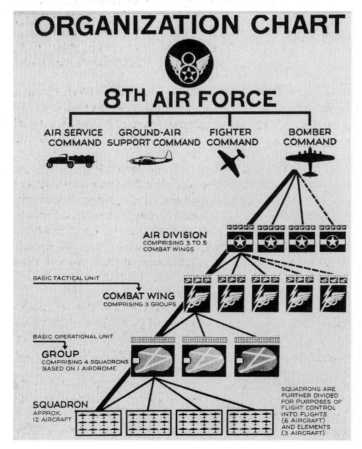

Organisational chart of the 8th Air Force as originally planned, prior to restructuring to accomodate a tactical Air Force - the 9th. (USAAF)

theatre. To try and supplement the shortage of men knowledgeable in the ways of the army, commissions were offered to many career non-commissioned officers to improve the situation. Things were still difficult through the early summer of 1942 and many departments were only brought up to anywhere near the strength required just prior to embarkation for Britain.

Much the same story can be applied to equipment, and although progress was made during the early summer to at least provide everyone with the basics, some units still went overseas without their full allocations. This led to a situation which became referred to as 'reverse lend-lease' or reciprocal aid, whereby British forces and agencies had to supply the Americans with huge amounts of equipment to enable their operation to literally get off the ground.

While all this was going on training continued apace for those who were actually going to wage the war, and squadrons and groups were worked up into cohesive fighting units. Much work was done to bomber and fighter units to work more effectively together, especially with the more tricky aspects of formation flying, not only for their role in future combat missions, but also as it had been decided that that was how the first waves of aircraft would get to Britain – fly. Not too much of a problem for a four-engine-long range bomber with a ten-man crew including a dedicated navigator, but for a fighter with a single crewman, a bit more tricky. The plan, therefore, was to shepherd several fighters with one bomber which did the navigating.

The Bomb Group

Within each numbered air force in the Second World War, the 'group' was its basic combat unit: the air force equivalent of an infantry regiment. Groups could comprise bomber, fighter or transport aircraft, but within each group all would be the same aircraft type and have the same role. Usually commanded by a colonel or lieutenant colonel, a group acted as the basic tactical control and administrative unit, serving in all theatres in the Second World War.

Bomb groups were classified into five types: very heavy (VH), heavy (H), medium (M), light (L) and composite, which combined bombers of differing categories. Bomb groups were all numbered, those assigned to the 8th AF in Britain for its strategic operations were latterly all heavy bomb groups and operated either the Boeing B-17 Flying Fortress or the Consolidated B-24 Liberator.

Bomb groups were all organised in a similar manner, according to US War Department tables of organisation and equipment (T/O&E). These tables laid out explicitly for every unit the exact quantities of personnel and their skills and allocation of equipment, to enable them to operate. Heavy bomb groups were originally tabled to operate three squadrons. In 1942 all existing groups were expanded to four squadrons, which is why some of the earlier groups created have one non-sequentially numbered squadron within their organisation. At this time squadron size also increased from twelve aircraft to eighteen. The net effect of this was that when the US entered the Second World War a heavy bomber group could field thirty-six aircraft; by the end that total had risen to seventy-two.

In addition to the combat element – the squadrons – each group comprised a number of support units, which handled all the specialist functions required to keep the group operational. Each of these units would be self supporting according to its particular T/O&E listings. Once within the group structure many of the personnel within the units would be pooled and used wherever their specialties were required.

The USAAF, like most military organisations, operated to a system known as the 'principle of command'. Within that system each of the separately numbered air forces operated in a similar way. In basic terms it meant that the operating structure was very similar to that in any multinational corporation comprising many companies and subsidiaries. All the component companies within such an organisation would possess their own individual boards of management, but ultimately the company chief executives would report back to 'head office', through their reporting chain. The major difference was that the USAAF wasn't in the business of creating wealth but of systematically removing the elements of the enemy's war-making machine.

Alongside the separate numbered air forces, the USAAF had several additional commands, including Training Command, Material Command and Air Service Command, among others. These also all had their various reporting structures based on the same principle of command, up through to USAAF High Command. The crucial point to make here is as these commands provided services and support, they operated alongside the numbered air forces but were not subordinate to them. Many of the support units allocated to a bomb group reported directly to their own commands. This structure caused problems within individual bomb groups particularly in the area of supply, due to support units having to serve two masters: their parent command and the group they were assigned to.

The situation was finally resolved right at the end of the war in April 1945. An Air Service Group (ASG) was created at each 8th AF station, taking control of all support groups on a base except the combat squadrons and Group Headquarters. This new unit then fell wholly under the command of the Group Commanding Officer (CO) and his headquarters staff, more of which later.

Functionally, a group would be divided into an air echelon, comprising all aircrew, and a ground echelon, which was much the larger group and comprised all the ground support staff (which really meant everyone else who didn't fly). All the support units would form part of the ground echelon by 1945. The total strength of most 8th bomb groups was around 3,000 personnel. The elements of a bomb group comprised:

Headquarters

The Group Headquarters was its management unit, provided with four separate administrative departments. In addition to various component support units of the group, a number of other specialists appropriate to the various support units would also be assigned. With these ready-made elements, a group would be able to establish itself and become operational fairly swiftly.

Squadrons

Just like all the other units that formed together to create a group, a squadron was a self-contained military organisation capable of supporting itself for short periods. As well as aircrew, it contained enough personnel to administer and furnish its own necessary ground services.

The squadron also comprised an air echelon and ground echelon. For administrative purposes both echelons were further divided into four departments. Air had administration, technical, tactical and service. Ground had headquarters, technical, tactical and service. Each of the four departments was further divided into functional groups, all responsible for an essential part of the end product: flying a combat mission.

The flying element of a squadron was divided into 'flights'; anything from two or more aircraft formed a flight. At the outset of the Second World War a USAAF heavy bomber squadron comprised three flights of four aircraft each (A, B and C flights). T/O&E for a heavy bombardment squadron was structured to supply manpower and material to support these twelve aircraft. According to the tables, manning strength for the squadron was 420 men, sixty-six of whom were officers and the rest enlisted men. This further divided into the air echelon of thirty-nine officers, 114 enlisted men and the ground echelon, which had seven officers and 240 enlisted men. With the introduction of another squadron and more aircraft, the workload increased as these manning levels stayed fairly static.[1]

Support Units

Although bomb groups all had a similar number and type of support units, within the 8th no two groups were exactly the same. Due to the rush to get groups established in Britain many of these units were created much later and were therefore much later in deployment. The 8th Group structure was still very much a work in progress and it was not fully clear until they had been in Britain for some months where the strengths and weaknesses lay; hence, when each group is studied, variations can be seen. Some units were drawn from the regular army, and some were raised as aviation specific. This is particularly evident in some fire fighting and ordnance units. After retraining of personnel and changes to equipment allocation, some units had their designations changed after having been in Britain for a period of time. Some of the smaller organisations may not have featured in the make-up of all groups while others were only part units or detachments as they were spread between several groups. Typical of this is the 18th Weather Squadron, which had a detachment with every 8th bomb group.

The structure for most groups for most of the war was as follows:

Engineering Support

Originally this was provided by Service Squadrons, though within bomb groups from the autumn of 1943 these were replaced by new Sub-Depots. Although part of 8th AF Service Command (VIIIAFSC), the Sub-Depot was under the day-to-day command of the Group CO to which it was assigned. This turned out to be one of the most problematic areas of split reporting.

Their main role was servicing, repair of combat damage and provision of Engineering Support beyond the scope of the squadron ground crews. Sub-Depots also supplied all technical stores relating to flying missions, such as spare parts and fuel. After April 1945, this element of a bomb group became part of the new Air Service Group.

Station Complement Squadron

This was generally considered the station 'housekeeping' unit. It comprised personnel with a variety of skills not only to maintain a station but to run many of the essential elements. Typical of station complement personnel would be catering staff, flying control personnel, carpenters and electricians, transport drivers and telephonists.

Medical Dispensary

Organised and operated the station sick quarters.

Ordnance Supply & Maintenance Company

Operated the base munitions dump and maintained all the vehicles in the station motor pool.

Chemical Company

Operated all gas defences on station and handled chemical weapons such as incendiary devices like napalm, as well as the more noxious forms of ordnance.

Quartermaster Company

Dealt with all non-technical stores on site, particularly those of a more domestic nature associated with day-to-day living.

Fire Fighting Platoon
Provided fire and rescue services for both domestic fires and aircraft crash rescue.

Military Police Company

Provided base security.

Then followed a number of specialist groups that generally, but not always, included such things as a finance section, weather detachment and a postal detachment.

Although obviously an independent non-military organisation, the American Red Cross (ARC) also featured highly within a group's supporting units once deployed to theatre. Much like its international 'parent', the ARC was born from the heat of battle during the American Civil War. Among its many programmes, it grew to find itself brought in wherever disaster and conflict struck to support without prejudice those involved. Much of this experience, that it was to use so effectively to support troops and civilians alike, had been gained during the First World War. Further strengthened by its work during the inter-war period, the organisation was instrumental in providing a wide range of support programmes to American servicemen during the Second World War, particularly USAAF personnel.

Once operational, due to the pooling of resources and personnel from its component units, many parts of a group would break down into a series of functions rather than along predetermined organisational lines. Some of these included engineering, ordnance, transportation, training, medical and messing. Consequently, the demarcation between various units often became hazy, but all to the benefit of the group.

During late 1944, a large number of ground personnel were transferred back to the ground army to make up for shortages in Europe. This was an unpopular move all round. At the very least it meant that those individuals concerned had to move to less pleasant surroundings, but it also created manpower shortages within groups at a time when both mission and aircraft numbers were increasing.

Expansion into Great Britain

Popular lore suggests that the December 1941 attack on the US Pacific Fleet caught the United States completely unprepared for war. The historical truth behind the rapid build-up of forces after this event tells a different story. Although President Roosevelt's administration was still projecting an outwardly isolationist attitude to the populace, the planning for the material build-up in Europe had begun months before the Pearl Harbor attack. The origins for expansion were in fact grounded in 'war games' played by the US military. As early as the 1920s, complicated scenarios of global unrest were played out and resulted, by the late 1930s, in creating strategies for industrial as well as just purely military planning.

In early 1941 the US conducted secret meetings with the British and Canadian military leaders with regard to military co-ordination should the US enter the war. Following these meetings, known as the ABC-1 (America, Britain, Canada) Conference, the US issued its final plan in April 1941, thus helping to guide the mobilisation of economy and manpower for the upcoming war. The initial part of the plan called for the creation of advanced bases for US build-up in Europe. Northern Ireland was chosen for this purpose as the new force established there could act in a defence role for Ulster. That would free up British forces for use elsewhere, as well as providing valuable lessons in future force expansion.

In May 1941, a Special Observer Group was set up in London under Major General James E. Chaney. In June, a contract was awarded to US contractors to start building naval facilities in Northern Ireland for the US Navy. Shortly after this, Chaney submitted to Washington preliminary estimates of troop and aircraft numbers to be based in Northern Ireland. In early September, the Special Observer Group sent back their first official report on the situation and among its recommendations was that an aircraft repair base be set up at Langford Lodge, Northern Ireland, for the repair of US aircraft – probably the first airfield to be allocated to the USAAF in Europe.

The first movement of troops to Northern Ireland began in January 1942 under the code name MAGNET force. This initial implementation phase was underway even as the ARCADIA talks were still taking place. By early March 1942, the number of US servicemen in Northern Ireland had already risen to over 100,000. While events were escalating in Northern Ireland, the USAAF began assembling on the British mainland. On a grey day in late February 1942, seven men arrived at Hendon an airfield in North London. The party, led by Ira Eaker, was the advanced guard of what was to become the 8th AF Headquarters. They had flown in from Lisbon via what was to become known in the years that followed as the Southern Ferry Route.

The group's primary task was to start proceedings for the reception of American forces and, in particular, the USAAF, into Europe. Eaker was actually personally carrying the first hard copy of the plans for initial build-up to reach London. Initially it was suggested that the USAAF operate solely from Northern Ireland. It was swiftly realised, however, that to have any chance of success, given the additional flying distance involved, combat groups would have to be located as close to the east coast of England as possible, as had the RAF. Therefore the airfields given over to the USAAF in Northern Ireland would be mainly utilised to train new crews in the peculiarities of the European Theater of Operations (ETO) and British practices.

Out of convenience – it was close to his RAF opposite numbers – Eaker established his Bomber Command headquarters in an evacuated girls' school in High Wycombe, Buckinghamshire, approximately 30 miles west of London. As Eaker had drawn much of his initial staff from former civilians rather than career military officers, the group became known as 'Eaker's Amateurs'. Eaker, however, wanted a more flexible team unencumbered by traditional military thinking, to make things happen, and fast. Eaker named his initial team Bomber Command Shadow Staff, as essentially that was their first priority: to shadow RAF Bomber Command and learn from them. Much work was done to create operating procedures for the new air force, drawing heavily on RAF methods in order to allow the two forces to work together.

Spaatz arrived in Britain in late April 1942 and established an administrative headquarters for the 8th at Bushey Park in North London in order to prepare the infrastructure for the arriving air force. Eaker was able to inform Spaatz during the middle of May 1942 that headquarters should be ready to control and operate bomber operations by the beginning of June. By that time links had grown so close as to enable the two allies to start planning future combined strategies, and 8th representatives were invited to attend the RAF Bomber Command daily conferences.

There were differences of opinion on various issues, and the role of fighter aircraft was one such. Spaatz defined their role as bomber escort and support, but the RAF was hoping to use them in a defensive role. A compromise was eventually found with Spaatz promising their use if the British mainland was again severely threatened.

The most publicised disagreements though were over the method of the Americans' strategic bombing campaign – in daylight. The RAF had tried daylight bombing early in the war, had taken fearsome losses and moved to night-time area bombing. They wanted the 8th to have no part in it, but the Americans disagreed. This they felt was what they had been training for, it was the bedrock on which their bombing strategies were based and they were convinced they had in their aircraft, men and equipment a way to provide a swift knockout blow to the German war machine.

In a memo to a sceptical Winston Churchill, Eaker stated that he felt the American and British approaches complemented each other. He concluded: 'If the RAF continues night bombing and we bomb by day, we shall bomb them round the clock and the devil shall get no rest.' Churchill apparently so liked the concept of round-the-clock bombing that he was persuaded by Eaker's arguments.

In his report, 'Work of the Advance Echelon', to General Spaatz of 19 June 1942, General Eaker had this to say about the relationship built up between the 8th and their RAF opposite numbers:

> The British, in whose theatre we have been understudying and operating for the past five months, have co-operated one hundred per cent in every regard. They have lent us personnel when we had none, and have furnished us clerical and administrative staffs; they have furnished us liaison officers for Intelligence, Operations and Supply; they have furnished us transportation; they have housed and fed our people, and they have answered promptly and willingly all our requisitions: in addition they have made available to us for study their most secret devices and documents. We are extremely proud of the relations we have been able to establish between our British Allies and ourselves, and we are very hopeful that the present basis can be continued, and that all incoming staff and tactical commanders will take the same pains we have to nurture and maintain the excellent relations which now exist.[2]

Once through this intense period of planning, Commanding General of the USAAF 'Hap' Arnold was able to present RAF Air Chief Marshall Charles Portal the schedule for the build-up of the US air forces into Britain, to planned strength, by March 1943. Eaker now had to make it happen.

Much of the early preparatory work for the invasion of northern Europe was conducted under the code name BOLERO. In recent times this operational name has been incorrectly attributed purely to the actual building up of air power in Britain. However, for the purposes required here, the example of previous commentators shall be followed and Operation BOLERO will be used as a generic title for the implementation of the 8th's mission.

The massed movements were now underway and the first troopships started to sail in May 1942, carrying the initial ground echelons. Ships used to carry the bulk of the personnel were mostly converted liners, such as the Queens, *Elizabeth* and *Mary*. In the Battle of the Atlantic the fortunes of war were starting to turn in the Allies' favour, allowing large convoys of material to be attempted again. The liners, though, generally sailed independently; their main defence was speed: the ability to outrun enemy warships and more importantly, U-boats. Vigilance on these sailings was still vitally important, as the sinking of one of these vessels packed with thousands of soldiers (GIs) would have been a disaster of a magnitude not seen before and a propaganda coup for the Germans. The prestige liners became known as the 'Grey Ghosts' due to their wartime paint schemes and the way they swiftly plied their way back and forth across the oceans. Fortunately all the liner sailings arrived safe and well although the *Queen Mary* in particular had a couple of close calls. In one incident, she collided with the British light cruiser HMS *Curacoa*, which unfortunately sank with considerable loss of life. On another occasion, on one of her crossings in December 1942, nature nearly did what the Germans couldn't when a freak wave almost swamped her during a storm.

It was possible for both of the Queens to carry around 15,000 troops each per sailing, completing the crossing in around six days. It has been estimated that RMS *Queen Elizabeth* for instance carried over 750,000 troops, covering 500,000 miles during her war service in all theatres. For those that came over on these sailings, the cramped conditions on board were a far cry from the ships' civilian days of opulence; still the experience of travelling on one of these great ships was not lost on some. Master Sergeant Lawrence J. Scholze, a mechanic with the 335th Bomb Squadron (BS), 95th BG, remembers his experience fondly:

I was very happy we were going to England, a country where they spoke English! We sailed out of New York Harbor in March [May] 1943 – on the big luxury liner the *Queen Elizabeth* – WHAT A SHIP!!! We landed in, I think, Clydebank [actually Greenock] Scotland 4½ days later.

Staff Sergeant Art Watson, a bombsight technician with the 335th BS, 95th BG, was on the same crossing:

In the last [days] of April 1943, the flight crews flew to England and the Ground Crews went by train to New Jersey, where we assembled and were then sent to New York Harbor to board the *Queen Elizabeth*. We left New York and in about 5 or 6 days, anchored in the Firth of Clyde, between Gourock and Greenock.

For others the trip over was to be by means of slightly less prestigious and slower craft. Corporal Richard Creutz, an aircraft sheet-metal specialist with the 457th Sub-Depot, recalls his sailing with less pleasure:

I left the U.S. on the 21st October 1943, on HMS Orient, a British ship [possibly RMS *Orion* as the Royal Navy didn't have an HMS *Orient*]. It was a 13-day crossing, in a convoy of many ships surrounded by the U.S. Navy destroyers and an aircraft carrier. We had an uneventful crossing. We were starved, getting only 2 meals a day – they called it rationing! We slept down below in hammocks. We landed in the Firth of Clyde and were herded into railroad cars as we unloaded from the ship.

2nd Lt Paul Kovitz, Engineering Officer with the 569th BS, 390th BG, also had mixed feelings about his means of deployment:

After we got into the 390th and got so we were ready to leave, the airplanes from each squadron went to a different place in the mid west. They then went on their way and we got on a train to our point of embarkation. We set off by ship and landed, I think, in Liverpool.

On the way over they put the officers in charge of the enlisted men. Officers had there own quarters and enlisted men theirs. We had to check on life rafts and stuff like that. During our patrols we had to walk past the vegetable stores, without any refrigeration they started to smell bad very soon! We used to go on deck to get fresh air at night and watch the fluorescence in the water as it was dark with everything blacked out. We got a lot of wave action and sitting at tables everything would slide back and forth. It wasn't much of a luxury ride over but we made it.

While the ground echelons started deploying, the air echelons began gathering at airfields on the north-east coast of the US. They were preparing to fly what became known as the Northern Ferry Route. They departed the US from airfields in Maine, heading for Newfoundland, Greenland, Iceland, then Northern Ireland or Scotland. By the end of August, Operation BOLERO had flown 386 aircraft to Britain and by the end of 1942, 882 had arrived.

Tragedy was unfortunately ever present for those that managed to make the Atlantic crossing. One B-17 from the 401st BS, 91st BG, crashed into a hillside in Northern Ireland in fog, having just made landfall after enduring the arduous ferry flight. Eight of the crew were killed in the impact.

By December, the Northern Ferry Route had to be closed due to winter weather and all transfers of aircraft were concentrated on the south route. Although it was almost twice the distance of the northern route, the Southern Ferry Route did pass through some slightly warmer territory! The route headed south from the US to the Caribbean, then

B-17 down on the ice in Greenland. It was anticipated that during ferry flights, a loss rate of 10 per cent would be acceptable. In the event, figures were much lower. The largest loss was a group of two B-17s and six P-38s forced down in Greenland through lack of fuel, after turning back due to navigational and weather problems. All crews were rescued but the aircraft were abandoned. (USAAF)

across the Atlantic via the Azores to North Africa. After gathering in North Africa, flights then headed for Britain, making a wide detour of the Spanish, Portuguese and French coasts, out into the Bay of Biscay. In the spring of 1943, the northern route became usable again. In general, during 1943 the weather conditions were better on the northern route than the previous year thereby allowing more flights.

As with all best laid plans, however, during the first year of expansion things didn't or couldn't go as projected and figures had to be revised downwards. Frustratingly many new aircraft were routed to the north African campaign and even worse, in November 1942 the 8th's first, and to that date most experienced bomb group, the 97th, was also reassigned to North Africa, taking with it a wealth of knowledge.

Ultimately, the 8th was able to grow steadily. Through 1942 and 1943 development was at times exceedingly difficult, but into 1944 the pace quickened. Known for his brevity, in a short speech he made to dignitaries in High Wycombe after setting up his 8th Bomber Command headquarters in the town, Ira Eaker said:

> We don't do much talking until we have done more fighting. We hope that when we leave you will be glad we came.

Infrastructure & Support

Accommodating the USAAF

As we have seen, planning for the establishment of US air forces in Britain had actually begun in 1941, with the US government allocating $40 million towards the cost, but it was to put an additional burden on an already struggling construction programme. To give some idea of the task, in September 1939 the RAF had 116 airfields in Britain, 100 of them built since 1935. From 1939 to 1945, a further 444 airfields were built with paved runways, each costing about £1 million. At the peak of construction, during 1942, one airfield was completed every three days. In addition to this, sixty-three existing permanent stations had major extension programmes undertaken usually to provide surfaced runways and associated trackways.

This task was completed with a peak labour force of 60,000 people employed exclusively on construction projects related to the air war. Most of these were civilian workers employed by British construction companies, although US Engineer Aviation Battalions (USEAB) built fourteen of the airfields and carried out modifications to many more.

Even more airfields were planned, but on 16 December 1942 the British Government decided to indefinitely postpone construction of those where significant construction had not yet commenced in a necessary drive to conserve resources and manpower. The majority of those postponed had been provisionally allocated to the 8th as part of its projected final growth. As the war ended before they were required, construction never resumed.

By the end of the war, the total number of airfields of all types in Britain was well over 700. Of this number the USAAF inhabited around 150.

834th EAB constructing an airfield at Matching Essex, 26 May 1943. Originally intended for 8th AF medium bombers, it was passed to the 9th AF due to restructuring. It would appear that the farm has been left as undisturbed as possible. Usable farmland was kept available around airfields for food production as well as aiding camouflage. (USAAF)

The Airfield–Building Programme

Britain's first major airfield-building programmes had been for the First World War, however by the mid-1920s the majority of the approximately 300 constructed, being of a very temporary nature, had reverted to their previous use, mostly as pasture. Only a few more substantially constructed sites were to survive, Duxford being a prime example.

By 1924 Britain had twenty-four service and seventeen civil airfields left. After the guns had finally fallen silent at the end of 'the war to end all wars', the desire of the majority was to never have to return to such a situation again and militarisation declined. However, changing political conditions during the latter part of the 1920s and early 1930s suggested that future conflict could come from the direction of France. The strategies based on these theories largely dictated that a new set of frontline airfields should be constructed around the south-east and south coast of England. By 1934, the year before the first major expansion period of airfield building, the number of RAF aerodromes had risen to fifty-two, based mainly on this premise.

By the middle of the 1930s the political situation was changing again, with the rise of Nazi Germany, and this led to another change of policy. The Reorientation Scheme of 1934 introduced the largest airfield-building programme to date. What became known as the expansion era began in 1935 and provided a whole series of new, permanent airfields and facilities. The scheme, unknowingly at the time, introduced the largest single civil engineering programme Britain has ever seen. Rather fortuitously as it turned out, the expansion era sites as well as those provided for earlier contingencies complemented each other. Even though when war came it was with Germany, the attempted invasion was to have been through France and the Low Countries. The spread and location of airfields, to a degree unintentionally, was perfectly planned. It also established the English east coast, between the Humber and the Thames, as 'bomber country'.

A Standard Layout

Before 1939, the design of airfield layout and construction had remained fairly static. Until that time a typical RAF airfield was arranged around a large grass flying field. The average size of a pre-Second World War airfield was around 250 acres, roughly circular in form. Advancements in technology, in particular the introduction of the Lorenz blind approach system in the late 1930s, necessitated the establishment of defined airstrips. The grass field itself was then normally laid out to include four overlapping strips orientated with the most favourable wind conditions. At the time there was seen to be little requirement for surfaced runways.

By 1939 only nine airfields had paved runways of any sort and this was due largely to the RAF's heaviest aircraft of the time, the 'Wellington' bomber. The Wellington was a twin-engine design with an operational weight of around 32,000lb. It could be considered at the time to have been at the cutting edge of British heavy bomber design, and in wet weather especially it made many a grass flying-strip unusable! As all-up aircraft weights were only going to get heavier, more than doubling by the end of the war, a radical rethink of runway policy was required.

The arrangement of structures on a typical expansion era station would usually be divided into three separate functions, flying, technical and domestic. The flying site would usually be bordered radially around one 'quadrant' by a number of aircraft sheds or hangars, normally four or five. The thinking behind this layout was that enemy aircraft would be unable to make a straight attack run as the target formed a curved alignment and thereby lessened any impact. These hangars, along with several other special purpose buildings, provided the technical accommodation. All other station buildings and domestic structures were neatly grouped in rows, in close proximity behind the sheds. This type of combined layout, it was later realised, did make for a compact potential bombing target!

These factors ultimately necessitated a rethink of airfield layout, firstly to provide paved runways and secondly to remove close groupings of station facilities. This new approach resulted in what became known as 'dispersed airfields', the vast majority of which were built as temporary stations.

Through a series of programmes beginning in May 1939, runway size and layout increased until, in late 1942, a standard was agreed; this became the basis on which all 'heavy' airfields would be either built or modified to until the end of the war in 1945. This became known as the Class A, Air Ministry Directorate General of Works (AMDGW) Standard for Heavy Bomber Stations, or more simply just 'Class A'. It was a specification that would provide for the requirements of all contemporary heavy bombers, especially the American types that had been arriving in Britain since earlier that year.

As previously stated, the number of airfields under construction at this time caused an enormous logistical problem. In addition to all the new airfields that were waiting to be constructed, many previously built stations from the expansion era would have to be brought up to Class A standard. All major airfield modification or construction would be limited to bomber fields, both operational and training. Unless already having surfaced runways, many fighter airfields would remain grass or, at best, use one of the temporary metal surfaces. Elementary flight-training school fields and the like tended to remain as grass strips throughout the war.

Allied to the hard surfacing issue was the need to provide parking for aircraft around the airfield. Just as they couldn't possibly land on a grass surface, neither could they be

Aerial picture of Horsham St Faith (Norwich), with runways and perimeter track under construction in 1943. Originally opened in June 1940, the original crescent-shaped group of five 'C'-type hangars can be seen in the lower left-hand corner, along with all the other station buildings, typical of a non-dispersed permanent pre-war airfield. (USAAF)

regularly parked on one. Hard surfaced dispersals, or 'hardstands', were another feature of a Class A field that went through several iterations before a final design was settled on.

To address the issue of the vulnerable camp layout in stages through the metamorphosis to Class A, the buildings of the camp area were gradually broken down into functional groupings. These groups, or sub-sites, were moved out from the main airfield site and dispersed into the surrounding landscape.

With the onset of war the constructional methods for all structures on military sites became more utilitarian, due to shortages of materials and the need for expediency of construction. Engineers involved in site layout used methods that were the very antithesis of traditional military thinking and went to great lengths to make clusters of buildings appear as haphazard as possible in order to further blend them in and avoid establishing patterns that could be interpreted by enemy aerial reconnaissance.

The Concrete

The first thing to remember about the Class A airfield is that the standard parameters really only applied to the hard surfacing, and in particular, the runway size and layout. Secondly, every airfield was different in all other respects, as there was no standard layout with regard to airfield building infrastructure. Rather, an airfield would tend to receive a number of certain building types to suit the function the Air Ministry had initially planned for it, be it an operational bomber or a transport station, for example. Although modifications occurred all the time they were generally minor when placed in the context of the whole site. By the time the station was built it was usually too late to restructure what was there. This was particularly true with regard to airfields allocated early in this war, although the later arrivals from the US tended to be provided with fields constructed more specifically to their requirements.

All the airfields allocated to the 8th AF were built during a ten-year period (1935–45). As this was a period of rapid development, it led to innumerable plan changes. However, by detailed site analysis, the airfields under examination in this work appear to fall into four distinct bands.

Band 1 –   Expansion era grass runways, updated to or near Class A hard surfacing, built from 1935 to 1939 with non-dispersed administration, technical or living sites. C-type hangars.

Band 2 –   Built early war, 1939 to mid-1942, with runways later updated and extended to or near Class A. Temporary brick structures. T2- or J-type hangars. Partly dispersed technical and living site.

Band 3 –   Built to Class A, late 1942 to mid-1943, with temporary brick buildings and hutting. Two T2-type hangars and fully dispersed sites.

Band 4 –   Built to Class A, mid-1943 to the war's end with T2-type hangars. Fully dispersed sites with buildings, especially accommodation, becoming of even poorer quality.

It can be seen that the 8th AF inherited a wide variety of station types for its heavy bomber operations, from the formal style of the pre-war airfields, to the extremely austere wartime construction of the later sites.

The essential parameters for Class A standard were the provision of three intersecting hard surfaced runways. The main runway had to be a minimum 2,000 yards long, with the other two a minimum of 1,400 yards long. All runways needed to be 50 yards wide.

As the main runway would see primary use, particularly in poor weather conditions, it was deemed to be the instrument landing runway and as such, wherever topography allowed, would be aligned with the prevailing wind, generally NE/SW. The runways were encircled by a perimeter track, or taxiway, 50ft wide, which joined the end of each runway. The perimeter track had a total length of around 3 miles.

The other large areas of concrete provided were the aircraft hardstands. For the same reason as for the policy for arriving at the dispersed airfield, it was also realised that parking aircraft close together was not a good idea for survivability in the event of attack. Therefore aircraft storage became dispersed over a wider area too. Hardstands were built branching off the perimeter track at various points along its length. Although not strictly falling within the requirements of the Class A specification, they too went through their own evolutionary process before the final design was agreed upon.

Bob Clarke, in his book *The Archaeology of Airfields*, suggests that the chronology of hardstanding or dispersal type is a good indicator of when in the wartime period an airfield was originally laid down, particularly when a former airfield no longer exists and is only visible as crop marks on the ground. The earliest hardstand design was a circular pad of concrete, 125ft or 150ft in diameter. Several hardstandings branched off a main access leading from the perimeter track, and were randomly placed around the perimeter of the airfield. It was realised that this design had a potential major flaw in that if the track was blocked at its initial entry point, either by damage or aircraft breakdown, it could trap several other aircraft behind it. The original requirement for RAF use was for thirty, then later thirty-six hardstandings per airfield. At this stage in the war it was the design of hardstandings rather than the quantity that was of concern; this thinking was later to be partly reversed.

The second design was a variation of the first type but this time each circular pad would have its own access to the perimeter track. Due to its shape on the plan, it became known as the 'frying pan' type. This design also had shortcomings; the severe 360-degree turn that an aircraft had to perform to enable it be parked the correct way round to exit put a huge strain on tyres and landing gear, and caused many failures. Other factors that would lead to another change were also becoming apparent. With newly arrived USAAF bomb groups increasing in size to four squadrons, there was now a requirement to increase the number of hardstands to fifty.

In late 1942 the loop or 'spectacle' design was introduced and became the standard for the rest of the war. This permitted a separate entry and exit point as well as the possibility of storing more than one aircraft per dispersal. This was rather fortuitous as in 1943 8th bomb groups again grew in size, this

The three types of dispersal and runway extensions also shown is a typical extension pattern to a runway extended to Class A standard. (After R. Clarke)

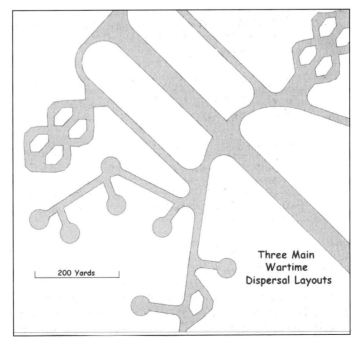

200 Yards

Three Main
Wartime
Dispersal Layouts

time to four squadrons of eighteen aircraft. Space for dispersing seventy-two aircraft caused yet another headache for hard-pressed USAAF commanders and Air Ministry planners. In some instances, such as at Framlingham, older 'frying pan' dispersals were increased in diameter to enable more than one aircraft to be parked on them, but that situation was far from ideal. Aircraft of over 100ft wingspan became common, requiring a much larger turning area, and as a consequence the new type of dispersal needed to be constructed rather rapidly.

According to an Air Ministry memo dated 27 October 1942, ninety-one airfields that had been or were intended to be allocated to the USAAF required dispersals bringing up to the loop type design. Interestingly the list includes a number of those sites which were planned but never built. The same document also contains a memo dated 3 November 1942 from Headquarters Bomber Command that states:

> It has been decided that dispersal schemes at all aerodromes occupied or intended for use by, the U.S.A.A.F shall be prepared by the Americans and submitted direct to this headquarters through the appropriate American channels...[1]

To speed up the decision process, what the Air Ministry required were plans for suggested hardstand layouts to be submitted to them for approval from individual airfields. This was where the problems began. Various USAAF commanders, tired at the slow turning of Air Ministry 'wheels' and desperate to get accommodation for their ever expanding air fleet, took matters into their own hands. It would seem that some took this instruction too literally and went ahead and simply organised construction of significantly more than the permitted fifty, and often to their own designs. The need for an approvals panel was to enable all interested parties to agree that the schemes were workable, both from a location and operations point of view. There was particular concern that sites might be constructed in the vicinity of facilities housing such things as the radio direction finding equipment that could be seriously affected by spurious radio interference. The British authorities were also particularly keen that loop types were neither constructed in groups of more than four, nor in a 'cul-de-sac' form, thus leading to the shortcomings of the original dispersal design and additionally maintained a minimum of 50 yards between parked aircraft.

Squadron Leader Eric Benson seems to have been the officer appointed to act as liaison between the USAAF and RAF and Air Ministry regarding the dispersal expansion issue. In an extract from a memo dated 13 April 1943, he appears to be extremely exasperated by the fact that elements of the USAAF apparently wanted to go it alone and not comply with Air Ministry requirements. He continues:

1. As you know we have been concerned for some time when agreeing to the sites proposed by the Americans for dispersal points to replace existing standings. I think we can honestly say that whenever this has been done, we have explained to the Americans that we are not in a position to authorize this work and that our approval merely stated that the sites proposed were regarded as satisfactory but that approval to construct anything beyond the first 50 standings would have to be obtained from Air Ministry.
2. I think the Americans have understood this position but I am not at all happy that this is actually being done and I feel that if plans are handed to a resident engineer with the signatures of 2 Colonels and a Squadron Leader on the bottom he will build a whole layout without question!'[1]

Eventually, as with all things, the pressure of war dictated the issue eventually resolved itself nd all heavy bomber airfields used by the USAAF were modified to a minimum of fifty hardstands. Some had more than fifty, in particular those airfields constructed or modified by the USEABs. These were probably the main culprits causing the above problems, as being US military units they saw their mission slightly differently to those of the British civilian contractors employed elsewhere. It was also quite probable that if the local topography could cope and there was available space, more hardstands were laid out, especially as some airfield modifications resulted in the loss of previous hardstand types as they were swallowed up by loop-type designs.

The 'frying pan' shape did not completely die out, and at least one example still appeared at the firing butts even on the later stations, for testing aircraft guns.

Airfield Site Layout

As we have seen, station forms varied considerably, with no two alike. This was partly because of continual evolution, but fundamentally due to the landscape that they were constructed within. During the process of laying out a site, it was topography that often dictated layout. By not conforming to a standard pattern this further aided the concealment process.

Much like and partly because of the development of the hard surfacing, the area taken up by the average airfield had increased to around 600 acres by 1945. The number of dispersed sites varied, using, where possible, natural cover from woodlands and hedgerows as camouflage. A whole airfield could have as many as twenty dispersed functional sites, but most tended to have around fourteen. Generally it would have a main technical site with hangars and workshops close to the perimeter track, with a smaller secondary one on the opposite side of the flying field. These would be within the boundary of the main site. Also within the airfield itself would be a small cluster of buildings connected with flying control centred, unsurprisingly, on the control tower.

The headquarters would normally be the first site away from the airfield, as at Podington and Ridgewell for example, but again variations can be found, such as Great Ashfield where it was attached to the main technical site. Further away would usually be two communal (living) sites and between five and ten domestic (accommodation) sites and further away still, a sick quarters and sewerage disposal site. Often, at the point of the airfield furthest from any human habitation, for obvious reasons, the ordnance stores or bomb dump would be constructed, though not always, as at Thorpe Abbotts and Bassingbourn where they were inside the airfield perimeter. In some instances there could also be a separate instructional site, but most of the heavy bomber airfields combined instructional buildings with the main technical site. Including all the dispersed sites, a complete airfield could now be spread well over a square mile.

Early plans for the dispersal of domestic accommodation suggested it be divided into sites for 150 personnel of all ranks and to be no closer than 800 yards from each other and the main site. These distances were unworkable, however, in terms of administration and

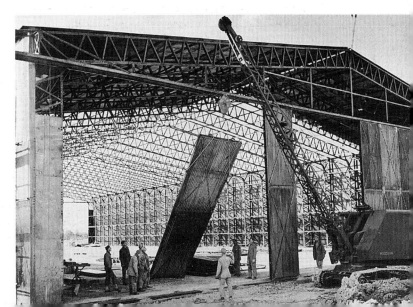

A T2 hangar under construction, the 'T' for transportable types. Assembled from pre-fabricated steel sections, these could be constructed far faster than their robust but expensive predecessor C and J types that were found on permanent stations. (USAAF)

Nuthampstead Airfield, Hertfordshire, 15 March 1944, a typical later dispersed site having virtually all loop-type hardstands. The various dispersed accommodation sites can be seen towards the bottom right half of the picture, the bomb dump in the top right half located in woodland. Just to prove that there was no standard airfield layout, Nuthampstead's two T2 hangars can be seen in the centre of the picture located on just one large technical site. (USAAF)

operational efficiency. The allocation was changed to 250 to 400 personnel, depending on vulnerability to the main site, and 200 yards away from each other. Obviously all these sites had to be connected and so a network of roads and paths were constructed. Existing roads were used where possible and pre-existing roads were often closed to public traffic, apart for local access, for the duration of the war.

As the war progressed and more temporary airfields were constructed, even the larger structures on an airfield became more utilitarian. Hangar type in particular became standardised at the T2 type.

One hangar was usually located on each technical site on opposite sides of the airfield. The original plan had been to provide four hangars, as had generally been the case on the pre-war sites. Two were provided to start with for expediency, with the intention of adding a further two once the airfield had opened. However, this rarely happened due to material shortages and time constraints, and most sites remained as built until the end of the war.

Generally as the construction programme evolved, building construction became further rationalised, partly through constructional necessity but also due to the fact that as technology evolved some of the earlier functions were no longer required.

Deployment and Allocation of Bases

Although originally intended to depart America at the end of March 1942, the first heavy bomber groups did not arrive in Britain until July. After the original plans to operate from Northern Ireland were abandoned, the USAAF wanted to locate itself in east Yorkshire and Lincolnshire. This was mainly because this was closer to the selected sites for air depots at Wharton and Burtonwood in Lancashire, although regarding Langford Lodge in Northern Ireland this made little difference. This area of England, however, was already

Map of south-east England showing the location of bomb groups and major headquarters for the 8th Air Force's strategic operations. (After D.A. Lande)

firmly established as RAF Bomber Command's territory. With so many airfields already operational, moving would have been impractical. Instead East Anglia was offered as is it was less heavily populated by the RAF and those squadrons that were there could be moved. There was also room for expansion as there were a number of airfields either newly constructed or under construction. This was accepted by the Americans as a workable solution, particularly for combat groups.

It was, however, another group of airfields that were first allocated to the 8th AF. According to the earliest records regarding the USAAF build-up in Britain, these were eight airfields located in the east Midlands, at Polebrook, Grafton Underwood, Chelveston, Podington, Molesworth, Kimbolton, Thurliegh and Little Staughton. All of these, with the exception of Little Staughton which was later handed back to the RAF, became heavy bomber stations.[2] These had been constructed to early wartime patterns that generally corresponded with details of band two, identified previously. As such they required quite considerable amounts of extra construction work to bring them up to, or close to, Class A standard. This caused a degree of inconvenience as they were already in use by the RAF. On these airfields the concrete pattern of perimeter track differed from the later standard and the extensions to runways were very obvious. Probably the best surviving example of this arrangement is at Podington. The start line of the current 'Santa Pod Raceway' is located on this area of the airfield and the pattern still shows in aerial photographs.

It was to these airfields that the first 8th AF heavy bombers started to arrive during the summer of 1942. Initially the 8th AF comprised a number of commands: bomber (comprising both medium and heavy groups), fighter, support (transport) and service. With the eventual reallocation of medium bomber and transport groups to the 9th AF, this left the 8th with just heavy bombers and fighters.

The original plan had been to follow a practice similar to that of the RAF: grouping airfields in threes, having one as a base station and two satellites, with the base station having greater technical facilities. Initially the idea was that two groups could operate from three airfields, using the base station as its primary maintenance site. This would work, due to aircraft numbers, for medium bomber, transport and fighter groups, but one heavy bomb group required a single airfield. It was soon realised, however, that this would be impractical as the projected number of groups to be sent to Britain far outnumbered the available airfields if such a method of organisation was introduced. Although many airfields at the time had nowhere near the space required, as we have previously seen, plans were put in place to expand airfields to accommodate just one group per airfield. This system would also ultimately lead to the restructuring of maintenance arrangements.

The composition of the three Bomb Divisions of the 8th Air Force, including the group's primary location while based in England their headquarters location and group code letter as applied to the aircraft. (Author)

Combat Wing	Lead Group	Second Group	Third Group	Fourth Group
US Eighth Army Air Force Heavy Bombardment Groups Great Britain 1942 - 1945				
1st Bombardment Division – B-17s – Triangle symbol Headquarters - Brampton Grange, Huntingdonshire				
1st Wing	91st BG – A Bassingbourn	381st BG – L Ridgewell	398th BG – W Nuthampstead	
40th Wing	92nd BG – B Podington	305th BG – G Chelveston	306th BG – H Thurleigh	
41st Wing	303rd BG – C Molesworth	379th BG – K Kimbolton	384th BG – P Grafton Underwood	
94th Wing	351st BG – J Polebrook	401st BG – S Deenthorpe	457th BG – U Glatton	
2nd Bombardment Division – B-24s – Circle symbol Headquarters - Ketteringham Hall, Norfolk				
2nd Wing	389th BG – C Hethel	445th BG – F Tibenham	453rd BG – J Old Buckenham	
14th Wing	44th BG – A Shipdham	392nd BG – D Wendling	492nd BG – U N. Pickenham	
20th Wing	93rd BG – B Hardwick	446th BG – H Bungay	448th BG – I Seething	
95th Wing	489th BG – W Halesworth	491st BG – Z N. Pickenham		
96th Wing	458th BG – K Horsham St. Faith	466th BG – L Attlebridge	467th BG – P Rackheath	
3rd Bombardment Division – B-17s – Square symbol Headquarters – Elveden Hall, Suffolk				
4th Wing	94th BG – A Rougham	447th BG – K Rattlesden	486th BG – W Sudbury	487th BG – P Lavenham
13th Wing	95th BG – B Horham	100th BG – D Thorpe Abbotts	390th BG – J Framlingham	
45th Wing	96th BG – C Snetterton Heath	388th BG – H Knettishall	452nd BG – L Deopham Green	
93rd Wing	34th BG – S Mendlesham	385th BG – G Great Ashfield	490th BG – T Eye	493rd BG – X Debach

Eaker did, however, decide to continue the RAF policy of controlling groups of airfields with a local headquarters. The bomb groups of the 8th AF were organised into a number of air divisions; originally planned to reach five, only three were formed before the end of the war. Each division comprised twelve to fourteen groups, which were further divided into combat wings, made up of three and sometimes four groups. The 1st Air Division was located in the English east Midlands, the 2nd in Norfolk and the 3rd in Suffolk. Each group was identified by a single capital letter on a white background painted on each aircraft's tail and wings. The 1st Air Division was a triangle background, the 2nd a circle and the 3rd a square.

Maintenance System of the 8th Air Force Bomber Command

In the pioneering days of aviation, aircraft construction was fairly simple, requiring few specialists. However, as technology advanced, the systems and materials involved required a new breed of engineering staff to support them. Following on from fairly primitive arrangements utilised during the First World War, the procedure for maintenance of US military aircraft was streamlined. Post-war, a new Air Service plan for the supply, salvage and repair of aircraft was instigated. One aspect of this plan was to establish tiers or echelons of maintenance, becoming the basis for the accepted structure and location of implementation, for differing degrees of aircraft servicing.

The plan called for a network of bomber and fighter groups supported by a system of maintenance units located at dedicated air depots around the US. For most of the inter-war period, a three-echelon system of maintenance evolved: the first echelon was daily maintenance undertaken by aircrew, the second was the regular servicing, inspection and repair work by squadron ground crew, and the third was major overhauls undertaken by air depots.

Further advances occurred during the 1920s both in the administration of aircraft maintenance with the introduction of aircraft record keeping, as well as massive technological advances in aircraft design and construction. With the coming of the Air Corps Act in 1926 and its slow but steady evolution during the inter-war years, the AAC was able to use both its combat experiences of the First World War and expanding peacetime role to develop a more comprehensive process of maintenance and support.

The AAC was, even as late as 1939, still relatively small, with an inventory of fewer than 2,000 aircraft. Maintenance facilities had been established over some years and could cater for this number of aircraft and twice the number of engine overhauls. Just five years later in 1944 – the peak year of aircraft production – the USAAF had, in all theatres, a total number of aircraft nearing 80,000. Obviously the impact of the coming conflict was about to cause massive changes to the then system of maintenance.

It was not really until the effects of the appointment of General 'Hap' Arnold to the post of chief of the Air Corps in 1938 started to be felt that a profound change in organisation and emphasis occurred within these areas of operation. Arnold was well versed in the workings of this area of the service, having previously held commands within the field of maintenance. He once describing an air force as: '... a balanced compound of three essential elements, airplanes, combat and maintenance crews and air bases'.[3] Just like many other areas of which he had control, he intended for maintenance of aircraft to be not found wanting. However, due to the AAC still being a 'twin pronged' organisation, two distinct policies had emerged on how support and maintenance of aircraft should be carried out.

GHQ Air Force restructured its own maintenance arrangements by forming what were termed 'Base Air Groups', to perform third echelon tasks at establishments still under its own command within the continental USA. Its requirement was for a flexible system, able to follow a mobile tactical air force. In contrast, Maintenance Command under

Arnold's jurisdiction preferred a more static system, of the sort it had been developing for some years using its network of fixed permanent air depots. When the two arms of the Army Air Corps were finally amalgamated, becoming the Army Air Force in June 1941, the existing Maintenance Command took over responsibility for all aircraft maintenance. In October 1941, Maintenance Command was re-designated the Air Service Command (ASC) and assumed responsibility for third echelon maintenance and supply for all the Army Air Forces.

Due in part to the increased complexity of aircraft and the adoption of a more stringent maintenance recording and inspection system, as well as vastly increasing aircraft numbers, the new command expanded the maintenance system from three to four echelons. The new system came into effect from February 1942. The major repair functions of the existing air depots now became the fourth echelon and a new third echelon was introduced primarily to oversee the heavier requirements resulting from prescribed servicing intervals for aircraft. To provide this new third echelon at 'fixed' bases, these new units became known as Sub-Depots, and would see many new facilities built at existing US airfields due to an urgent need for expansion space. The new units would be run by civilian organisations, initially those already allied to the civil aviation industry but overseen by commissioned USAAF officers from Air Service (Maintenance) Command. As time went on, more civilians were trained and this had the effect of releasing increasing numbers of skilled air force personnel back to front line work, both at home and overseas.

The echelons of maintenance were now defined as:

First echelon comprising daily checks and light maintenance that could be performed by the crew of an individual aircraft, such as servicing, refuelling, pre-flight and daily inspections. It also included minor repairs such as tightening bolts, hose clamps, adjustments and replacement of minor parts. All tools and equipment required had to be transportable by air. In practice however, this was generally performed by squadron ground crew but could be done by the air crew of a particular aircraft when necessary.

Second echelon was routine servicing at prescribed intervals. The ground crew of the combat unit that the aircraft was assigned to generally performed this function. Tasks were generally limited to those which could be accomplished with hand tools or equipment which was air transportable. Second echelon service normally encompassed repairs that could be completed within a limited time, usually around 36 hours.

Third echelon work was considered to be the preserve of the Sub-Depot or equivalent organisation. It generally required teams of specialists with fixed or mobile heavy equipment to carry out the tasks, which by its nature required shipping by means of surface transport. It included field repairs and salvage, removal and replacement of major unit assemblies, or fabrication of minor parts and repairs to aircraft structure, often quite considerable in a combat theatre. Third echelon sometimes included operations, especially overseas, that would normally be handled by an air depot.

Fourth echelon servicing called for major airframe and component overhaul which would be carried out at a 'rear' air depot. Their remit was generally the complete overhaul and reconstruction of an aircraft due to life cycle, combat damage or both. The depot's role also included overhaul of assemblies, components and systems, as well as fabrication of new parts to supplement normal supplies. In addition, the depot system also carried out technical modifications on aircraft and components.

Realising that there were now requirements for both fixed and mobile methods, the ASC now took elements from both systems to suit both a static home air force and also the necessities of a mobile overseas force. To this end, in June 1942, all of the previous maintenance groups in the continental US were transferred from the former GHQ Air Force operations to the jurisdiction of the ASC. They were then reassigned and re-named service groups. From then on all service groups, both existing and newly created, were trained to carry out the same function as Sub-Depots: third echelon servicing but for overseas duty and comprising of service personnel only. The work of air depots in the US continued with the fourth echelon role, and the overseas fourth echelon functions were left in the hands of the air depots that Maintenance Command had originally created nearly a year earlier for just such a task.

In little over a year the new organisation, Air Service Command, had grown from a minor offshoot into a fully functioning command in its own right with responsibility for third and fourth echelon maintenance and supply for all the Army Air Forces at home and overseas. However, the system of maintenance and servicing that ultimately evolved in Britain, took elements from both the mobile and fixed models developed in the US. While the 9th and to a degree the 12th and 15th AFs that were also serviced from Britain required a mobile system, the 8th moved partly to a fixed system.

Realising, rather fortuitously, that for the mission they had been set, and the predicted amount of combat damage, aircraft would require a much faster turnaround, 8th AF HQ decided to go against the prescribed structure described above. To this end, each group had a maintenance unit attached to it. At the outset these were the service groups as had been created for air forces operating overseas, but from late 1943, using the term for fixed third echelon units, new Sub-Depots started to replace them within bomb groups. Initially these new organisations were created by reorganising service group personnel and providing them with improved allowances of equipment that were necessary for their more exacting role. This situation, however, only applied to bomb groups and fighter groups still retained their service groups.

Although US air forces operating from Britain were considered to be overseas, the reality was that given the distance from the US, it was better to establish a quasi-domestic system to oversee their supply and servicing arrangements. Three locations had been initially chosen for establishing air depots to provide fourth echelon facilities. These were sited away from combat zones to minimise the threat of air attack and close to port facilities for easy transhipment of stores, and the delivery of aircraft. The increasing pace of expansion, however, dictated that these be converted to virtual aircraft factories, supplying complete aircraft and parts. Air depots required for fourth echelon servicing were now established closer to the combat airfields and the original three sites at Langford Lodge, Wharton and Burtonwood were reassigned to be Base Air Depots (BAD). Burtonwood, BAD1, became headquarters of the Base Air Depot System, and specialised in US radial engines and aircraft that used them. It was this BAD that was largely responsible for supplying all of the 8th's bomber fleet both in terms of replacement aircraft and parts. Wharton became BAD2 and specialised in US in-line engine aircraft, particularly the P-51 Mustang. Langford Lodge (BAD3) was used for additional aircraft assembly and modification.

The facilities for fourth echelon functions now became known as Strategic Air Depots (SAD). These were established alongside existing operational airfields that for the most part had not been converted to Class A standard but had the room for expansion. Although part of their parent station they were given new names to distinguish them from the main site. SAD1 was Troston, part of Honington in Suffolk and served the 3rd Air Division's B-17s. SAD2 was Abbots Ripton, part of Alconbury in Cambridgeshire. Alconbury was a Class A station but had been utilised for experimental bombing methods so was not home to a permanent operational group. Its main function was to look after the B-17s of the 1st Air Division. SAD3 was Neaton, also referred to as Griston, part of Watton in Norfolk. It oversaw the maintenance of the 2nd Air Division's B-24s.

Although not directly connected with the subject matter of this publication, two more SADs were operated by the 8th: SAD4 at Hitcham, part of Wattisham in Suffolk, serviced and supported USAAF fighters. SAD5 was put into action in northern France in December

1944. Its duties, among others, were to provide a forward base for aircraft damaged in combat and unable to make it to home base to land for repairs.

The agency tasked with responsibility for service and supply in Britain was the 8th AF Service Command (VIIIAFSC). It was they who controlled the air depots as well as forming the direct command structure for the Sub-Depots. However, the Sub-Depot's day-to-day allegiance was to the bomb group to which they were assigned. It was this split loyalty that was responsible for the many problems concerned with supply that was only finally resolved in April 1945 with the creation of Air Service Groups.

One issue that aggravated the supply problem was the operation of two heavy bomber types by the 8th AF. Originally the B-17 was to be the preferred aircraft to operate from Britain but supply of adequate quantities dictated that they be supplemented with the B-24. The initial groups were B-17 outfits and formed the 1st Air Division. The second batch of groups flew the B-24 and they were formed into the 2nd Air Division. Further expansion came with the 3rd Air Division, comprising of groups flying both types. In order to standardise for supply and spares reasons, the 3rd Air Division converted fully to the B-17. When General Jimmy Doolittle took over from Ira Eaker in January 1944, as commander of the 8th, he wanted it to become a B-17-only air force, but the 2nd Air Division resisted as they felt B-24 was the aircraft of choice. As there were already two air divisions of B-17s, it made sense to change over completely to the B-17. It was also well known that Doolittle preferred the older proven design of the B-17 as it was relatively easy to fly and structurally superior.

Both the B-17 and B-24 had very different flying characteristics. The B-24 could carry a greater bomb load but didn't have the altitude of the B-17. When comparing the two types flying deep into Germany, the B-17 carried about half the bomb load of a B-24, as due to its less advanced wing design it wasn't as fuel efficient. However, even though the design of the B-24 wing was more fuel efficient, it could not fly at the altitude of the B-17, and was thus more vulnerable to enemy anti-aircraft guns. The argument over which was the better aircraft continues to this day!

In the event, the 2nd Air Division's faith in the B-24 held and the 8th remained a composite bomber force until the end of the war in Europe, although still compounding supply problems.

Moving In

Once an airfield had reached the stage at which it could be considered usable, the first personnel to arrive would normally be an RAF equipment officer and his staff, making preparations to equip the site and work it up to operational status. Very often this occurred as building construction was still ongoing. Sometimes the accommodation was still a long time coming. As with most building projects, the last trades usually left on site were the plumbers, electricians, carpenters and painters. Electrical trades were kept busy not only wiring buildings, but also fitting the new runway lighting systems that were coming into use. Painters also had a lot of work to do giving each building its interior coat of standard ministry blue and white, and some form of camouflage scheme outside.

Even so, a lot of finishing was left to the new inhabitants, particularly constructing pathways to avoid the mud that tended to be left behind by the contractors. Mud was a constant problem on many airfields during the war and much time and effort went into its elimination, particularly on runways and perimeter tracks. Colonel Hubert 'Hub' Zemke, commander of the 56th Fighter Group told of his experiences when setting up a new base at Halesworth in July 1943:

> While the contractors continued construction of accommodation and other facilities, mud was a constant nuisance. The soil, being of a heavy clay texture, was not free draining. When dry it was hard as rock but even after a summer shower the vehicles

churned the surface to a glue-like substance that clung to tyres and shoes getting everywhere. One of the first things we had to do was get a line of our boys to sweep the perimeter track clear of the mess left by the contractor's trucks. I was constantly protesting to the RAF liaison officer about conditions and the contractor's slow progress. He did his best but the contractors were a law unto themselves. Their men seemed to be always sitting around drinking tea. Once I remonstrated with a group, pointing out that we were trying to fight a war and they should make an extra effort to help. Then I discovered they were Irish as were most of the contractor's workforce. It wasn't their war and they were there for the money ... [4]

Once completed, much re-seeding of grass was carried out as part of attempts to make airfields less obvious from the air. One such idea was to re-mark hedge lines that had been removed during construction by spraying tar or paint on the ground to replicate their former positions. But due to the obvious scars on the landscape from construction, it would take some time for them to fully blend in. Once this point was reached, the new occupants would soon appear.

The arrival of American units tended to be a fairly ad hoc arrangement. Sometimes the ground personnel of a group would arrive first and sometimes it would be the air echelon with their aircraft. In many instances a base would first be inhabited by support units not yet assigned to a group and often a unit or group would just get settled in before having to move on again. Art Watson was already a member of the 95th BG, which arrived with their ground echelon:

As we went through the midlands, I really enjoyed the beautiful scenes of the hills and waterfalls and flocks of sheep. Besides England was where my roots were, in as much as my grandfather and grandmother were born there and through them and my father became quite accustomed to some of the ways of the English. They loved their tea, spoke English and not American and used many descriptive words with which I wasn't familiar.

The train carried us to Framlingham, where we were based for about 2 months and were then sent to Horham in Suffolk, which became our permanent base.

Richard Creutz on the other hand, although ending up at Horham with the 95th BG was a member of 457th Sub-Depot and at that stage was unaware of which bomb group they had been allocated:

After we landed in Scotland we didn't have much time to make much of an impression of the place as we were shipped to a former British base the US used as a distribution centre, I think it was near Liverpool. I stayed there for three days and was then taken by truck to the 95th at Horham.

Generally once a suitable number of HQ personnel were available then an official ceremony would take place, handing the keys to the camp to the new inhabitants and changing the RAF pennant for the Stars and Stripes. Each station retained an RAF liaison officer to smooth the transition of control as well as a mainly civilian engineering team, who were kept busy finishing construction work as well as attending to many repairs that became necessary.

On some stations it wasn't long before the first problems began to manifest themselves. It was discovered that on some of the earliest stations to receive hard surfacing the concrete wasn't thick enough to withstand heavier aircraft landing on it. This often became obvious once the first B-17s arrived in Britain. Poor quality work and thin concrete started leading to runway breakthroughs on landing and takeoff. Much damage to men and machines was caused, resulting in closing stations temporarily for rectification work to be carried out.

The 91st BG moved from its originally assigned base at Kimbolton to Bassingbourn for just such a reason. Kimbolton hadn't yet been upgraded to Class A standard at that time, and the runways were not strong enough or long enough to support heavy bombers. Rudi Steel, a sheet-metal specialist with the 322nd BS, 91st BG, remembers:

> We arrived at Kimbolton after arriving from the U.S. with the first group of ground staff. We weren't their very long, a matter of a few weeks. My lasting memory from that time was getting hauled in to help clear up after a lot of the guys got sick with a stomach upset – not a nice job!
>
> We had to move out in a hurry after the runways got damaged and stopped flying. We got word to move out virtually overnight ...

Following on from this, the story goes that the commander of the 91st BG, Lt Col. Stanley T. Wray, was so annoyed at the likely injury to be caused to his men if they continued to fly from Kimbolton that he went out looking for another airfield and effectively 'stole' Bassingbourn, vacant at the time. He apparently did so without asking the Air Ministry for permission, moving the entire group and its equipment from Kimbolton to its new home in a day. His hunch that once they had moved in the Air Ministry was unlikely to move them out again, paid off. The 91st BG remained at Bassingbourn, a pre-war permanent station, for the duration, enjoying the relative luxury of the vastly superior facilities.

Concrete break-up was also a problem on some of the later airfields constructed by the USEABs. Possibly through attempting to complete the job ahead of schedule or through ignorance of soil types and geological conditions, or both, it became apparent that the surfaces were breaking in an even more catastrophic manner. On further investigation it was found that the engineers involved had been failing to put any form of hardcore sub-bed down, preferring instead to lay concrete straight onto compacted soil, as was the policy in many areas in the US.

Perimeter tracks became similarly afflicted at many airfields, aggravated by fully laden taxiing aircraft, as well as heavier road transport such as the large US articulated fuel trucks coming into use. The civilian maintenance crews retained on virtually every airfield during the war had more or less a full-time job keeping the hard surfacing in usable condition.

Once a group had fully assembled at its new home, it had to work up to operational status in very short order. Air crew training would begin and practice flights would be made, stores and equipment unpacked and the whole process of supporting the mission would begin.

Probably the airfield worst affected by concrete break-up was Debach, the last 8th AF heavy bomber base to become operational in Britain and constructed by the 847th EAB. The 493rd BG moved in during April 1944 and began operations on D-Day, 6 June. Problems began to arise more or less immediately. Later in the year the group had to move out while the runways were completely re-laid, only moving back to see out the last two months of the war. The HQ convoy of the 493rd BG returns to Debach on 1 March 1945. (USAAF)

3

The Airfield

The main component of any airfield site was obviously the flying field with runways, perimeter track and aircraft dispersals. However, to begin with, a look at this overall entity. In this chapter the function of those organisations working around the periphery of the main site are examined.

Security

Although the dispersing of airfield component sites offered improved protection from bombing, it did however give rise to another significant problem, that of security. Nowadays we are used to seeing high security fences around many facilities, not just those of a military nature. This was also certainly the case pre-Second World War: the compact nature of airfields and other military installations made it fairly simple to enclose a single site. Once dispersed, though they covered a large area, often having existing communities, such as farms, hamlets or even whole villages as at Nuthampstead in and around them.

Some form of control had to be applied to secure the requirements of the military community. Period photos show that wartime-built airfields generally didn't have miles of high fence around them, as often there simply was no time or resources available. Instead use was made once more of the local environment, with natural obstructions utilised where possible. Coils of barbed wire were strung out at vulnerable points and check points were placed at all roads leading to the main site, with most roads leading through the camps having been closed to all but essential local access. Each dispersed site would have its own sentry point or picket post, so those entering or exiting would have their credentials checked. The majority of these buildings took the form of a small brick-type shed but often on later sites some were constructed from packing crates to save on vital materials.

Guards were often placed at aircraft dispersal areas out on the airfields, particularly at times of heightened security risk, but what must be remembered is that the airfields were rarely quiet. Due to the nature of the daylight missions the USAAF undertook, aircraft

1 January 1944, Pvt. Haydn C. Williams, a guard with 1199th MP Co. with the 401st BG Deenthorpe, mans his post at the far end of the camp. His tiny visitor is from a neighbouring village, the official caption says. (USAAF)

maintenance was mostly carried out at night, making the aircraft dispersals normally very busy places during the small hours, thus aiding the security aspect. All picket posts would be linked by telephone with their operation controlled by the main guardroom.

Even with all this security, stories told by civilians, especially children living in the locality, seem to suggest that they often, unofficially of course, had quite free access and many friendships were built up among the local communities and servicemen due to their close proximity.

Main Gate

The first point of contact for any airbase would be via the main gate. If it was a permanent station, the main gate would be a formal and rather grand arrangement; a later temporary airfield would have something a little more rudimentary. No matter which type of site, the main gate would be the camp's official primary entrance and the first building would be the Guardhouse. From this area, the main site road would lead through to the airfield, more often than not via the main technical site. If it was a pre-war station then the Guardhouse, along with many other buildings, would be constructed in a neo-classical style with columns to the front supporting the roof; if it was a wartime site it would normally be a somewhat more mundane Nissen hut!

Both buildings, despite looking completely different, would fulfil a similar function and contain similar facilities. The building would comprise a reception area, offices, toilets and cells. A pre-war site would also contain accommodation for the fire fighting party and an attached building for emergency vehicles. On a wartime-built station these facilities would normally be situated close by, again of a more utilitarian nature, normally temporary brick structures or more Nissen huts.

Outside the Guardhouse would be the obligatory flagpole on which the Stars and Stripes would be hoisted in the morning and lowered in the evening. Personnel were expected to stop and stand to attention when this daily ritual was occurring, but as many veterans recall, it was always best to avoid the area at these times so as not to get caught in the open, especially when it was raining!

The fire party based at the main gate would in the main be the domestic arm of the base fire service. The other element, dealing with aircraft fires and crash rescue would normally be situated in the vicinity of the control tower. Control of the site's fire alarm system would be

King George VI in the uniform of an Air Chief Marshall inspects MP Guard of Honour outside the Guardhouse at Bassingbourn after visiting the 91st BG, May 1943. Note ornate nature of Guardhouse edifice, compared with that at Framlingham, p44. The building in the background is the station headquarters. (USAAF)

from the guardroom. On pre-war stations these systems could be quite extensive, making use of electrical controls, but on the wartime sites services were still often summoned by a hand bell. The station's air-raid warning system would also be controlled from here and linked to picket posts on all the dispersed sites. Any station lighting existing outside of blackout restrictions were controlled from the guardroom, again so they could be extinguished from a single central source in the event of air raid warnings.

As is still the practice, anyone entering or leaving the camp would have to report to the guardroom to verify their identity and inform security personnel that they were on or off the station. New arrivals would report for duty and station personnel would check in or out whenever entering or departing the camp. If they were taking leave then all passes would have to be checked and details recorded as it would be important to know if anyone had overrun their leave period or was absent without leave (AWOL).

Leroy Keeping spent a night in the lock-up at the Guardhouse at Framlingham after being caught AWOL but under slightly different circumstances. Outside each squadron's HQ building, on the technical site would be a flagpole on which was hoisted a red flag on evenings prior to missions being flown. This was to warn all personnel to be back on base in time ready to undertake their duties. Leroy continues:

My pal was dating a girl from Framlingham, one day he said to come along as she had a sister; I did and started dating her. We got married in 1944 at the Saxmundam registry office. After we married I was still supposed to live on base. However I used to stay down in town with her. I had an arrangement with an orderly room attendant on camp who I used to call up in the evening to see if there was a raid on the next day. He would give me the coded message, 'she wears red knickers' (referring to the red flag) if he knew there was something imminent. Once I got caught out, when having said there was nothing doing, the weather changed and a raid was rescheduled, which found me AWOL in the morning. All in all I was AWOL four times and got caught twice, which resulted in me being confined to camp for two weeks. One time I got caught I was seen at a dance when I shouldn't have been, by a guy who also shouldn't have been there. He outranked me and got away with it, not so fair I thought! I got to spend a night in the cell. If you go up to the camp, the old guard house is still there, you can see the cell room, it's still got bars on the window!

One other feature of the standard Air Ministry layout of a station Guardhouse would be the provision of a prophylactic store. Due to the high incidence of venereal disease, airmen, both RAF and USAAF, as well as other servicemen, would be well provided for with the necessary items to avoid obtaining any unwanted 'souvenirs' from their off-duty liaisons!

It was important that personnel on duty operated in a smooth, professional and business-like manner; after all it was never known when the 'top brass' might make a surprise visit!. The unit charged with all these responsibilities would be the military police company attached to the bomb group. For the first groups to arrive in England, such as the 91st BG at Bassingbourn, many of these duties, like so many others, were handled by RAF security for the Americans. Some early groups had to arrange security in other ways. For the 303rd BG at Molesworth, security was originally controlled by a lone base Provost Marshall, with security personnel drawn from squadron strength. Later, once sufficient military police companies had been established, they started to take on the duties at all USAAF airfields.

A military police company (aviation) was tabled to comprise ninety-seven enlisted men and four officers. The commanding officer would usually be a captain supported by 1st and 2nd lieutenants. The unit would be self supporting, with administration clerks, drivers, mechanics and a cook. During the early USAAF build-up it was often the practice to split a military police company between two nearby bomb groups, again until unit quantities increased.

Military policemen's duties were very similar to those of any police organisation except their 'beat' was normally just the airfield and related property. Their primary role was to

The Guardhouse at Framlingham, 1 July 2006, as used by the 390th BG. This is the very same building from Leroy Keeping's story. (Author)

provide round the clock protection for the station, but to achieve this required an almost infinite variety of tasks. The base perimeter would be patrolled by jeep or motorcycle; entrances were manned at all times and the keys to all of the site's buildings would be held at the Guardhouse for issue and control. Aircraft would require guarding on certain occasions not only on the airfield, but also, prior to clearance, at crash sites. Guards would be provided for briefings and other such operations and the military police would also provide escort duties for visiting dignitaries.

Another important function was to investigate crimes or breaches of the peace alleged to be perpetrated by US service personnel from the group. Any such individuals would be detained by the military police until presented to the base CO or for court martial, depending on the seriousness of the misdemeanour. If convicted, perpetrators of crimes would again be the responsibility of the military police. Prisoners could be detained on camp and given anything from a few days of hard labour to extra duties, such as helping in the kitchens, censoring letters or having privileges taken away. Miscreants would also have to report to the Guardhouse at regular intervals during the day. If offences involved British civilians then the military police would have to liaise with the relevant British civilian police force.

As with any police force, a large percentage of time would be exhausted on traffic control and regulation enforcement, particularly with so many vehicles being used on an airfield every day. A number of traffic accidents occurred and were often attributable to the fact that US vehicles were left-hand drive and in the US they drove on the right, the direct opposite to Britain. It would have been very easy to stray onto the wrong side of the road. Blackout restrictions also caused numerous motoring problems due largely to the limited amount of illumination vehicles could use. A strict speed limit, usually around 20mph, would have been imposed on the airfield and enforced at all times. There would have been a constant movement of vehicles, many carrying fuel and ordnance, so obviously the potential for a serious conflagration was ever present. Art Watson remembered that his only brush with the military police at Horham was for speeding on the perimeter track.

Another traffic related duty would be overseeing the bicycle 'population' on the camp. As the airfields covered such a wide area, the first thing a serviceman would try to do would be to obtain a bike for getting around. There would be a number of official RAF bicycles on the stations, but if these were unavailable then one would have to be acquired, either through purchase or other means. Registers of bikes were kept by the military police and sometimes it would become necessary to have a 'round-up' to try and return cycles to their rightful owners, especially after a busy period of asset reallocation had occurred!

Inspections of the station and quarters would also have to be carried out. A lot would depend on how busy the group was or even how much of a stickler for military procedure the base CO was. If there were regular inspections they would often be scheduled to occur on Saturday mornings. Sometimes these would be instigated by a purge on the use of unofficial equipment, particularly electrical items that had a habit of overloading the station's power supply and causing outages.

As an example of the wide variety and often bizarre occurrences that a military police company could expect to deal with in their daily duties, the following events at the sick quarters at Ridgewell serve well:

We had a little excitement this morning for an unwelcome change. During the night, Cpl RWM, whose sanity we have been investigating, jabbed himself in the left hand with a stick and a pencil which he said was a suicide attempt, which we doubt. He remained in sick quarters overnight and pulled the old gag of climbing out the latrine window when the guard was standing at the door. He took off across a pea patch and it looked for a while as if he had made good his escape.

The author was surprised at the fortitude shown by the individual and admittedly a bit amused at the consternation of the military police from whom he had escaped before. However, the amusement was cut short when the author found out the responsibility was his as much as the military police. Not being an alarmist, the author called out the station defence, Home Guard, civilian police and as many men of the squadrons could supply. The area was searched and after about two hours the prisoner was returned. Captain Porter, the CO of the military police was with me and I don't believe I have seen him so happy.

To add further to our misery, someone stole an American ambulance from the front of Station Sick Quarters late last night and within 45 minutes had wrecked and abandoned it. We are carrying out a search for the driver. The damage is estimated at about $300.[1]

Law and Order

The military police would also have responsibility for policing US servicemen while they were off duty in towns and villages in the locality of their home camp, particularly during officially organised 'liberty' runs. Generally members of the USAAF were well behaved, but problems that did occur with US forces often involved combat troops prior to the invasion of Europe. Airmen, having been stationed in an area, tended to mix well with the locals and develop an affinity with their local town. These sorts of problems were, in the main, limited to areas in southern England where greater numbers of troops were massing, but some towns gained a reputation for problems and required additional policing.

Expecting considerable problems occurring between Americans and the local population, one of the issues the US military had addressed prior to its build-up in Britain was that of law and order. From July 1942 to October 1944, the headquarters of the American military justice system in Europe was based in Cheltenham, Gloucestershire. Officially designated the Branch of the Judge Advocate General, its job was to deal with the more serious crimes that might occur with so many personnel being channelled through Britain and into mainland Europe. Initially a facility in Northern Ireland was allocated to house prisoners, but from mid-1942 Shepton Mallet prison in Somerset was handed over to the American authorities for the punishment of offending US service personnel. In the event crime figures were far less than expected and no worse than those typically occurring within the civilian community, however a number of rapes and murders were perpetrated. In all, nineteen US servicemen were executed in Britain for their crimes, and two of those were members of the USAAF. Both were tried and subsequently hanged at Shepton Mallet.

These were the worst cases and very much the minority. In fact the figures speak highly of the US military selection process in that many other unsavoury types were discounted for service at an early stage. The majority of indiscretions caused by service personnel in their locality were of a minor variety, and often no more than could be expected of service personnel anywhere exercising a little initiative for living off the land. Such things as poaching and removal of firewood were commonplace and the sorts of issues that could be dealt with by the military police, and with a placating word and a spot of compensation from the base CO. Relationships within the areas of the airbases must have been fairly good judging by the strength of goodwill still felt towards the American servicemen more than sixty years later.

Base Defence

Having looked at base security it is now worth investigating arrangements for the defence of an airfield in the face of a more determined attack. From the outset of the Second World War British authorities had been acutely aware of the chance of an airborne invasion of the country. Areas of open flat land had had obstructions placed upon them to make any such occurrence more difficult. The most obvious areas, however, to land troop-carrying gliders and airborne troops, would be the burgeoning quantity of airfields. To counter this threat, each airfield as constructed also had a series of structures provided to defend the site should such events occur.

Every airfield would have had a battle headquarters built partly underground, and a series of pillboxes. These structures would have their fields of fire for the most part looking inwards on the airfield, although many pillboxes, particularly the 'mushroom type', were constructed with a clear 360-degree view. The defence network was designed to operate independently of the other systems on the camp, the whole idea being to prevent an invasion force moving out from the airfield.

All service personnel, with the exception of chaplains and some medics , were combatants and would be expected in event of enemy attack to draw weapons and ammunition and meet the aggressor. Therefore it was essential that the occasional practice on the shooting range took place to re-familiarise personnel with arms and shooting technique.

After the fall of France following the Normandy invasion in the summer of 1944, there was an increased expectation of a German counter attack, which may have consisted of airborne or sabotage attacks on British airfields. To counter this threat, increased guard duties were placed upon station personnel. Rod Ryan recalled these duties at Chelveston:

> Around mid-1944, we were given additional duties. We had to guard aircraft out at the hardstands. I think this was because high command considered there was a greater threat of German counter attack after D-day. We had to work at nights. We would go on guard duty a half hour before sunset and remain at our posts until a half hour after dawn.

Airfields also had to be prepared for the ever-present threat from attack by German aircraft. As part of preparations for this eventuality, significant quantities of blast shelters were constructed all over British airfields on all the dispersed sites. After the air raid sounded, base personnel were supposed to go to one of the shelters. Later in the war, due to the limited number of attacks on airfields, many personnel became blasé about the threat, particularly at night, and stayed in bed against orders!

Although raids on British airfields never again reached the extent of those during the Battle of Britain, some were attempted, particularly on stations close to the North Sea coast. None were particularly heavily orchestrated, more hit and run in nature, but they were nevertheless a considerable nuisance. One of the more successful, as far as the Germans were concerned, was on the night of 23 May 1944 when a direct hit on a hangar at Great Ashfield damaged the hangar and destroyed a 385th BG B-17 inside.

Bomb damage to 385th BG hangar at Great Ashfield after German air attack on 23 May 1944. (USAAF)

Another tactic occasionally practised by German pilots was to follow a returning bomber stream home – particularly later in the day when visibility wasn't as good – and join in the landing circuit, thereby placing itself perfectly to attack the unsuspecting bombers. One of the worst attacks of this kind occurred at Mendlesham on 7 June 1944 when enemy aircraft shot down four 34th BG B-24 Liberators in a matter of minutes over the base.

Airfields, particularly those along the east coast of England, came under the defence areas of the British anti-aircraft batteries and the 'heavy' air defence was provided by these units. During the early part of 1944, prior to the invasion of France, there was an increasing provision of air defences on the camps themselves, and the 390th BG at Framlingham was typical. Heavy machine gun posts were constructed using .50 calibre machine guns similar in type to those carried in the aircraft themselves. In fact several machine gun posts were constructed from complete turrets salvaged from B-17s and mounted on the ground or in a machine gun pit.

Framlingham, being close to the coast, also lay under the flight path of German V weapons coming from the Low Countries during their use later in the war. Several airfields including Framlingham had close calls when V1s fell short of their intended targets. During this period several of the US EABs were drafted in for airfield defence as the role was part of their remit. Because to this, they already had some of the necessary equipment including a number of armoured half tracks. To supplement these, local conversions to jeeps and trucks were often made for additional anti-aircraft protection, with .30 and .50 calibre weapons being mounted onboard. Air defence organisation at this time was also often improved. All the machine gun pits and defence sites around the perimeter were linked to the HQ by phone line. In the event of an attack and phone wires being cut, military police on motorcycles were expected to act as dispatch riders to carry messages between the defences. Until it was considered that Germany no longer posed a threat in this manner, defence drills were held regularly.

One other precaution was the provision of facilities for use in the event of chemical or gas attack. There had been widespread concern at the outset of the Second World War in Britain that Germany might resort to using these sorts of weapons. Up until the Allies return to France they hadn't, but once again concern arose that an increasingly desperate enemy might resort to these tactics.

The majority of 8th bomber bases had a Chemical Company stationed on them as one of the group's component units. A Chemical Company had, in fact, two functions. One was the preparation and handling of chemical weapons, including not only gas warfare munitions, but any ordnance that contained some form of chemical agent such as incendiary munitions and petroleum based explosives like napalm. This function would have been carried out in the area of the bomb dump. The unit's second function was to provide preparation for and decontamination in the event of a chemical weapons attack. They organised gas mask drills and other training connected with chemical attack, such as decontamination should it prove necessary.

Each station would be provided with a gas defence centre: a windowless brick building for decontamination. It had an air-locked entry system and contained showers, cleansing equipment and dressing rooms. The building would also be used for gas mask drills. Personnel would be required to experience using their gas masks and by passing them through a smoke-filled chamber inside the building, enabling them to experience the difficulties of working while using such equipment.

The Chemical Company would also operate the gas clothing and respirator store located on the technical site. This building was usually used as a store of clothing and a maintenance facility for equipment used by the gas defence personnel. Fortunately, none of the gas defence equipment was ever required to be used for its intended task.

The Bomb Dump

All operational airfields had a bomb store both to provide a buffer stock during periods of high usage and to enable munitions to be kept relatively close for loading into the aircraft.

Structures and Facilities

The airfield expansion era heralded an increase in the quantities of bombs that needed to be stored. It was soon realised that established criteria for ordnance storage would be impossible to meet in terms of land required for storage. A new system based on grouping certain tonnages together and estimating projected crater size in the event of an explosion now dictated space requirements. These later bomb store designs went through three basic changes of form: pre-war era, early war and later war. Pre-war stations comprised two sets of six detached brick and concrete high explosive stores, symmetrically laid out in two rows of three back to back. Each store was completed with its own gantry system for lifting and moving bombs. Stations laid out during the first two years of war had detached open stores of around 30ft by 30ft protected by earth banks. Each store was capable of storing up to 24 tons of bombs.

The last type of store was of the kind found on the majority of 8th bomber stations. This was a complete redesign of previous layouts and allowed for much greater handling efficiency. This was required as greater bomb loads now needed to be transported around the airfield and out to the waiting aircraft by 'trains' of bomb trailers. The store consisted of four or five storage areas each slightly separated and each individually comprising four storage bays all divided by earth banks. Each of the storage bays could hold around 50 tons of bombs. A double system of roads through the store allowed trucks to unload ordnance deliveries from one while bomb loading vehicles could load trolleys from the other. The delivery road was usually at a slightly higher level then the removal road, allowing gravity to assist when rolling bombs in the store piles.

Bomb stores were laid out to provide storage for such ordnance as high explosive bombs, incendiary bombs, fused bombs, bomb tail units, small bomb containers and components. However, aside from the bomb stores on pre-war stations, structures on the site were usually extremely sparse in their provision with much of the ordnance simply stacked outside.

Rod Ryan was an ordnance technician with the 1,632nd Ordnance Supply and Maintenance Company, 305th BG, at Chelveston:

> On the bomb dump we were out in all weathers, but we had a shack for when we had to do guard duty. Trouble was if you got wet, there was nowhere to dry your fatigues, so it was out the next day in wet clothes. There wasn't much cover and there wasn't much netting (camouflage) either.

The bomb store at Bassingbourn comprised both the early and later designs. Seen in this aerial view, 7 February 1944, the early type to the top right looking like blocks of chocolate and the later type, three rows to the left. A one-way road system through the bomb dump negated the need for trains of bomb trailers to be reversed. Bassingbourn was unusual in that it also had its bomb dump located within the perimeter track. Various types of aircraft dispersal are also visible in this photo. (USAAF)

Several huts were provided particularly for administration but the only covered accommodation for ordnance would have been for pyrotechnic storage for smaller items such as incendiary components and bomb fuses.

The Air Ministry specification also called for two 36ft-long Nissen huts to be provided for bomb fusing once bombs had been loaded on their trolleys. However, this was not often used for its intended purpose as although RAF trolleys could pass through, it was too small for the American trailor design. After several devastating accidents in the early summer of 1943 when previously fused bombs exploded after being dropped during handling, it was decreed that fusing wasn't to be carried out until bombs were loaded into aircraft. The huts provided would often then be used for additional storage. Other Nissen huts stored the 0.50 calibre ammunition for use in the aircraft guns and other munitions required for base defence. Although there was no specific quantity of ordnance to be held on a base, during heavy operational periods as much as 2,000 to 3,000 tons of bombs could be in store on each airfield.

Camouflaging of bomb stores was accomplished in several ways. Those at sites such as Nuthampstead and Grafton Underwood were constructed in local woodland and much use was made of natural cover. On other sites the actual stores areas were often covered by frameworks and camouflage netting in an effort to hide them.

Ordnance Supply

Bombs and other munitions were shipped from the US among all the other equipment being moved across the Atlantic. Much of it would arrive in Britain through the port of Liverpool. From there they would be moved by rail and stored in centralised ammunitions storage areas. Several main ordnance storage depots were provided for the USAAF, close to groups of their airfields. Sites such as Sharnbrook near Bedford, Barnham in Suffolk and Lords Bridge near Cambridge supplied airfields in their locality, the whole system operating like a huge cross-country conveyor carrying the vast tonnages on a daily basis to the end user.

Such was the volume of traffic to be handled that bombs often made their final journey to the individual airfields by civilian haulage contractor. Those being delivered to the 92nd BG at Podington, for example, were often transported in trucks belonging to the London Brick Company, who operated a number of brickworks in the vicinity.

Rod Ryan continues:

> I was involved with bomb dump admin. We received the bombs and fuses in from the main bomb dump near Bedford, they were usually delivered by civilian contractors. We then organised them by bomb weight in holding areas. When required we booked them out to the squadron armourers. The squadron men used their vehicles and trailers to lift and load bombs.

The early bombs used were older types taken from US stocks but these were exhausted by the autumn of 1942 and the new standard army/navy series bombs came into use. These came in five general purpose types: 100lb, 300lb, 500lb, 1,000lb and 2,000lb, the latter three being most used against industrial targets and the smaller sizes against airfields.

The first incendiary bombs used by the USAAF were British, mostly of the 250lb type; however, during the winter of 1942, the 4lb US magnesium incendiary arrived firstly in 100lb clusters and shortly after in 500lb form. Other types were introduced and developed in smaller quantities through the war and ordnance personnel would be required to familiarise themselves with the peculiarities of handling all these and other designs. Other types of ordnance available to the USAAF in Britain included napalm bombs, fragmentation bombs and poison gas bombs, as well as other early types of controllable-guided types of bomb.

Members of the 1751st Ordnance Company S&M unloading bombs in the bomb dump of the 92nd BG Podington, 19 February 1945. (USAAF)

The last type of ordnance handled by bomb dump crews, although non-explosive, would have been leaflet bombs. These special operations 'weapons' were often disliked by many crews, ground and air alike, who considered them a waste of effort, although those controlling the psychological aspect of the air war obviously thought they had merit.

Bomb Dump Operation

Two of a bomb group's component units would normally operate from the bomb store. Conventional munitions were handled by the Ordnance Company and chemical weapons by members of a Chemical Company. Ordnance companies went through a process of development and generally appeared in two formats. Some were established to handle aircraft ordnance and others had an initial role of vehicle maintenance. Through various mergers during the course of the war most ordnance companies were joined with other units to become 'Ordnance Companies Supply and Maintenance' (Aviation). They then covered the dual role of both ordnance handling and vehicle maintenance. Once formed as such the unit would be split between a station's bomb store and its motor transport workshops.

As units were combined some personnel had to be reassigned or retrained to tasks that most suited their new function. As a supporting unit, daily command was through the Group HQ, although once again they would have been controlled by 8th AF Service Command.

The section of the Ordnance Company operating in the bomb dump was tasked with selecting the correct bombs, dependent on the mission target requirements from HQ, and loading them onto trailers or trolleys so they could be delivered to the aircraft. Some groups preferred the bomb tailfins to be fitted at the bomb dump and others at the aircraft dispersals. On some stations each of the four bomb storage areas in the dump would be allocated to an individual squadron, to ease administration.

In April 1945, ordnance companies became part of the new Air Service Group structure.

A train of RAF C-type bomb trailers hauled by a Chevrolet M6 bomb service truck prepare to leave the bomb dump at an unknown station. The bomb load is being checked against that of loading orders. (USAAF)

Chemical Weapons

The second group of personnel present in the bomb dump would be members of the Chemical Company. In some instances, due to a shortage of trained personnel, a whole Chemical Company would be divided into detachments and spread between two or three bomb groups.

A Chemical Company would have previously spent many weeks learning to handle and load weapons, often wearing their restrictive protective suits to do all manner of tasks both on and off the job to acclimatise to their use. Regular day-to-day tasks that chemical personnel would have had to undertake would be the assembly and handling of incendiary and target-marking bombs. On average, one in three missions flown by the 8th AF involved carrying incendiary bombs. Later, napalm-jellied petrol bombs were introduced, and these too came under the jurisdiction of chemical personnel. If the worst did happen and the enemy used chemical and gas weapons against Great Britain, then it would have fallen to the personnel of the Chemical Company to prepare and load retaliatory munitions. The Chemical Company also comprised staff to oversee and maintain their own specialised fleet of vehicles, mostly required for decontamination purposes.

Although there were several devastating incidents concerning exploding ordnance during the 8th's residency in Britain during the Second World War, overall, considering how much ordnance was handled, these events were rare. More damage was done to hands and feet from incorrect handling, particularly during the long winter months when cold steel and bare flesh do not make for good bedfellows.

Rod Ryan finishes his recollections about his time at Chelveston:

> Generally base morale was very good; no one worked nights on my section originally but once the 422nd squadron started flying night missions, (leaflet dropping) then some people had to support this. There were no accidents at the bomb dump we had a pretty good safety record.
>
> I did once however pull out in front of a taxiing B-17 by accident, with a tractor and a train of loaded bomb trailers, the pilot had to stop, 'cos I couldn't go back, he sure wasn't pleased about that, and I caught hell when I got back to the dump, from the officers!

Armourers of the 878th Chemical Company attached to the 390th BG Framlingham fill napalm bombs, loaded on a USAAF M5 bomb trailer, 15 April 1945. (USAAF)

Base Utilities

When a new airfield was planned, one of the first tasks to be completed, during the establishment of the site's suitability, would be the assessment of service provision to the site. Most airfields were located in parts of the country that hitherto had little or no mains drainage and sometimes not even mains water supply. Depositing what amounted to small towns so swiftly in these locations required careful planning to avoid all sorts of public health issues arising. Once the go-ahead for construction was given, electricity, water supply and sewerage disposal infrastructure were more often than not the first construction jobs to be implemented.

After the war local communities often adopted utility supplies, normally with official sanction, after an airfield closed. For example, the sewerage site at Ridgewell continued to be used long after the airfield ceased to operate and served a local village for many years.

Water Supply

Prior to 1939 the procedure would have been to assess whether the local water authority could provide adequate fresh supplies to a new airfield. However, rapid expansion of both military and industrial requirements made it more difficult to obtain supplies this way. After 1939 other sources had to be investigated to provide an airfield with its own source of pure wholesome water, as even any existing supplies would prove inadequate. New sources would include drawing water from local rivers or, if necessary, the sinking of dedicated boreholes. Whatever the supply, one of the first structures to be installed would be the high-level water tower and pumping equipment. Pre-war stations once again had rather grand water tower designs, with the tank actually concealed behind a brick edifice.

Temporary stations normally had steel panel tanks supported on a girder framework 50ft to 60ft high. As these services often remained in use post-war, many survived a lot longer than other structures on abandoned airfields. As improvements to water supply in rural areas have occurred, many tanks have now been removed. Framlingham until very recently still had its tank, but it has now been dismantled even though the pump house site is still operated by the local water company.

The water tank would be sited to give best possible delivery, with a secure gravity flow to all parts of a station. With this tank normally placed either on the technical site or one of the communal sites. The average daily water requirement for a typical station was considered to be 100,000 gallons. The tank provided would be designed to give sufficient storage for peak period consumption, but as most tanks were in the 50,000 to 80,000-gallon range it must be assumed that some form of rationing would be implemented during times of emergency. The water distribution system around the camp was designed to provide sufficient quantity and pressure head for each end user, be that technical, domestic or fire service. Aside from the tank and pump house, the water system comprised of other facilities, in particular a chlorination plant for water treatment.

On pre-war stations all the water pumping and treatment equipment would be grouped together with the water tower. This group of buildings formed a works area along with extra stores and workshops operated by the Air Ministry Works Directorate (AMWD), the site maintenance section. This would normally be operated by civilians. Staff working here would be fully trained to monitor the water supply and make adjustments where necessary. On temporary stations these facilities could be a little more spread out depending on where the water supply was situated. Monitoring of issues essential to health, such as water quality, often fell to the medical detachment. According to records from the medical detachment assigned to the 381st BG at Ridgewell, between July and September 1943, the group had several outbreaks of illness attributed to poor water quality as no chlorination plant had been installed at the time. Equipment was duly ordered and installed but by the following July problems were still occurring. It wasn't until the divisional engineer inspected the chlorinator that it was realised that it was not working correctly due to an incorrect chemical balance.

One other form of water storage existed on most camps, although it was not for drinking. These were pond-like structures located at various areas on all sites, constructed for additional emergency water storage for fire fighting.

Once a familiar sight in the British landscape, airfield water tanks are now disappearing. Two of the few remaining examples on 8th AF sites are at Glatton and Metfield. Virtually all the steel tanks supplied to the Air Ministry in Britain were manufactured by Braithwaite of Newport in south Wales, who are still manufacturing tanks of a similar design to this day. Pictured is the tank at Glatton in 2008, one of the few original structures remaining at the airfield and now dedicated as a memorial. (Author)

Electricity

An adequate electrical supply would also be one of the first services to be installed on a new site, essential for contractors setting up the rest of their construction plant. For most Class A airfields the supply would be spurred into the site from an existing high voltage network. Robert Gould was a civilian electrical engineer during the Second World War. He was foreman of the construction department working for Edmondson's Electricity Corporation, starting work with them in 1937. Although working in the Wessex and Cotswold areas of southern England his experiences would be similar to those of engineers working in other areas of the country. He recalled that laying cables to new airfield sites was performed in a very hurried and 'shoddy' manner. Cables were normally brought in on poles but sometimes they were just laid along hedgerows, such was the speed with which they were expected to be installed, using a Fordson tractor to drag cables across country to sites.

This was often the first electricity supply to some areas, as few rural communities had mains electricity at that time. Some of these poor installations didn't come to light until years later, by which time supply lines had been absorbed into the National Grid. Local electricity boards had often adopted the infrastructure for domestic use. A lot of supply problems that plagued the networks in the post-war years were attributable to poorly installed wartime cabling.

Electricity was used for a multitude of tasks on an airfield: lighting of buildings, runway and approach lighting, wireless, radar, direction finding, machine and power tools, water and sewerage pumps and the ventilating plant. However, it was not normally used for heating or cooking.

Outside supply was normally taken at 11kV, occasionally 20kV, and transformed to 3.3kV for distribution. Voltages would have been at 240v for domestic supply or 415v three-phase supply for workshop plants. As sites grew in size the average demand rose from 100kW to 300kW, largely due to the requirements for airfield lighting. Standby power plants were normally provided for use in case of power cuts, but could only cater for essential services and were designed to throw off any overload beyond their standard capacity. Housed in a large brick building, usually situated on the main communal site, they were provisioned to have two or even three generating sets, but due to wartime shortages, most only ever received one set, normally rated around 185kVA.

Only certain buildings qualified for emergency supply as it would be impossible to supply all. Usually it would only be the control tower, briefing room, operations and speech broadcast buildings, airfield lighting, sewerage pumps and petrol installations that maintained supply. The base sick quarters would also sometimes be included in the list, but many often had their own emergency generator. Some buildings also were provided with emergency battery-powered lighting.

Station telephone systems were normally installed by the General Post Office (GPO), although contractors would often install the basic infrastructure during the construction of camps.

Sewerage

Most airfields constructed during the Second World War in Britain would have been provided with one and sometimes two sewage treatment plants. Those that weren't so equipped tended to be airfields that were never constructed or improved to the Class A standard, such as some of the smaller fighter stations and those constructed for short-period use like the advanced landing grounds prepared for the invasion of France in 1944. Leiston in Suffolk, home of the USAAF 8th AF 357th Fighter Group, was a good example, its sewage waste being collected by truck for disposal off site, often at a point where it could be used as fertiliser on local farmland. The father of local resident Bernie Fosdike drove a truck and Bernie remembered travelling with him to collect the contents of the 'honeypots' from Leiston!

On those sites that had mains sewerage disposal installed, the systems were of the single type, in that they only carried foul drainage and not storm water. Few buildings, due to the expediency of construction, had any form of guttering and in wet weather standing water and mud were constant companions for those travelling around a station.

Initial construction plans made no provision for mains drainage from domestic sites on dispersed camps; only the main airfield and communal sites were to be so provided. Distances between sites and relative heights were considered prohibitive for the efficient installation of sewerage systems. However, in 1942 drainage on domestic sites began to appear, due to a new type of pumping station being introduced that permitted longer runs of pipe to be laid.

A new enlarged standard of treatment plant was introduced by the Air Ministry during the war, and this may have been in response to public health issues that were beginning to emerge at airfields such as Podington. Coinciding with the arrival of the 92nd BG in September 1943, complaints started to emerge about the contamination of local water courses. The first incidences were at trout ponds at several locations close to the airfield, in particular Hinwick Hall, killing commercial fish and eel stocks. As the situation worsened, reports came in of the village becoming affected and contamination leading to the death of cattle on local farms. The problem was traced to untreated sewerage being released directly from one of the airfield sewerage sites, spreading into much of the locality.

One local resident, a Mr J. Graham of Elston Lodge, was similarly affected described the situation in correspondence to land agents on 28 December 1943:

> I have been at Hinwick during Christmas and there is an unholy stink in the grove and it actually reached the house ... It is undoubtedly a menace to the health of anybody living nearby.

The Air Ministry outwardly did very little, save making a few modifications to pipe work and outfall arrangements, although USAAF medical personnel did take samples and have them analysed in their laboratory. Behind the scenes however, it would seem that changes were being made at other airfields based on experience. The Podington situation continued for the duration, only stopping after the 92nd BG left in mid-1945. The ramifications of this particular situation, however, rumbled on for several years with the local MP, the Rural District Council, several government ministries and of course solicitors looking to apportion blame and gain compensation.

What the situation did suggest was that the sewerage disposal facilities initially provided on camps were nowhere near adequate once increased numbers of American servicemen arrived due to the expansion of heavy bomb groups.[2]

Boiler House

Due to their more compact layout, pre-war permanent stations normally had a central boiler house to provide all of their heating, cooking and hot water requirements. Buildings were sited close enough together to enable pipelines, normally laid below ground, to be run to most facilities. Once again the move to the dispersed layout of temporary stations made this difficult. Instead, individual solid fuel boiler rooms were constructed adjacent to any buildings requiring a constant supply of heat or hot water, such as mess halls and ablutions blocks. Some specialist workshops also had similar provision, such as paint and dope workshops and parachute stores, where heating was essential for their operation. Instructional buildings, where possible, were also heated in a similar manner. These smaller boiler units would supply the heat to operate calorifiers or small heat exchangers. Most of this equipment would have been of British supply to standard designs and installed by British contractors. Boilers would normally be maintained and operated by British civilian workers, often drawn from the local community.

Domestic Fuel

An airfield normally used three types of solid fuel for its domestic requirements, which were mostly heating and cooking: house coal, steam coal and coke. The Air Ministry made contracts with the Ministry of Fuel and Power on behalf of the USAAF. It was they who established the allocations to stations from the collieries. The authorised amount for winter consumption was 8lb per man per day. During the winter of 1944/45 a 50 per cent raise in allocation was provided due to the severity of the weather. Summer authorisations were considerably less.

Local transport companies were usually contracted to carry fuel from a nearby rail yard to a base. Most important in order of priority was coke, then house coal. The Quartermaster (QM) Company oversaw the delivery and distribution of solid fuel on each camp. Each dispersed site would have a walled or fenced coal yard and all supplies were strictly rationed and controlled, and as such became quite a valuable commodity with the capability of 'walking' if not monitored!

Salvage

Salvage reclamation or recycling was probably as important during the Second World War as it is now. All reusable materials were collected, sorted and passed on through a very efficient collection service to various part of the country. Salvage collection and organisation on the stations came under the control of the Quartermaster Company. Salvage was sorted into three classes; A, B and C. Class A included aluminium and other non-ferrous metals, plexi-glass, batteries and aircraft tyres and tubes. Class B covered several items, the most important being used aero engine oil, textiles, partly-used dry batteries and toothpaste tubes. Class C comprised waste paper, ferrous metals, scrap rubber, petrol cans, oil drums, leather, used motor oil and re-usable bottles.

Organisations on the base such as ordnance, engineering, and Sub-Depot supply either disposed of their salvage through their own channels or deposited it at the Quarter Master dump. Here it was segregated according to classification. Rubbish was picked up from the various dispersed sites of the camp by station utility staff and delivered to the dump, where recoverable salvage was removed. Anything not salvageable was either burned or buried. Such was the amount of salvage generated that on the average station, trucks often carried up to four loads a week to British disposal yards. Aluminium and plexi-glass were shipped by rail to British salvage centres specialising in that type of material. Waste paper was normally collected by British contractors. Receipts were obtained for all salvage and were forwarded to higher HQ where they formed part of the accounting process for the lend-lease system.

Site Maintenance

Due to the unique way in which the USAAF became established in Britain, airfield site maintenance was one area that constantly remained in British control throughout the

Second World War; USAAF T/O&Es never provided staff for maintaining someone else's home. The closest a bomb group got to having official maintenance personnel would normally be a few staff assigned within the Station Complement Squadron to oversee work of a more minor nature. Instead each airfield would have an AMWD team, headed by a British officer or NCO, normally an engineer. Under his control would be a staff of around twenty British civilians, undertaking or overseeing most of the maintenance work on a site.

Some bomb groups would set up a base utilities section drawing together those specialists from the Station Complement Squadron and some from squadrons that might be spared, to liaise and add extra manpower where required under the direction of the AMWD personnel.

As we have previously seen, on pre-war stations the AMWD maintenance works were located around the high-level water tower. On wartime airfields things were more rudimentary, usually with an area more reminiscent of a building site with huts and materials stored, waiting to be used.

Once the bomb groups started to expand in squadron strength, there was an additional strain put on accommodation and domestic structures. As well as the aforementioned problems with concrete, continuing camp construction and building remodelling became the norm on many sites through the war years. Building new hutting, showers and latrines or modifying interiors for such things as club use, as well as general plumbing, carpentry, electrical work and painting kept all the site maintenance tradesmen constantly busy. John Sloan had this to say about maintenance work at Podington:

> March 1945. In keeping with the changing season, the base continued to improve in appearance: street signs were installed; the 325th Squadron erected a distinguishing sign; signs appeared on Senior and Junior Officers messes. The Air Ministry undertook a building waterproofing program, spraying roofs with a bituminous black paint which

US maintenance crews repairing broken concrete on a taxiway at Thurleigh, 1 May 1943, under British supervision. The poor state of the surface can be seen in the foreground. (USAAF)

Ridgewell, Essex, looking north-east from the main entrance through the tech site. The Guardroom is the Nissen hut at an angle in the centre of picture nearest the camera. The group of buildings in the lower left half is the work services unit; building materials can be seen stored around the outside. Two high-level water tanks can be seen in the centre-left of picture and one of the hangars, top left. (USAAF)

glistened attractively in the spring sunlight. Fencing continued to be erected all over the base; the wits murmured that the Cole Porter hit 'Don't fence me in' might well be the 92nd Group theme song. None could deny that the base had never looked more attractive.[3]

As well as all of the building work, the utilities plant had to be maintained. Water and sewerage equipment needed to be kept in first-class order and the standby electrical generating sets serviced and running correctly in case they were required. All the heating, ventilation and air conditioning plants required occasional servicing and/or repair. Then there was the seasonal grounds maintenance: grass had to be regularly cut in summer and sometimes local farmers would be allowed to remove this for hay. Leaves and fallen trees and branches would have to be kept clear of taxiways in autumn, and snow and ice, in addition to their impact on water supplies, would have to be dealt with in winter. Art Watson said about Horham:

When we arrived at Horham, the base had been occupied by the RAF, so we found it in a very liveable condition and it accommodated our need very well. We had British and Irish maintenance people who helped keep the base in excellent shape.

4

Headquarters Site

On pre-war permanent stations, the headquarters was usually the first building to be reached once passing through the main gate. Normally facing out from the camp, it comprised a two-storey office block, flanked either side by a single-storey annex. To the rear would have been a single-storey operations block. Sometimes, as at Bassingbourn, a meteorological unit extension would be added above the second storey. The building's function would obviously have been laid out to suit RAF organisational requirements, but would have contained all the necessary elements to suit the USAAF once they moved in. Inside there would have been offices for the CO and his staff as well as accommodation for finance and other administrative departments. The operations block would have rated a higher security status, as that was where all flying missions would have been planned and co-ordinated.

When the move towards dispersing elements of an airfield was first implemented, the headquarters was one of the first site types to be relocated in such a way. On temporary stations the headquarters, sometimes called the admin site, would be situated close to the main airfield. Occasionally this would be as an adjunct to the main site as at Great Ashfield, or, at stations such as Ridgewell, as a separate unit a little distance away. It would also have warranted the highest security status on an airfield, with its compact form helping to preserve that necessity, and was guarded at all times.

The headquarters understandably would have been the nerve centre of a station, home of the group's management team. It would have been here, under direction from Division HQ, that mission planning and preparation would have taken place and been overseen. It would not just be the operational function that would have centred on this site, however; the complete day-to-day running of a station would have been controlled from offices within the headquarters.

A headquarters site on a temporary station would have contained a small number of buildings, and would be very much more functional and utilitarian than on the pre-war stations. The structures on the headquarters site would have centred on an operations block: a large, windowless, single-storey building of brick or concrete construction. Fronting the operations block and linked via a corridor would have been a pair of station offices, either Nissen huts or temporary brick buildings. Adjacent to this group would be another hut in a style and size similar to the others constructed. This would have been provided originally as a crew briefing room. A speech broadcast building would often stand close by, housing the equipment to run the tannoy or public address system around the station for communicating with personnel in all departments. The last building, normally placed with the headquarters grouping would be the bombsight building, another highly secure unit.

As with all other areas of the station, the headquarters site would also contain its own picket post, latrine block, electrical substation, coal store and blast shelters, affording staff working within its less sturdy buildings a little protection in the event of an air raid.

An aerial picture of the HQ site at Ridgewell, Essex. The large flat-roofed building is the operations block, the twin Nissen huts are the station offices, the single Nissen the briefing room. The smaller flat-roofed building at the top is the Norden bombsight building. The speech broadcast building is the small flat-roofed building on the right-hand side, next to the operations block. (USAAF)

Group Headquarters

The main occupants of the site would be drawn from the bomb group's headquarters unit. Like all of the units that made up a bomb group, it was structured by allocations according to the T/O&Es and contained all the necessary staff to fill and support all of its roles. Normally a headquarters unit would be tabled to have twenty-nine officers and seventy-four enlisted men. In practice, not all members of each headquarters unit worked on the headquarters site; a senior officer may have had an office there but commanded a unit working somewhere else on the camp.

A bomb group was structured such that below the commanding officer there would normally be two assistants or executive officers, one for ground operations and one for air operations. All USAAF units from group level upwards would have a general staff of four reporting through the executive officers to the CO. The standard army staff positions were personnel, intelligence, operations and supply; at group level they were usually referred to as (S for staff) S-1, S-2, S-3 and S-4 respectively. These four senior staff officers headed departments that handled the administration and operation of all the elements of the group.[1]

The S-1 department administered everything that affected the living and working conditions of officers and men within the group. It was responsible for securing and assigning all the personnel required. It organised all the things a personnel department would be expected to do, such as wages, personnel records, training and awards. S-1 also oversaw the work of the Special Services Squadron, the chaplain and the Red Cross, as these elements were connected with the moral and pastoral care of personnel on the station.

Another department that came under the control of S-1 was statistical control. It was they who maintained the status boards in the operations room, recording aircraft and crew strength at all times. They also maintained the statistics of all that occurred on a base, such as aircraft and crew losses, quantities of fuel used and ordnance dropped etc. All this information would be passed back through the chain of command to 8th HQ, to gain a clear picture of the progress of the whole operation in Britain.

To ensure that all domestic facilities were kept in good order on the camp, a small administrative inspectors department kept a check on the relevant departments, such as the messes and living accommodation, at regular intervals.

The S-2 section was tasked with co-ordinating and recording all intelligence material pertinent to the operation of the group. When the US entered the Second World War, they did not possess the necessary intelligence services essential to conducting a war in Europe, and the USAAF had to play catch-up very quickly. Fortunately much of the pioneering groundwork performed by Ira Eaker and his staff during their initial visit in early 1942 had been to establish close links with the RAF for the provision of such facilities to train the necessary USAAF personnel in such matters. The S-2 section of every group worked hard to collect as much material for this task as it could and pass it back to higher authorities. This included photographic intelligence and reconnaissance, post-mission interrogation or debriefing of air crew and collating all aspects of enemy operations necessary for mission planning. S-2 personnel were heavily involved with day-to-day issues of mission planning and implementation and it would be S-2 staff that carried out the briefing of air crews prior to missions. As well as combat crews, S-2 staff would often give lectures and talks to the wider group personnel to inform on the progress of the war from the group's perspective.

S-3 was the group operations department, and they were housed entirely in the operations block over the course of the working day. It was they who established the framework of a mission once the target objectives had been received from Division HQ. The operations team worked closely with the group bombardier; the whole structure of the mission, route planning, lead crew selection and so on, would be based on providing the most effective means of dropping bombs as accurately on target as possible. For this task they worked very closely with the S-2 intelligence staff.

The S-4 department performed the staff functions pertaining to the supply of all items necessary for the group to operate, from pens to planes and everything in between. S-4 oversaw the quartermaster and technical supply element of the Sub-Depot and was often caught in the fight between supply requirements for the group's objectives and those of the Sub-Depot's controlling organisation, 8th AF Service Command.

A bomb group HQ was also tabled to have various other specialist staff officers in sufficient numbers and relevance who all reported, via the executive officers, back to the CO. Many of these would have to create their own departments using the staff pooled from all the component units of the group. Specialist staff usually comprised an armament and chemical officer, a communications officer, a group surgeon (from the medical corps), a group dental surgeon (from dental corps), a weather officer, an engineering officer and a chaplain (from chaplain corps).

Group HQ normally also contained a small number of rated flying officers of which the CO was usually one.

Operations Block

As stated previously, the operations block was a windowless, airtight structure with air-locked entrances. Therefore an essential element for the day-to-day existence within the operations block was an efficient ventilation, heating and air conditioning system, linked with the anti-gas measures. This would have been one of the few buildings on an airfield to have such provision.

The operations block was one of the most secure structures on the site, containing offices for the intelligence staff and their records as well as the main operations room. Sometimes it would also have contained a small canteen and toilets, but normally just rooms for wireless telegraphy, teleprinter, batteries, the private branch exchange (PBX), station telephone exchange and a meteorological office. As the building was one where women, either WAAFs or WACs, often worked as plotters or telephonists, there would be one annex containing women's WCs as well as two others, one containing heating boilers and the other air conditioning plant. The main operations room would have been dominated by the operations board along one wall providing up-to-date information on the group's aircraft, aircrew and their operational status.

Mission Planning

Orders usually came through on teleprinter from Division HQ in the evening indicating a mission and a chosen target for the following day. Division HQ would have been informed of each group's likely combat strength after returning from the previous mission. As most missions involved only three of the four squadrons, one rested in rotation, unless a maximum effort was requested. Therefore the first thing to happen would be the flying of red flags, indicating an impending mission to the relevant squadrons. Telephone calls to and from the base would now be limited and monitored and guards increased at the HQ site.

S-2 and S-3 departments would work hand-in-hand on mission preparation. Intelligence staff would busy themselves by interpreting orders from higher command into workable solutions for the mission. They would bring together all of the material they held on the proposed target such as photographs and other reconnaissance material. Other information useful for planning the likely route to and from the target would also be assessed, such as known enemy anti-aircraft gun positions, fighter strengths and locations.

Access to the operations room, normally tightly controlled, would become even more so with only those directly involved with mission preparation allowed anywhere near. Staff would normally work through the night, often having last-minute variations to plans sent in from Division HQ. Once the plan framework was in place, the route would be posted on the large map board on one wall of the operations room, normally by the S-2 duty officer.

Group navigational officers and bombardiers would by now be involved with the planning: briefing the lead crews ahead of the other crews. This was often the case if they were acting in a pathfinder role using some of the later electronic navigational and target acquisition devices such as GEE, OBOE or the H2X ('mickey') system.

Information based on target details would be passed to various departments. The ordnance section would prepare the bomb type and loads for each aircraft. Distances would be given to the squadrons to enable them to tell the fuel dump operators how much fuel to deliver. If the mission was to be a maximum effort then every effort would

401st BG operations room
Deenthorpe, 13 January
1945. Note the system of air
conditioning and ventilation
ducting on the walls.
(USAAF)

The official caption states: On the telephone is S/Sgt John H. Finitzer, Cleveland Ohio, checking on details of weather and notifying ordnance to load up the ships, while Lt Co. Addison E. Baker, Akron Ohio, calls the combat crews over the public address system to attend the briefing. Some of the many details to be attended to before B-24 Liberators of the 93rd BG take off again over enemy territory. Hardwick, April 1943. (USAAF)

be put into getting as many serviceable aircraft prepared as possible. All this information would need to be disseminated to wherever it was required to pull the mission preparation together. Carlton M. Smith, a photographic interpreter remembered, his part in mission planning with the 303rd BG at Molesworth:

> I dealt with mission preparation and the paper war that supported combat. The dedicated performance of duty by the ground support units cannot be over emphasized or praised. By special permission I flew five missions and thus experienced the combat side of the war. Flying as an observer or photographer, I was in various positions in the plane and in various slots in the formation, from deputy lead to tail-end Charlie. I returned better prepared to brief the bombardiers on target identification, interrogate crews on mission results and interpret the strike attack photos.
>
> On two occasions I put the whole package together over a period of almost 24 hours. When the field order came in around 0200 hours, I prepared the bombardier's briefing and conducted it about 0600. I flew the mission (8–10 hours) and after the quick shot of Four Roses or whatever it was, I interrogated the crews. By that time the strike attack photos were in from the photo lab and it was time to put on my photo interpreter's glasses. Several hours later I issued the PI Report to the Group and Squadron Commanders. I hadn't felt any lack of sleep during this time because there was so much activity and so much to do, but eventually I sacked out like a rock. Unlike the crew I had just flown with, I could sleep in the next day – they weren't as fortunate.
>
> After a few hours of well-deserved sack time, they were aroused with the familiar you're flying today. Breakfast at 0400; briefing at 0500. The Intelligence did a lot of report writing which eventually became history-recording. I did my share of it, but I wished I had kept more notes and was more mature at that time.[2]

Others, such as the meteorological staff, would have been preparing their charts, assessing the expected weather conditions along the route and over the target in readiness for briefing the air crews. Operations room staff would prepare the large map boards with route details and fighter and flak known locations for setting up in the briefing room. Once the map was assembled in the briefing room a curtain would be drawn across it to keep it from prying eyes. Beforehand it would have been ensured that all blackouts were in place on all the briefing room windows.

Once the operation planning was at a suitably advanced stage the briefing officers were called in. They would have to familiarise themselves with the operational details of the mission, prior to briefing air crews. Once a mission was underway many of the planners would try to get some sleep before the aircraft returned. Later, before the aircraft landing, they had to prepare for debriefing the fliers regarding the events of the day. Those working the day shift would either monitor the progress of the mission or catch up on the daily task of administering and filing the paperwork from previous operations.

Briefing Room

As first designed, the purpose-built briefing room was part of the HQ complex, usually beside the operations block. As station strength grew this often proved too small and briefings were carried out on or near the technical site, sometimes in a new, larger building although in some instances one of the crews' locker and drying rooms was used.

The briefing took place after breakfast and prior to dressing for the mission. Some groups had primary briefings for all crew members and then secondary briefings for navigators, radio operators, etc. to give them the specific mission maps, routes and radio frequencies. In some groups, gunners attended a separate briefing in which expectation of enemy aircraft opposition was assessed. In certain instances, one of the officers briefed the gunners at the plane just before take-off; gunners usually arrived at their aircraft earlier to be able to mount and set up their guns and perform ammunition checks. Standard operational procedures varied from base to base and group to group, often dependent on the CO's preference.

2nd Lt John Borchert of the 18th Weather Squadron, served on detached service with three bomb groups, the 306th at Thurleigh, the 93rd at Hardwick and the 392nd at Wendling, as well as 2nd Air Division HQ. His recollections of a typical briefing:

> Pre-dawn briefings, dead-serious business as the group navigator and intelligence went over the route and target material with the flying officers and crews, and I laid out the weather forecast. For the sake of order, the group weather men like me were not allowed to deviate from the division/bomber command forecasts for the mission route

Photographic intelligence staff inspect aerial photos in preparation for another mission, 379th BG Kimbolton, 12 March 1945. (USAAF)

379th BG Kimbolton control boards in the operations room, 29 January 1944. The boards contained all the essential information about the station, the one in the centre about the airfield and the large board on the right about all aircraft and air-crew status details. (USAAF)

and target. However, we were allowed to present our own forecasts for our local base weather at takeoff and return.

On a few occasions my synoptic analysis, and resulting forecast, were not consistent with those at higher headquarters. On those few occasions there was tension-relieving laughter when I'd go through the headquarters' route and target forecast and explain it, and then present a local forecast which said that obviously I didn't think they could possibly take off for the mission. There were always good reasons why the forecasters disagreed, and it actually gave the crews more confidence to get some insight into the complexity of the situation. A couple of times our commander called the Division commander and asked him what was wrong: [stating] 'My weather man knew damn well this mission was going to have to be scrubbed.'

The debriefing when a mission returned was another memorable event. The guys were always exhausted; sometimes effusive, sometimes sombre, depending on the success of the mission. Sometimes they knew they had demolished the target; other times they knew they had missed, or were even uncertain that they had bombed the right location; sometimes they were just purely uncertain of any results, pending the post-mission reconnaissance photos. They were always interested in the weather and anxious to talk about it, tell me what had been right and what had been wrong; and we'd interpret it together. It was a priceless teaching experience.

Just before the arrival of the air crews back at the briefing rooms, the interrogating officers were assembled and given their own overview of the mission to enable them to be able to extract the correct sorts of information during questioning. Once the air crews had returned to the briefing room it could often descend into a mass of noisy confusion as relief spread through the returnees, especially if it had been a difficult mission. It was here that the skill of the interrogating officer came into play as he had to keep on subject by asking specific questions and not allow himself to be distracted by peripheral chatter. Information such as flak density and fighter tactics, weather conditions and details about aircraft that were lost from the group or other groups, such as any parachutes seen, were all the sorts of detail that an interrogator needed. All of this information was gathered, collated and later assessed and cross-referenced to enable a detailed picture of the mission to appear.

Visual target bombing information would be backed up by evidence from the aircraft strike cameras once the photographs were developed. Gunners would give their version

Pre-mission briefing, 390th BG, Framlingham. Preparation for briefings was completed under total secrecy but once in the briefing the better briefing officers tried to introduce a little 'theatre' into their presentations to make the information a little more memorable. (USAAF)

of any aerial combat and any claims of enemy aircraft shot down. These would be logged and later verified or discounted after analysis of all the data supplied. Once the interrogation was completed all of the information was assimilated and passed on to divisional HQ for further assessment. Often as crews were arriving back at the briefing room for interrogation they were given a shot of whisky, and there would also frequently be coffee and doughnuts or sandwiches waiting for hungry crews. The following from the medical detachment diary of the 381st BG Ridgewell provides an interesting view of the practice:

> The liquor ration was issued to combat crews at the briefing block hut just before they were interrogated. Most of them seemed to like the idea, but I am not convinced that it has the real value, nor am I convinced of the idea of having the medical department associated with a bottle of whiskey. At the present time we are doing about as much catering as we are medical work and at every mission we dole out carbohydrates, coffee, cookies and now whiskey.[3]

One of the American Red Cross (ARC) operations was the 'Clubmobile' programme, delivering welcome doughnuts and coffee to service personnel at their various postings. Using requisitioned British buses, fitted out with the necessary doughnuts-making equipment, many visited USAAF airfields, providing much needed refreshment.

Angela Petesc arrived in Britain in May 1943. In her memoirs she described the daily life of being a member of the ARC in a series of letters home to her family in Chicago. For a while in 1944 she operated a Clubmobile around Sudbury in Suffolk, where she had a lot of contact with air crews. She explained that at an airfield they visited (possibly Sudbury Suffolk) they transferred their doughnuts, coffee and other supplies from the Clubmobile to a crew room, so they could provide refreshments during debriefing. She described how she and her crew had to 'sweat out' the return of the bombers from a mission along with the ground crews. Describing how sullen the crews were when they first entered the briefing, she felt rewarded after they received their warm coffee and food, and was much relieved to see how their work seemed to lift the men's spirits.[4]

Being a Red Cross girl was not a task suited for all, and girls were carefully selected for the task. For most of the time they had to provide a cheery welcoming face wherever they were working, often working to keep a light-hearted atmosphere, but they also had to be ever watchful and judge the situation correctly, for there were many times that such joviality was totally inappropriate. Girls had to be on their guard not to misjudge the timing of comments when interacting with their customers, especially at times of high stress.

After interrogation, air crews handed in their flight equipment at the relevant store and were then free to relax somewhere like the combat library, a room set aside for crews to unwind post-mission, or to go and get a hot meal in the combat mess.Many just needed a good night's sleep.

Station Offices

These buildings would have contained the head offices for the four general staff officers' sections and also sometimes those for some of the specialist staff officers. One side of the block was also normally the location of the CO's office and sometimes his quarters and those of the executive officers. One more department normally operating from the station offices, though not strictly part of the headquarters unit was the finance section. Not all groups were allocated a finance section, but where they were attached to a group, such as the 390th at Framlingham, they worked in close co-operation with the S-1 section. Many of the men working in finance sections were drawn directly from equivalent civilian occupations and provided with minimal military training. Often they were somewhat older than the average GI.

The finance section's main task was the handling of wages and other financial allotments to personnel. Around a quarter of a million dollars in cash would be brought to each camp every month from a local British bank to make up the wages. Of that, almost half was sent home to the US by servicemen to their families using a money order system. In addition to that, the average monthly deposits in the soldiers' savings fund and cash purchase of war bonds could often exceed $15,000. The finance section oversaw all of these transactions. Art Watson recalled the procedure for being paid at Horham:

> Pay was dispersed on the last day of the month, generally. We were paid in a room off of the supply room in our squadron area. The first Sgt of the squadron and an Officer would have the men line up by last name and would dispense the money due to the individual. Some of the squadrons had a man stand by with a gun as a guard.

It was also the finance section's job to acquaint all new arrivals with the British pre-decimalisation currency system in use at the time. During the Second World War, the British pound was stabilised at $4.03. This meant that the shilling was worth 20¢, the threepenny bit a nickel and the penny roughly 2¢. In addition to British currency they also at times had to deal with those from other Allied countries, especially when some of the close co-operation missions were flown involving countries such as Russia.

Another office that became established and evolved during the course of the war was the public relations department. Normally the task would be given to an officer from intelligence. Its inception at group level came about to offset much of the bad press the 8th was getting about its mounting losses in Europe. Due to tight censorship GIs were unable to write about their exploits and so it was felt that an official department was required to fill the gap and put events, as they unfurled, in a more positive light. Much use was made of army and air force 'in-house' papers such as *Stars and Stripes* and *Yank*, to positively promote the activities in Europe as well as elsewhere. In fact the USAAF were very good at recording events in Britain as they occurred; many of the photographs in this publication bear testament to this fact!

As well as stills photography, at a higher level the 8th AF made use of publicity from the silver screen. Much use was made of the skills and talents of Hollywood and the USAAF even formed a motion picture unit, employing many famous names from both

Pay day at Ridgewell 381st BG, September 1943. (USAAF)

sides of the camera. Among other stars, Clark Gable was based in Britain with the 8th AF, primarily at Polebrook. Gable, who had joined up after the loss of his wife Carol Lombard in a plane crash, was considered too old for combat, although he did fly on at least two missions. However, he mainly utilised his charismatic personality both on and off screen to help with the training of air gunners and on general morale-boosting visits.

Many officially sponsored propaganda films were made in all theatres of the war to explain to the folks back home how things were progressing. Then, as now, these films were often used to put some positive spin on things when they weren't going so well. One of the most famous films of this nature was the original *Memphis Belle*, produced by noted Hollywood director William Wyler. During the first year of the 8th AF's strategic daylight campaign, losses to air crews were so great that it was considered by some to be impossible to complete a tour of twenty-five missions. The film was produced to sell the idea of daylight precision bombing at a time when the whole concept was thought to be flawed and was at risk of being abandoned. Wyler was brought in to try to explain what was going on to American citizens thousands of miles away from the fighting. The result was hailed as a hard-hitting masterpiece, much of it filmed by Wyler and his film crews on actual missions. The difficulty faced by aircrew was savagely brought home to everyone by the fact that at least two of Wyler's film crew were also lost on combat missions during filming. The starring aircraft herself, of course, went on to be an American icon, now residing at the USAF museum at Dayton, Ohio.

Bombsight Store

As we have seen, a vital component of the strategic bombing campaign was the Norden bombsight. Because of the importance and sensitive nature of the technology, the Norden bombsight was a closely guarded secret. Nevertheless, it didn't stop Britain, early in the war, from trying to obtain the sight for use by the RAF. Having failed to get anywhere through normal diplomatic channels, the British Prime Minister, Neville Chamberlain, was persuaded to write to President Roosevelt to apply a little more pressure, so important the device was thought to be. Attempts were also made to trade British secrets such as ASDIC/Sonar for the sight using the lend-lease agreement.

10 Downing Street
Whitehall
25 August 1939

My dear Mr President

The secretary of state for air informs me that the United States Navy
Department have developed a new type of automatic air bombsight known
as the Norden bombsight, and I understand that this sight (together
perhaps with a similar development of the United States Army Air
Corps) is the most efficient instrument of its kind in existence. We
are therefore most anxious to obtain details of the sight and have
enquired urgently through our Air Attaché in Washington whether they
can be given to us. For reasons which I can readily imagine the Air
Authorities of the United States have not felt able to accede to our
request...
... Should the war, which threatens break out, my advisors, tell me
that we would obtain a greater immediate increase in our effective
power if we had the Norden bombsight at our disposal than by any
other means we can foresee. Air power is, of course, a relatively new
weapon, which is so far untried on a large scale; there is a danger of
unrestricted air attack, which we for our part would never initiate. I
am however most anxious to do all in my power to lessen the practical
difficulties which may arise in operations even against legitimate
military targets, and I feel that in air bombardment accuracy and
humanity really go together. For this reason again I am certain that
you would render the greatest service if you could enable us to make
use of the magnificent apparatus which your Services have developed.

Yours Sincerely
Neville Chamberlain[5]

However, Sumner Welles, one of FDR's trusted foreign policy advisors drafted a reply for
FDR, indicating that the British authorities were not going to get hold of the Norden any
time soon.

August 31, 1939

My Dear Mr Prime Minister

The initial survey which I have made of the situation and which I have
myself studied very carefully leads me to the conclusion that under
the existing legislation of this Government the request you make could
not be granted unless the sight desired by the British Government were
made available to all other governments at the same time it was made
available to Great Britain. This certainly would not be in the interest
to the United States, nor for that matter, I believe you will agree, in
the interest of Great Britain...

Believe me
      Yours very sincerely
                        FDR[5]

All was to no avail, and it was not until the US became involved in the war that some of the secrets of the Norden were revealed. Speaking in a taped interview some years after the war, former chief of staff George C. Marshall gave a little more insight into the reasoning behind what appears initially to have been a strange decision of FDR's advisors not to let Great Britain have access to the Norden bombsight.

There was a great concern at the time among US politicians that FDR might give too many secrets away to Britain. With the US not being in the war at the time they understandably considered it folly to give away materiel and secrets to things they might very well need themselves shortly. Marshall and others considered offering the Norden to be one step too many. They were not only concerned it might fall into the hands of a potential enemy (both Nazi Germany and the Japanese were mentioned), but worse: if British authorities had access to it they would be obliged to let the French, as their ally, have access to it as well. It seems that elements within the US government of the time considered this to be even more dangerous than it being obtained by the two previously mentioned enemies![6]

Eventually, of course, once the US entered the war information on the Norden did get traded. It had to be; one of the things that the bombsight required once in service was a secure maintenance and storage facility, and due to it being a high precision instrument this required the provision of special conditions.

The USAAF had already designed purpose-built structures on US bases for storage of the Norden. Initially these were wooden structures with internal strong rooms. As its potential began to be realised a type of concrete second-generation vault started to appear. This led to a requirement that similar facilities be provided on each bomber station the USAAF would inhabit in Britain. The Air Ministry had to develop a standard building type for this function and implement their construction. It is from this second-generation US vault that diagram 1906/43, the standard bombsight building design, evolved. The UK type, however, provided a larger maintenance facility as well as storage.

Due to the bombsight's top-secret status, it was decided the best place to locate the store was the HQ site, and many stations, including Podington, Framlingham and Wendling were thus provisioned. From mid-1943 the security level on the Norden site was downgraded from 'secret' to 'restricted'. This may be one reason why on some of the latter airfields constructed, such as Debach and Snetterton Heath, the bombsight store starts to appear on the technical site instead. Because the shop had to be warm in order to calibrate the sights, the building was heated and kept at a constant temperature. Like the operations block, the building was also air conditioned and had a ventilation and extraction system to keep the air as clean as possible to avoid dust and dirt damaging any of the sight's intricate workings. Art Watson was a bombsight technician at Horham:

> My job was maintenance on the Auto Pilots and Bombsights. The bombsight was the top secret of the Air Force, so every time we installed a bombsight for a mission, we had to be taken to the ship by an armed guard, and he stayed with the ship until the crew designated for the mission arrived. This later changed and we didn't need the guard because the clearance was changed to confidential instead of secret. We had a vault that was for storage and also was the shop in which we worked. It was all concrete and had air filtration and air conditioning, so that the dust or the condensation did not affect the efficiency of the sights.

While any aircraft fitted with a Norden bombsight was on the ground, the sight had to be removed and locked away. Later in the war every, not aircraft was so fitted, but normally only the lead and deputy lead aircraft within each squadron would have one. The procedure then became such that all other aircraft flying with the group would drop their bombs visually, once the lead aircraft had acquired the target and released their ordnance.

Norden bombsight building at Debach, June 2005. The Norden bombsight store only appears on sites inhabited by or provisioned for the USAAF. If a building of this type is seen on a British airfield it would be a clear indicator that the site was allocated or used by any of the USAAF bomber groups, heavy or medium. (Author)

A bombsight measured about 16in long, 10in wide and 10in tall. The complete sight comprised two main pieces: the stabiliser and the bombsight. The stabiliser on which the sight mounted was fixed in the aircraft and normally stayed in position as it was linked to the autopilot and other flight control systems. It was the bombsight optical head assembly that was removed after each flight.

A group's supply of bombsights at any one time was limited, certainly not enough for each aircraft, and probably fewer than twenty. That would give enough for two aircraft per squadron as well as a number of spares. The building as provided would never have been big enough to accommodate many more and provide workshop facilities as well.

Bombsight mechanics were often required to make major repairs on the instrument. Because of the violent manoeuvring after a bomb drop and rough landings due to damaged aircraft, the sights were often out of adjustment. There was a caging device that was used to protect the sighting mechanism and gyroscope, but this was not 100 per cent effective. When sights came in for repair, the procedure was to visually inspect the exterior. Damage was assessed to determine if they warranted further inspection. If exterior damage was so great and could not easily be put in order, the sight was shelved for possible use for parts. The sight would now be tested for accuracy by mounting it on a heavy cast-iron calibration stand. The bombsight had to be set perfectly level to be zeroed and calibrated, using a mirror and bubble level. This was a difficult procedure and was hard to maintain due to vibrations from heavy trucks and planes taking off and landing nearby. Someone, however, had the idea of putting a small deep saucer-type dish with a quantity of mercury in it under the sight and this became an 'ever-level' mirror. Art Watson continues:

As maintenance men, we had to work in shifts and handled the bombsights as precious watches. Before each mission, we were given the number of sights and the

Inside a bombsight building, this is the 386th BG 9th AF at Great Dunmow in Essex but is typical of all Norden maintenance operations in the 8th and 9th AF, 20 August 1944. The instrument calibration stand is in the centre. Again note the HVAC ducting on the ceiling. (USAAF)

number of the planes in which they were to be installed. We checked each sight and made sure that it was ready for the mission. After the sights were ready, we would take them out to the planes and install them and recheck them. They were then attached to the stabilizer gyro and then covered with a cloth cover and they were ready to go. The bombardier came with the crew and he rechecked the sight and stabilizer gyro for any possible problem. When the crew arrived, we went back to the vault and worked on other sights. Most of the equipment that we used was standard hand tools, but we had separate tools to check the sight for general maintenance. We also had a 'grid stand' which was used to check the precession of the gyro that was part of the bombsight. When the ship returned we were at the hardstand to retrieve the sights and return them to the vault and recheck them. We were also responsible for the maintenance of the Automatic pilot. Much of our time was spent on the ship cleaning and adjusting the AFCE (automatic flight control equipment). Each of the men were well trained in their job and we had very few problems on the mission because they were well maintained.

I was assigned to the 335 Sq, but we were all working from one shop with one officer in charge. Though we were assigned to squadrons, we worked as a group entity.

90,000 Norden bombsights were manufactured during the war, each weighing about 40lb and costing over $1 billion. Despite the controversy surrounding the instruments' effectiveness, there is little doubt that it was a very important step in the development of ballistics delivery and control systems.

Aircraft Dispersals

The vast open expanses of a British Second World War airfield can be fairly unforgiving places at any time of year. Open to the elements, they are exposed whatever the weather conditions. With little in the way of shelter, this was the 'workshop' allocated to ground crews of the four bomb squadrons that made up each heavy bomb group of the 8th AF.

Concrete and Structures

The main 'structure' available was the concrete hardstand. Although these tended to be spread out equally as best as possible around the perimeter track, they were approximately divided into groups, initially three and later four, each group being given over to a single squadron. Aside from these areas of concrete the only other fixed structures this far out on the airfield were a few scattered Nissen huts. Generally there were one or two huts per squadron area. Paul Kovitz recalls:

> Our Squadron offices for 569th squadron were between hardstands 16 and 19 at Framlingham. There were two Nissan huts, one for engineering and one for supply staff.

Unfortunately this small amount of accommodation provided nowhere near enough shelter. With most airfields that were inhabited by the 8th having only two hangars, they were usually reserved for repairing the most severely damaged aircraft. Even on the older stations that had up to five hangars, there still would not be enough covered accommodation for up to seventy-two aircraft. Besides, the logistics of moving aircraft

The 401st BG at Deenthorpe, 12 January 1945, with several B-17s undergoing maintenance outside, illustrating the less than ideal conditions ground crews had to work in for much of the time. Typical ground-crew tents can be seen, providing a little respite from the elements. (USAAF)

around the airfield and frequently towing them in and out of hangars (buildings not much wider than the aircrafts' wingspans) would have been virtually impossible to co-ordinate, leaving little time to fly missions! Due to material and labour constraints there was little that could be done to improve covered space for working on the aircraft, so the next best thing was provided: shelter for the men.

The whole American concept of strategic bombing was based on flying daylight missions to enable precise target acquisition, which meant that take off for missions would, on average, be around 8 a.m. depending on distance to the target. This would require ground crews to work at night to ready an aircraft for the coming mission.

Quantities of standard US Army 16ft x 16ft 'pyramid' tents started to appear around the dispersals. During downtime and the long nights, these tents provided somewhere to warm up or brew some coffee. Where there were insufficient quantities of tents then the resourcefulness and ingenuity of personnel came to the fore. Complete 'line shacks' were created from surplus materials, with some quite elaborate examples appearing. Eventually nearly every hardstand was equipped with a home away from the regular barrack site. The tents were often individualised to the ground crews' taste, with flooring and walls made more robust with timber salvaged from surplus bomb and spare parts crates. Many started to sport homemade heating systems, usually constructed from oil drums and designed to use waste engine oil as fuel.

Paul Kovitz explained that ground crews would often mix the oil with 100-octane fuel in a tank outside the tent, then pipe it into a homemade stove made from a 50-gallon oil drum. The mixture would then be dripped onto a hot plate at the bottom of the stove, providing a more than adequate source of warmth! There was also very little provision for latrines out on the far flung corners of the airfield; usually the most convenient 'conveniences' were placed close to the hangars on either the main or secondary technical sites. This situation led some to take things a step further in providing temporary toilet facilities closer to the work area. In his story, Ken Lemmons described how he constructed a 'one holer' out of some bomb boxes over a flowing ditch near the flight line at Thorpe Abbotts to create a convenience![1]

Some shacks ended up being more comfortable than the regular billets, and due to the distances that were involved in travelling across the airfield, many ground crew ended up living at their hardstands most of the time, only travelling to use mess halls, ablutions facilities or for social functions. Crews also became fairly self sufficient and often provided their own meals. Eggs and chickens were traded with local farmers, pheasants and other forms of game were 'acquired' on occasions, and all supplemented by items from standard issue ration packs or other tinned goods that might be traded with a sympathetic member of the mess hall staff. Air crew, while waiting to board their aircraft before a mission, also appreciated the warmth the shacks afforded, especially when due to weather or other situations, delays to the schedule were incurred.

Not only did much of this maintenance work have to be carried out at night, but also under blackout conditions and sometimes in the most severe weather. Usually only the light of a torch could be used to see by. In extreme cases a tarpaulin would be pulled over the offending area of an aircraft to permit the use of more light or to give a little more shelter from the elements.

When the aircraft departed for a mission, ground crews used the time until the aircraft returned to catch up on sleep, meals, ablutions or necessary personal affairs and of course, 'sweat it out', hoping their individual charge would make it back to base. Arthur Ferwerda, a crew chief with the 409th BS, 93rd BG, describes life at Hardwick:

> The temperature could go as low as about -18 degrees F. This was not as low as we had sometimes in my home state of New Jersey. but when you are out in this weather all day and part of the night and then factor in the dampness that was always present in England, the coldness just got into your system and didn't leave. We used to build a small

Tail repairs to a B-17. The official caption states: 'as soon as the *Hit Parade* rolled to a stop, badly damaged after a raid, ground crews covered the tail in tarpaulins to protect themselves from the driving rain. Standing on scaffold is Cpl N.E. Welch from Melder, Louisiana, and assisting him is Pfc. G. Pairan from Lancaster, Ohio.' (USAAF)

fire and spend a few minute there to warm our hands. As you stood in front of the fire one could watch the steam being evaporated from your clothing. The only way that we could get the grease and oil off our hands was by dipping them into a bucket of 100 octane gasoline. Of course our hands got a little cleaner but as the gasoline evaporated very quickly, it only made them colder. We lived with the ship and the only respite we got was when the ship was on a mission. It gave us chance to take a shower (cold water). Later on we rigged up a boiler from a bombed out home in Norwich and set it up for heating some shower water. It also gave us some time to write a letter, take our laundry to the quartermaster hut to be sent out. That was one break we got. The women of Norwich would do laundry and were paid by the army.

Staff Sergeant Leroy Keeping, a power turret specialist with the 570th BS, 390th BG, has similar recollections from his time based at Framlingham:

I was here from July 43 to Nov 45, all that time I worked at the 570th Squadron hardstands. I worked on power turrets, ball, upper and chin. Working on drive systems, electric motor changes and wiring, and more rarely, worked on the hydraulic systems, which were generally very reliable. I also spent time checking and calibrating guns with gun sights at the firing in butts on opposite side of the airfield.

We worked out at the hardstands, two near the road to Parham, stand Nos 44 and 45 and two near the T2 hangar. All the time we were outdoors, never inside. We were outside in all weathers; the winter of 1944 was particularly bad. Later in 1944 we put up two pyramid tents at the hardstand area, near the armourers hut and set up temporary home here. We lived and slept there during busy times when there wasn't time to return to our billets and mess halls. Sometimes we were very busy, one time we worked two days and nights straight to turn round battle damage on several aircraft. Catching up on sleep was important then!

Even at Bassingbourn, which as a permanent airfield was better appointed than others, Crew Chief Whit Hill of the 323rd BS, 91st BG, remembers it being difficult out at the dispersals:

570th BS, 390th BG personnel construct a timber shell for their pyramid tent at their hardstand at Framlingham. Kneeling in the doorway is Leroy Keeping, this being one of the structures he recalled in his account. A completed tent can be partly seen to the left of the picture. (Leroy Keeping)

> Bassingbourn was a permanent peace time British airbase. We Americans arrived with each squadron having nine B-17s we later on increased to 18 per squadron. Except for major work, engines, landing gears etc, all work was out under the stars. We had no tents. When the US started shipping gliders, and if the crew chief was in the know, the glider crates were obtained converted into line shacks for the ground crews to warm up or dry off in. As in the old song 'Heart of my Heart' 'We were rough and ready guys'.

To add to their difficulties, over time the surface of a hardstand would become badly soaked and contaminated with spilt grease, oil and fuel, making it dangerously slippery, especially in wet weather. To remedy this situation, crews would back up a fuel truck to the empty hardstand and after notifying the fire department of their intent they would spray the area with 50–60 gallons of aviation fuel, before setting light to it and burning off the oil deposits. In a short space of time the hardstand would be clean again and a little warm on the feet!

Ground Crews

Each of the three flights within a squadron had a flight chief overseeing four crew chiefs, and these in turn were overseen by the squadron line chief. He was in effect the foreman of the ground trades, having all the additional squadron specialists reporting to him. Officially, according to the T/O&E, the line chief would have had a propeller mechanic, a sheet metal man, an electrical mechanic and a clerk/typist allocated to him. In turn, the line chief reported back to the squadron engineering officer. Each squadron engineering officer acted as liaison between group engineering and the squadron, enabling them to accurately plan missions based on numbers of operable aircraft and providing much needed help in areas such as the pursuance of vital parts shortages.

To support the air echelon engineering team, the squadron structure had a second and larger engineering department within the ground echelon element. Referring to the T/O&E again this group comprised:

48 aircraft and engine mechanics
2 aircraft inspectors
5 electrical mechanics
4 instrument mechanics
2 propeller mechanics
2 sheet metal workers
2 welders
2 motor transport mechanics
8 specialist vehicle drivers
1 carpenter
5 clerk/typists
1 supply technician

In addition the squadron armament section also had four power turret specialists as well as squadron armourers to call in for support.

The original theory with the squadron structured in such a way was that while the air echelon units worked the flight line with each crew chief allocated his 'own' aircraft, the ground echelon men would be the 'back room boys'. They would operate any workshop facilities available and provide a floating pool of labour to be directed wherever it might be needed most.

However, as a result of the introduction of the fourth echelon to the maintenance structure, an operational change occurred. As third echelon provision was now overseen within each group by a specific support unit, the squadron ground echelon engineers could be utilised in assisting with the additional workload that flying combat missions had

An example of the co-operation between ground crews and Sub-Depot was the regular task of replacing outer wing sections due to battle damage. Wing sections were repaired off the aircraft in the workshops. They were then transported out to the dispersal and lifted into place using specialist cranes, in this instance a Federal 606 wrecker, that were part of the Sub-Depot equipment allocation. Some groups used air bags to carry out the same task. (USAAF)

created, with the air echelon at the flight line. As with all other units forming part of the bomb group, the squadron support members not involved directly with either flying or maintaining aircraft were also pooled and sent to wherever their particular skills were required within other departments at the station. For the sake of simplicity, it could be said that the squadron ground crews looked after the maintenance of their aircraft while the system provided the repair function. The reality of the situation, however, meant it was never that simple.

As a 'rule of thumb', any job that was estimated to take more than 36 hours to complete would be handed over to the Sub-Depot. It is a great tribute to the squadron men that they worked tirelessly to see that this situation occurred as infrequently as humanly possibly. This was partly through pride in the job and aircraft and partly because they knew the pressure was also on for their colleagues. In much the same way, Sub-Depot personnel could be found regularly out at dispersals helping squadron ground crews repair parts of the aircraft that were way beyond their original remit.

As we have seen, the original allocation of men and equipment were formed to support the twelve-squadron aircraft, pooling the engineering function provided to each aircraft with a fixed ground crew of four mechanics under one crew chief. All the other aircraft specialists, such as the electricians and instrument specialists, floated between crews as and when their particular skills were required. However, high command upset this convenient division of squadron labour by increasing squadron strength from twelve to eighteen aircraft. Things now became far more difficult to oversee, as there weren't any more ground crew members allocated or available to help. In direct contrast to air crew where there was a continuous supply to make up for combat crew losses, essentially the ground echelon remained fairly static throughout a squadron's stay in theatre, having to make do with the personnel shipped out when dispatched to the ETO. Although not directly in the combat zone, the ground crews weren't immune to loss either. Men were injured and even killed in accidents around the airfields and again, unlike the air crews, these losses were rarely made up, especially in the short term, with tasks once again having to be spread more thinly. Occasionally when replacements were received, they had little in the way of trade training. Unless an individual had the aptitude and was a quick learner they would be considered more of a hindrance than of use. There was little in the way of slack time to train someone on the job and so the individual might find themselves being swiftly transferred to perform a less challenging task elsewhere.

The engineering section of the 569th BS, 390th BG was no different to any other. In a recent interview, Paul Kovitz, the engineering officer, likened his job of bringing all the elements of squadron engineering together and keeping them on track with their task to that of conducting an orchestra. With the crew chief and his crew assigned to a particular aircraft they would normally work on the same aircraft for the duration of its combat life. It was often said that the crew chief 'owned' his aircraft and only lent it to the air crew to fly, such was the affection felt by a ground crew to their particular machine. Each crew normally worked at the same dispersal point and an aircraft would generally return to the same position after a mission. If an aircraft failed to return its loss was felt throughout the base, but by none more so than its ground crew and chief. They would often be inconsolable and the grief felt added to the concern that it may have been something they did or didn't do that had contributed to the loss. Lawrence Scholze was one of many who had to endure that situation:

> When our planes came back we had to be up on the line to guide them in. It was tough on us when our plane didn't come back, for a few days, but then we would get a new plane and start the cycle all over again.

This occurrence, faced by many ground crews at one time or another, contributed greatly to their pride in the job and their professional approach to keeping their aircraft in the best possible flying condition. C.J. Leleux, a mechanic with the 715th BS, 448th BG at Seething, had similar experiences:

> We watched as the planes took off on each mission and waited patiently as the planes came back from each mission. In the early days, of my 448th BG experience, we had many days when many of the planes of our Group did not return. These were not days of joy and celebration but of sadness and sorrow for having lost close friends. We would unwind later at the pub.

During the course of the war, as squadrons were allocated more aircraft, the majority of crew chiefs ended up overseeing the upkeep of two or even three aircraft. The situation was eased slightly, Paul Kovitz says, by the reliability and relative ease of maintenance of the B-17. This statement can equally apply to the B-24, for those that worked on or with the later type also had a similar affinity to that aircraft.

Maintenance Procedure

Aircraft of any sort require constant maintenance and inspection to ensure their continued airworthiness. The following excerpt from *The Official Guide to the Army Air Forces*, published in 1944, sums up this process:

> **Preventative Inspection** – The basis of the AAF maintenance system is inspection of all parts to prevent accident damage or part failure before it occurs. For this purpose a detailed and systematic inspection procedure is prescribed and definite responsibility is fixed for different phases of each inspection. The Maintenance Inspection Record is a complete log book of each airplanes operations and maintenance. It contains the record of flying time and tells when an engine should be changed, when oil is to be changed and similar items.[2]

War Department Technical Manual TM 1-415 *Airplane Inspection Guide*, a slender 120-page document, laid down the criteria for inspection of all systems components and structures on any aircraft in the care of the USAAF. This book not only established the order, time schedule and process of inspection and components that had to be inspected, but also introduced the paperwork system for documenting all of these procedures.

Obviously this was only a baseline to work to, as a book this small could not contain all the peculiarities of every aircraft type. For this the engineering teams would have a mass of manuals from the aircraft manufacturers,containing the actual specifics for the type they were equipped with. Further to that, updates on procedure or processes were supplied either via technical or field orders from the overseeing air depots or company technical representatives based in Britain and operating under the air depot system.

TM 1-415 listed seven inspection record forms that cover the entire working life of every aircraft held by the USAAF. The two most important, as far as squadron servicing were concerned were:

FORM NO. 41B (Maintenance Inspection Record). This was the main aircraft logbook for any particular aircraft. It provided a complete history of the operation, maintenance, flying time and supplies that aircraft consumed. It was, in effect, the complete record of a particular aeroplane's life.

FORM NO. 1A (Airplane Flight Report – Engineering). This form conveyed to the pilot, prior to flight, the essential facts regarding the condition of the aircraft he was to fly. It also gave the mechanics, after the flight had been completed, information pertaining to the aircraft's performance and any work that had to be done on it after its flight, whether at its home station or stationed away from home.

Five other documents reported on: flight information (form 1); one-time changes of components on the airframe (form 60A) and engines (form 60B); a lifetime record for each propeller (form 61); and standard maintenance forms instructing on the best method and practice of maintenance for the type.[3]

Form No.1A tended to be used by the crew chiefs and ground crew members to assess and record their work requirements. The form No.41B was used by squadron engineering officers and aircraft inspectors to complete an individual aircraft's history. Forms 1 and 1A were where the mass of information for all the other documents was derived. In those pre-computer days, all this maintenance information would have to be transcribed and disseminated for use further 'up the tree' for statistical analysis and myriad other functions. This then is why a squadron and group required a considerable number of clerks and typists, to administer this and much other official paperwork.

Maintenance Periods

Again from *The Official Guide to the Army Air Forces*:

> Inspections are made before every flight, daily, after 25 hours, 50 hours and 100 hours of flight. At time of engine change, 25 hours after engine change and at special periods as required by the particular model of airplane. These inspections are progressively more detailed and thorough and by the time a plane has completed 500 hours every part and every accessory has been checked. Upon these inspections depend the lives of the crews and the success of the missions. A 25 hour inspection of a B-17 requires about 100 man hours and a 100 hour inspection may take 400 man hours.[2]

These prescribed tasks form the essentials of first and second echelon service, this being the squadron ground crew's primary duty. Due to slight variations in the inspection schedule, dependent on aircraft type, the 'Aircraft Inspection and Maintenance Guide for B-17 Series' dated 15 May 1944 lists the inspection schedule as follows:

PF	–	Pre-flight.
WU	–	During engine warm up.
D	–	Daily.
25	–	25 hours.
50	–	50 hours.
100	–	100 hours.
SP	–	Special.[4]

This put an additional level of inspection for the B-17 at engine warm up. Some of these checks involved items normally accessible to the air crew from the cockpit, including magneto and oil cooler settings and ensuring propellers were operating correctly. They were normally checked by the ground crew while running the engines up during the pre-flight procedure. During engine fire up and warming periods a ground crewmember normally stood close by with a fire extinguisher in case of engine fires. The maintenance schedule for a B-24 would have fitted into a similar pattern. Daily inspections were to be carried out unless the aircraft was unserviceable due to longer-term maintenance or repair.

The pre-flight involved a walk around to ensure that there were no obvious leaks or damage to the aircraft structure that had occurred since the last daily inspection, and then readying the aircraft for the crew by going through the engine start sequence: running up the engines to check all was well. Arthur Ferwerda describes the procedure employed on 93rd BG B-24s at Hardwick:

> As always we would start all maintenance immediately upon the ships return from a mission. There was always plenty of normal maintenance to take care of, but when you consider that in addition there was always battle damage there wasn't a lot of time to get the ship in shape for a mission the following morning. We were always running close on time. The last thing we did before quitting for the evening (which many times was only a few hours before briefing for the next mission) was to pre-flight the ship.

The 25-, 50- and 100-hour inspections were performed in a rolling fashion with the 50- and 100-hour inspections incorporating the requirements of the previous inspections within them. To allow inspection periods to fit in with the pressures of aircraft missions it was permitted for the inspection to be carried out over several sessions within a time frame of +/- 20 per cent of the particular inspection. Once 100 flying hours were reached the process would start again. Engine change intervals were as prescribed by an

Flight report, 'Form No'. 1A. When filling in any part of an aircraft's inspection paperwork, the crew member was expected to follow a rigid procedure. A set of symbols had been established to fully define the aircraft's serviceability status on the documentation and it was essential that these were correctly used to ensure all information on that particular aircraft was imparted. A series of vertical horizontal and diagonal lines in black or red ink would be applied to the various boxes on the forms as appropriate, as well as the initials and signatures of those that performed work and inspections. The most important symbols as far as indicating an aircraft's airworthiness were a red diagonal indicating a defect but allowing the aircraft to fly under certain conditions, shown centre left and a red X in the same box, which indicated a serious defect, rendering the aircraft unserviceable.

individual engine manufacturer's data and again there was a 20 per cent leeway either side of prescribed flying hours allowable, dependent on the condition of the engine at the time. The 20-hour post engine change inspection was a 'shake down' inspection to see all was well after refitting and to ensure any minor adjustments had been made. Again a leeway was permitted. The special inspection covered anything that might have had to be removed outside normal service periods, such as during an engine change.

Ground crews took great pride in keeping their aircraft serviceable and it was always with great regret that they might have to fill in the paperwork with a red line.

C.J. Leleux concurs:

We communicated continuously with the flight crews and particular the pilot and did so by word and by a flight sheet, which the pilot filled out after each combat mission. After each flight, the pilot would indicate any area of the aircraft that needed attention. We had access to the armament crews, the radio crews, the propeller crews and the fuel crews. We'd pre-flight the aircraft engines before each flight and during ground testing. We could red line the aircraft if we felt it was unworthy of flight. We did this reluctantly but on occasion it was necessary to do so.

Once repairs had been carried out to a 'red-lined' aircraft, the 'X' could be removed and the form signed as the aircraft being airworthy again. The aircraft would then normally be given a test flight, with the ground crew anxiously awaiting the pilot's seal of approval.

Combat Damage

In addition to routine maintenance programmes, in a combat situation the issue of combat damage had to be addressed. Combat damage by its arbitrary nature had an infinite number of variables. Once an aircraft returned from a mission, any damage had to be assessed. For this a category system for its evaluation was established:

Cat A	Minor, repair by combat unit within 36 hours.
Cat AC	Major damage requiring 36 hours or more to repair.
Cat B	Badly damaged requiring specialised engineering unit to repair.
Cat E	Total loss, E1 salvage for spares, E2 salvage for scrap.

Category A repair would normally be performed at a hardstand by squadron ground crew alongside routine maintenance. Category AC would be carried out either at a hardstand with ground crew assisted by Sub-Depot staff or, in very severe cases, the aircraft would be transported to the hangar. For category B it would depend on where the aircraft had landed but would generally come under the jurisdiction of the relevant SAD.

Working the Line

Although much has been said so far of working at night, work went on at the aircraft dispersals around the clock. Major repairs often had to be performed in daylight, especially on an aircraft requiring significant amounts of work. This was a far more practical and safe alternative, albeit that it required ground crews to work around the clock to complete other tasks elsewhere.

What has to be remembered though was that although the structure existed, it was very flexible. At times of high work load, such as during a maximum effort, when it was strategically imperative to get as many aircraft in the air as possible, men would assist with all tasks wherever required. Dayshifts did, however, tend to be more common for some of the other supporting personnel. Leroy Keeping explains the situation at Framlingham:

> We generally worked days; although that varied depending on how frequent raids were, using the tents to catch up on sleep when necessary. We obviously knew when a raid went out in the morning but were obviously not privy to its target. Later in the day we would be told through squadron HQ when to expect it back, so we would generally be at the hardstands waiting to appraise what was required to get things turned around.

Damage could occur virtually anywhere on an aircraft but typically some of the more common areas that needed attention included: structural components, electrical harnesses, fuel tanks, engines, propellers, tyres, brakes, wheels, turrets, oxygen systems, superchargers and sheet-metal work. Lawrence Scholze has similar memories of his time at Horham:

> I was involved in the complete plane and its engines; we worked out on the line, where we parked the planes. Rain or shine, dark or day light, we had to get those planes ready for the next day's bombing missions. Every evening we had to report the flying status of our plane, to let our command know it was ready to go the next day. I don't really have any anecdotal memories from that time; all we seemed to do was work and sleep!

Arthur Ferwerda describes some of his experiences dealing with the B-24 Liberator with the 93rd BG at Hardwick:

> Typical maintenance consisted of correcting any malfunctions that had occurred on the previous mission and as a rule there was always battle damage. We always worked outside, in all kinds of weather as there were only three hangars for about 60 aircraft. The only ships that were allowed hangar time were those that had major battle damage. We often had to work in darkness, in the early part of the war because there was still a possibility of enemy aircraft, so a blackout was imposed. I became quite good at working with a flashlight tucked between my chin and my shoulder!

As well as mechanical issues, aircraft sheet metal would require constant repair, as Whit Hill recalls at Bassingbourn:

> My Job as the 323rd Squadron sheet metal Crew Chief that consisted of eight sheet metal men, and we were responsible for cleaning up damage caused by Hitler's Troops and the Luftwaffe. We had a small office in the 323rd BS hangar, but most of our work was accomplished in the dispersal area, located on the property of the Wimpole Park Estate, owned by Rudyard Kipling's daughter. A memorial marker is located on the estate where the 323rd BS B-17s were parked. The other squadrons were parked in dispersal areas located throughout the Base. Aircraft damaged that required engine changes and lots of body repaired were transferred to the 441st Sub-Depot who were equipped to repair major damage such as engines, wheels, wings etc.
>   Our equipment consisted of a Jeep, and a portable sheet metal shop that our crew had designed and built up on a bomb loading trailer, that consisted of work bench, electric generator, flood lights which we had to turn off in the event of a night alert, air compressor to operate the pneumatic rivet guns, a couple of British pop rivet guns to be used in the event we could not buck the rivets by hand with a bucking bar. We worked under the wings, and until all the damaged aircraft were back and ready to go. Sleep was where you could get it.

Changing the inboard superchargers on numbers two and three engines on a B-17 was always considered a miserable job. There was extremely limited access inside the wing behind the wheel wells. As a consequence a squadron always liked to 'maintain' at least one small stature mechanic within its ranks, especially for this onerous task. Although such a member of the team would have been very popular with his colleagues at being allocated this job, due to the temperamental nature of the turbo superchargers, especially on the early models of aircraft, one would imagine the individual concerned would have felt rather picked on for this special duty!

Many ideas were tried by various bomb groups to speed up the process of getting damaged aircraft returned to service more efficiently. One job that required a lot of patience was checking the rubber de-icer boots, installed on the leading edge of the wings and tail, for flak damage. The boots were inflated with air and were used to break up any build up of ice on flying surfaces. It was very difficult to find any damage caused, as after flak particles penetrated the rubber, holes or tears would close over but not seal. Paul Kovitz elaborates on this and other solutions that he and his fellow engineers came up with to remedy these situations:

> Early aircraft came equipped with rubber de-icer boots in the leading edge of the wings, horizontal and vertical stabilizers. These were a nightmare to maintain. Eventually it was realized that missions could be accomplished without the boots. Existing boots were removed and installation of them during aircraft manufacture was discontinued.

Among the most common operations on all combat aircraft – and the B-17s and B-24s of the 8th were no different – were engine changes. Engines from new only had a finite number of flying hours available to them before replacement or reconditioning was required. Engine hours would be calculated by the manufacturer under ideal conditions. When in combat those hours available were greatly reduced as aircraft were flown fully loaded, hour after hour. Add to that the effects of combat damage and it becomes clear that ground crews spent a lot of time changing engines. Once refitted, they then had to be run in, or 'slow timed'. This was another process upon which all groups expended effort trying to speed things up; the 390th BG was no different. Paul Kovitz explains:

> Engine changes were a very common occurrence and each time a replacement engine was installed the aircraft was scheduled for a test flight to 'slow time' or operate the new engine under in-flight

A B-24 undergoing an engine change out at its hardstand. The new engine can be seen being prepared for fitment while still in its crate. The engine crane is a typical piece of equipment used for both B-17s and B-24s. (USAAF)

conditions to ensure serviceability. This tied up the aircraft and an aircrew until the test flight could be accomplished. The group took a war weary B-17 and used it as a test bed to 'slow time' engines so one was available for each of the four engine positions. The war weary aircraft and the combat aircraft were nosed together, the unserviceable engine was changed and the combat aircraft would be ready to return to duty after a ground run up check. Another engine would be installed on the war weary aircraft to be slow timed so that all four engines would again be available for replacement. The procedure was trialled by the 571st squadron and although it did achieve a measure of success, in that enabled a complete engine and propeller package to be changed in a few hours and without the 8 hours plus time taken to slow time the engine, it was discontinued in the end as in reality it necessitated a double engine change, which was less than popular with mechanics.

Another procedure to shorten down time was to build stocks of serviceable left- and right-hand outboard wing panels. These would have 'Tokyo' tanks, so named as when they were added to increase the fuel capacity of a B-17 it was said they could now make it to Tokyo and back, already installed.

These were built up and kept by the 458th Sub-Depot at Framlingham. Instead of tying up an aircraft to repair extensive flak damage to the wing structure or Tokyo tanks, the damaged wing was removed and a serviceable one was installed by the Sub-Depot. When the tapered pins that held the wing panel to the main spar were removed it sounded like a small canon going off!

Tapered pins were used to correctly align and positively mount the wing sections together. Once tightened, it took considerable effort to get them to part. A hydraulic extractor to aid removal of the pins was developed by S/Sgt Edward H. Nestor of the 458th Sub-Depot for which he was awarded the Bronze Star.

Engine Nacelle area cleaning was done with 100 octane fuel by using a hose hooked up to the engine fuel boost pump. A serviceable fire extinguisher was always available in the immediate area. Fortunately there were no fires and this particular procedure would be frowned upon today. 100 octane fuel was used to dry clean clothing with excellent results until certain smelly additives were included putting an end to that practice!

These and many other tasks went on around the clock, with the monotony only broken when aircraft left on missions. Often the only respite ground crews would get during a

busy period would be from the arrival of a canteen vehicle such as those operated by organisations like the British forces Navy Army Air Force Institute (NAAFI), the Church Army or an ARC 'Clubmobile' delivering much needed fortification in the form of tea, coffee and doughnuts to temporarily revive flagging spirits!

Preparation for a Mission

Those who lived or worked on or in the vicinity of a heavy bomber base during the Second World War say that it was never quiet. Standing in the rural peace of the English countryside near one of these former fields today, it is hard to imagine the unceasing work that went on. During the day the airfield was a veritable beehive. Aircraft came and went, vehicles drove around the site delivering supplies while men and women worked on the many sites, in offices, workshops and stores. At night, especially before a mission, many would still be hard at work, but due to the blackout conditions hardly a thing could be seen, save for the odd flash of a torch here and there. Whit Hill:

> Each squadron reported nightly to HQ, the flying status of each of their assigned aircraft, and an estimate of when the damaged ones would be ready to go, which they checked nearly hourly.

Mission preparation sequences varied slightly from group to group depending on local preferences. Variations on timings also existed, depending on factors such as target location, bomb load or aircraft type. The following is typical of tasks performed by ground crews in preparation for a mission using B-17 Flying Fortresses, interspersed with recollections by former Crew Chief Arthur Ferwerda on preparing a B-24 Liberator at Hardwick, in 1944:

> Whenever there was a mission scheduled for the following day, the term used was that we were on ALERT. If there was no mission scheduled, which was quite unusual in 1944, the term was we were on STAND DOWN. If a mission was scheduled for Germany and not to any of the occupied countries, the mission was never called off because of bad weather over the target. There was always a secondary target and if the weather was bad over that one, the ships would just drop their bombs randomly. Many mornings the

Opposite: An ARC 'Clubmobile' provides welcome refreshment to ground crews of the 493rd BG at Debach, 12 February 1945. The 'Clubmobile' is converted from an AEC Regal 10T10 bus, one of a number requisitioned for use by American forces from London Transport. (USAAF)

Right: An 8th AF ground-crewman warms his hands on a putt-putt. This was the term given to the small, engine-powered auxiliary generators, used to boost the aircraft's batteries when ground testing electrical systems. (USAAF)

weather at our base was so bad, that the visibility was zero. The ships would take off using only their compass and air speed indicator. They were flying blind, for they didn't have the technology we have today. They actually were going out on a 'wing and a prayer' in more ways than one. Preparation for a typical mission started very early in the morning. The ground crews were awakened around 5am. Usually we had only gotton to bed about midnight, because we had been getting the ship ready for the mission. When I went out in the morning to pre flight a ship, I would always take one of my crew with me. I would rotate them, so that the other two could get a few minutes more sleep. I went out every morning. The rest of my crew would usually come out about half an hour later.

Typically a jeep would pick us up and we would ride in any place that was available. Very often that was on top of the hood. This wasn't too bad when the weather was good. However when it was raining snowing or sleeting, by the time we got to the ship, we were cold wet and half frozen.

By the time they were at the hardstand the airfield would be alive with the sound of trucks in the distance indicating that the ordnance crews too were starting their morning duties of loading and delivering bombs from the bomb dump.

The first thing that we would do was to walk around the aircraft with a searchlight to see that everything was normal and intact and nothing appeared unusual. We were always aware that there could be some sabotage.

The crew chief would generally know the approximate mission departure time and experience would enable him and his crew to work through their schedule and have the aircraft ready for the arrival of the flight crew.

The squadron armament officer and crew would arrive at the hardstand and inform the crew chief of the bomb load and type. With the generator up and running and plugged in to the aircraft, the crew chief would enter the aircraft, access the bomb bay controls and open the bomb bay doors. The armourer would then run through a series of tests to ensure all of the bomb release system was functioning correctly. While this was going on, one of the ground crew would be removing the canvas covers from the cockpit and engines. These were an essential requirement for all but the warmest of summer months for the aircraft parked in the open and essential in winter to keep the cockpit glass from freezing over.

Loading bombs into a B-17 was a relatively straightforward process. As the design was a 'tail-dragger' the nose was high enough to wheel a loaded trolley straight under the bomb bay and winch the bombs up. Loading a B-24, however, was more difficult. Due to its tricycle layout, the B-24 fuselage sat lower to the ground thereby preventing a bomb trolley from being pushed underneath. Instead the bombs had to be lifted onto stands and manoeuvred under the bomb bay individually; the larger the bomb the more awkward the task. (USAAF)

2 March 1944, ground crew of 525th BS, 379th BG, at Kimbolton, fit chin turret guns, watched by an air crewmember. To fit the guns, the chin turret had to be rotated through ninety degrees. (USAAF)

The ammunition truck was normally the next arrival with boxes of 50-calibre ammunition for the guns. Ground crews preferred to get the ammunition loaded before the bombs went aboard as it was easier to access the front gun positions with the bomb bay empty. Ordnance crews would then arrive and leave a loaded bomb trolley at the hardstand ready for the squadron armourers to load the aircraft. Fins would be fitted to the bombs, and if the bombs were particularly muddy from storage, they would be cleaned so as to not allow mud to impair their fall characteristics when released.

A lot of care was required to avoid dropping the bombs or allowing them to swing and damage the interior of the aircraft. Once loaded, bomb fuses would be retained with safety wires and pins to prevent accidents during take off. The bombardier would only remove the safety pins and arm the bombs once in the air and on the way to the target. Generally the process of loading the bombs took 30–45 minutes per aircraft. If a mission was scrubbed the bombs had to removed, as they couldn't be left in the aircraft. Sometimes the bomb load might be changed at the last minute and the whole process had to be repeated as quickly as possible. All of this put immense pressure on the armament teams and, as well as being hard work, it could be very disheartening.

Once all the ordnance had been loaded aboard the ground crew would start to pre-flight the aircraft. This normally began with 'walking through the props'. Each propeller would be hand turned through at least three revolution turns to clear the cylinders of any fuel that may have drained into them. The crew chief would then get back into the cockpit. In a B-17 he would normally sit in the right-hand co-pilot's seat and go through the engine start-up procedure. First number one engine would be primed and then started. The sequence would be repeated for engines two, three and four. Once the engines had been running smoothly for a few minutes, each one would be run up to check all the items on the WU inspection schedule, such as magnetos and turbo superchargers etc. Fuel would then be cut off and the engines shut down. The engine run up and warm up would take about 15 to 30 minutes.

Having found everything in order, we would proceed to get into the ship and up on the flight deck. We would take our places in the pilot and co-pilots positions. (In a B-24) we always referred to the engines by number. Sitting in the pilot's seat, the farthest engine to our left was engine no. 1, then counting from left to right they were no. 2, no. 3 and no. 4. Engine no. 3 was always started first, because it was the only engine that had a hydraulic pump. This was needed to sustain the braking system and do other check functions during the pre flight such as flap positioning etc. It was usually still dark outside and in order to read the instruments there was a blue fluorescent light mounted on the ceiling and just behind our head that shone on the instrument panel. It was a pretty sight, as all the instruments were coated with a luminescent type of paint, which made the instruments readable. We had to run each engine individually and check all the various components by watching the gauges. It usually took about thirty minutes to pre-flight the engines, which consumed about 50 gallons of gas per engine.

If he was happy with all he had checked, the crew chief would start to fill in his form 1A on his clipboard. If there was still time he may run some checks on some smaller items that needed his attention that had been highlighted by the crew on their previous mission.

Around now another truck would arrive, delivering the heavy 'flak suits' – a form of body armour for the airmen – and the guns from the squadron armoury. The guns would have been cleaned and oiled since the last mission and be ready to go back into the aircraft. They were normally cleaned of all oil prior to fitting due to its tendency to thicken and jam the guns once in the cold air at high altitude. Normally the ground crew fitted the front guns, leaving the gunners themselves to mount their own guns in the rear, waist and ball turret positions.

Next to arrive would be the gas wagon to top up tanks after the engine test run. This was another operation strictly co-ordinated and overseen by the chief to avoid any overfilling or spills that could lead to engine fires. Normally it was only necessary to top up the Tokyo tanks. Last of all the crew chief would make sure all the filler caps were on and tightened securely.

Squadron crews would drive the fuel trucks, and would have been kept very busy during this period. A bomb group used on average around 70,000 gallons per mission. The trucks carried around 4,000 gallons, usually enough to completely fill only one aircraft. A B-17 held 2,780 gallons and a B-24 a similar amount, so the trucks were constantly shuttling back and forth from the fuel dump, which was normally located just outside the perimeter track. Class A airfields, as originally constructed, had one fuel dump of 72,000 gallons capacity. As it was soon realised that this could be depleted in just one mission, another was swiftly added, giving a site around two days' worth of fuel during a busy period. The fuel dumps had to be constantly replenished, usually by fleets

Men of the 392nd BG refuelling a B-24 from Wendling, in this instance as soon as it arrived back at its dispersal, after its return from a mission. Here, the tanker is one of the larger articulated trailers hauled by a Federal tractor unit. Air crew are about to be transported back to HQ for interrogation. 9 September 1943. (USAAF)

of British 'pool' petrol tankers running from nearby railheads. Some closely grouped airfields in East Anglia, however, were linked by a mains pipeline pumped from a central supply depot.

> As the war moved on and the missions became longer the gas load became very important. The first thing we always did when the ship returned from a mission was to refill the gas tanks. However as the targets selected were deeper inside Germany, the flying time became longer and fuel became a very critical matter. Because of this, we would always top off the gas tanks after pre-flighting. Those 200 gallons of fuel could be the difference between life and death on the return trip from the mission. As the gas loads became larger and hence heavier and with the normal bomb loads the runways became too short. More than once I had to pull small tree branches out of engine air scoops on my ship because they just couldn't get the required altitude immediately after take off. Real scary.

At some point during the early morning proceedings the Norden bombsight would be delivered out to the aircraft. Early in the war this was normally performed with an armed escort due to its secret classification. If it was left in the aircraft for any period of time, an armed guard would be posted at each aircraft thus fitted. Later in the war the classification was lowered and security was relaxed slightly, although the Norden bombsight remained a sensitive item for some years. Bombsight technicians would fit the sighting head and perform any maintenance required to the autopilot system that the bombsight was interconnected with, as part of the mission preparation.

As the crew chief performed a final walk round the aircraft, double checking for any major oil leaks and tyre condition, the oxygen team may well have arrived, to replenish the aircraft's oxygen system and check it for any leaks. The aircraft had a low-pressure oxygen system, vital for the survival of the crew when flying at anything over 10,000ft. The system was comprised of a series of fixed cylinders which had to be replenished after each mission, as well as a set of smaller 'walk round' bottles that enabled the crew to detach themselves from the main system and still receive oxygen when moving round various parts of the aircraft in flight.

> Usually someone was running up an engine late in the evening so I would wait until most of the noise had stopped or was distant and then I would go back to the ship early in the morning and try to find out if there were any oxygen leaks. First I would go to the various parts of the ship and listen. If I couldn't hear any I would go to various connections on the system and with a bar of Castile soap and some water I would coat the connection and look to see if any bubbles appeared. The reason we used Castile soap was because Castile soap was formulated without grease. Grease and oxygen form a combustive mixture and could cause an explosion.
>
> More than once I would see a pilot or other crew member who had been partying a little too much the evening before and with a hangover, standing by the ship with an oxygen bottle sucking in pure oxygen. Not good if he was the pilot!

Oxygen would be supplied from British sources, in traditional steel oxygen cylinders; these would then be transported to the hardstands to replenish the aircraft systems. Once emptied the cylinders would be returned to the suppliers for refilling.

As dawn broke over the airfield the aircraft was ready. About that time trucks would start delivering aircrews from their mission briefings out to the hardstands. While the air crews gathered around their aircraft making final adjustments to their flight clothing, the pilot would discuss the aircraft's condition with the crew chief and check over the form 1A. The pilot and co-pilot would then begin their checks of the aircraft, normally commencing with another outside walk round. They would again be looking for anything out of order; in particular making sure items such as the pitot tube cover had been removed to allow correct airspeed indication.

Meanwhile, gunners would be fitting the rest of their guns and connecting up the belts of ammunition and a member of the ground crew might be giving the cockpit glass and plexi-glass nose a final clean – vital for visual bomb aiming 25,000ft. Finally the air crew would load up their parachutes, adjust their parachute harnesses and get into the aircraft. After his inspection, the pilot would sign the form 1A, accepting the aircraft as mechanically sound, fill in the crew list, hand the form to the crew chief and climb aboard. It was now time for the pilot, co-pilot and flight engineer to perform their cockpit drill and checks. Once completed they would wait for the countdown to engine start time. This would normally be for a matter of a few minutes, but could often be the quietest time on the airfield, with every man seeming to collect his thoughts preparing for what lay ahead that day.

At the appointed time all the aircraft of the group would start their engines. At this time the crew chief and other members of the ground crew would take positions and stand by with fire extinguishers in case of an engine fire, something exceedingly undesirable with all that ordnance and fuel aboard! Once all engines were running and warm the pilot would indicate to the crew chief to remove the wheel chocks, something he would do carefully to avoid the rotating propellers. He would then stand clear and indicate to the pilot that all was okay and the aircraft would begin to move from the hardstand in preparation to join the queue of bombers taxiing around the perimeter track.

The last word comes from Group Engineering Officer Al Engler, 390th BG at Framlingham, regarding the auxiliary generator sets:

> The single cylinder two stroke engine driven auxiliary generators, called 'putt-putts' provided to check out electrical systems without running the engines and for starting engine were great! – If you could get them started. No statistics were kept, but it occurs to me that the auxiliary power units in each squadron required the equivalent effort of a full time mechanic. The power units expanded the swear word vocabulary of many mechanics and caused many a dripping sweat on cold nights from pulling on the starter ropes. Aircraft engines we understood and could cope with: auxiliary power units baffled us to the very end![5]

Danger

Although they may not have seen combat directly, ground crews saw its results on an almost daily basis. Life out on the flight line for any of the ground maintenance staff was hard, with superhuman efforts being performed daily to keep aircraft flying. Much has been written about the tough life of the combat flyer, and rightly so, but the men on the ground had a different but equally unpleasant job for much of the time. Although for the most part not being in the direct line of fire, there were still constant dangers. Working around big machinery in some of the foulest of weather conditions, particularly in winter, brought its fair share of dangers. Working at night by the light of a torch and struggling with cold metal and frozen fingers, or working in the half-light with all the inherent risks associated with rotating propellers, life out on the line wasn't without its hazards. Unfortunately accidents happen in any walk of life, but factor in working under pressure, lack of sleep, difficult working conditions and the often frantic efforts to ready aircraft for their next mission, then for the guys on the line they sadly came with the territory.

T/Sgt Walter Stubbs, Crew Chief 407th BS, 92nd BG, recalled some of these conditions and their consequences at Podington:

December 1944 was the coldest winter in England and Europe for fifty years according to the London newspapers and we felt they were 100% right. At each hardstand we had a tent to house our equipment and tools. In each was a bunk for the mechanic who was on duty a night. Each also had a stove of sorts for heat and also to serve as a stove to cook whatever we could scrape up. Tea was always heating up, eggs whenever someone could steal or bribe from a local farm and sometimes a rasher of bacon. Those that didn't have a proper stove made one out of a can of gravel and sand soaked with a mixture of oil and a little gasoline. One very cold night those that were on duty heard a whoosh from a nearby hardstand, a bright short-lived glow lit up a tent in the air. It settled down on the unfortunate occupant still on fire. Everyone ran to the site and I believe Sgt Hensler was first in his jeep. He pulled the tent aside and others pulled the man out and extinguished the fire. The man was badly burned on his face and hands but otherwise ok. He returned to duty after about 2 weeks in hospital. He told us the fire in the can went out while he was asleep. He poured fuel on it; steam boiled up from the can and that was about all he remembered. Still, the heat from these primitive stoves enabled us to warm our hands and continuing to work. Each morning, during this winter, we had to defrost the aircraft by climbing up onto the wing and spraying a defroster using an English stirrup pump. This was the same pump as used by the English fire wardens during the London blitz. I don't know of any mechanic that didn't slip off the wing at least once.

The following tragic accident, taken from the 303rd BG's records while based at Molesworth, grimly illustrates the fate that could befall unfortunate victims when they allowed their vigilance to slip. On 25 November 1943, a T/Sgt radio repairman with the 359th BS was killed instantly while working on a B-17 named *Knockout Dropper*. He tripped over a generator and fell headfirst into the revolving propeller of the number two engine.[6]

There were also losses in the air crashes. Paul Kovitz related how he lost one of his crew chiefs in an accident in June 1944, during a test flight to 'slow time' a newly installed engine on a B-17. Something went wrong with the flight, resulting in the aircraft crashing west of Woodbridge in Suffolk. All were killed in the accident.

Another major danger to ground personnel came from handling ordnance. Incidents of accidental explosion occurred at several stations during the 8th's tenure in Britain. Some of the worst happened at Deenethorpe, Alconbury and Ridgewell, when bombs exploded at the hardstands during loading. These incidents, not unsurprisingly, resulted in many deaths as well as causing immense amounts of damage and destruction. Probably the most devastating however, was the explosion that occurred in the Metfield bomb dump on 15 July 1944. At least five ordnance men were killed and five B-24s damaged beyond repair when a bomb detonated while being unloaded. The entire bomb dump erupted causing the site to be abandoned for a time until widespread repairs could be implemented.

Exploding bombs weren't the only danger from ordnance, as Arthur Ferwerda recalls, aircraft guns that hadn't been fully disarmed were another on the seemingly infinite list of things that could go wrong:

One morning when a mission had been scheduled for some unknown reason I went out to the ship alone. The ships were always parked on a circular hardstand and facing the runway. As I approached the front of the ship; I was about 50 feet away from the nose section when all of a sudden breaking the silence of the morning there was a loud report. I didn't realise what was happening but a single round of 50 cal ammo had just missed me. The nose gunner evidently had not cleaned his guns the previous afternoon on returning from the mission and had come to the ship early in the morning and before briefing. When he proceeded to clean his guns he left one live round in the chamber from the day before. When it happened I wasn't scared because I didn't know what had happened. A minute or so later when I did realise I began to shake. Then came the anger. My guardian angel must have been looking out for me because when I located the spot where the round hit it was about 12 inches from where I had been standing.

This incident was also sadly not uncommon and there were several instances recorded of this occurring, some with a less fortunate outcome. Ken Lemmons finishes with an account of one of the more harrowing aspects of the ground crew's work, that of cleaning the interior of an aircraft after a particularly bad mission, where casualties were suffered among the air crew:

> ... another plane from the group approached the runway for a landing. The pilot, a friend of mine, fired two red flares out of the window, which indicated a high emergency and gave the ship priority to land. I found out when I went with the medics, that it wasn't my friend that had fired the flares, but the co-pilot. A direct cannon explosion hit the plane at the pilot's window and his head had been completely blown off. The crew put a cover over the dead pilot and the brave twenty one year old co-pilot brought his ship back with his dearest friend still sitting in the seat beside him. It was a time I wish I hadn't gone in. The cockpit had blood and pieces of the poor mans skull all over the dash of the plane. After the medics and air crew left, we went in to scrub down the instrument panel with alcohol and gauze. My friend's blood had oozed down between the instrument panels and it was difficult to get out. But we did. In a case like this you just put your mind on hold and just scrubbed as hard as you could. The last thing the next young pilot needed to see when he climbed into this cockpit was blood on his instruments. Sometimes that was all we could do for them.[1]

The Lighter Side

One area, which in its association with the bomber aircraft of the Second World War has reached iconic status, is the subject of artwork, predominantly aircraft nose art, but also on camp walls, flying jackets and signage. Artwork first started to appear on aircraft during the First World War, the practice supposedly originating with German and Italian pilots. However, the conception and adornment of names and artwork on aircraft reached new heights during the Second World War.

As the USAAF geared up for war, within its compact squadron structure, crew members, both air and ground, were well acquainted, almost like a large family. This camaraderie led to various squadron aircraft gaining names from their crews, and artwork representing these themes started to proliferate. The early units arriving in Britain brought their aircraft with them and the crews generally stayed with the same aircraft. Some of the early aircraft gained their own unique personalities and some became celebrities in their own right.

When fresh crews were given a new aircraft in the US to fly to Britain and replace the aircraft and crew losses that were occurring, they too would often name the plane. However normal practice when they arrived was for the plane and crew to part. Crews would be pooled and sent to a group that required them while the aircraft was normally sent for field modifications to ready it for combat. Later it would be sent to wherever it was required. The process was quite arbitrary, any connection with that aircraft and its first crew being severed. New aircraft would be allocated to a group, often carrying a name, the relevance of which was already lost. Often they might be renamed, and sometimes the name was left and a new crew adopted its identity.

During the Second World War, the practice of painting names and images spread to many other locations. Air crews adorned their flight jackets with matching or similar work to that on their aircraft, road vehicles gained names and murals began to appear on walls of mess buildings and clubs at the various airbases. Normally these larger works started with representations of group or squadron logos and mottos and often led to more elaborate pieces of art. After the war many of these examples of wall art were left abandoned when the bases closed but in recent years work has been done to preserve as many of these examples as possible. Much of this is now considered as folk art, in many senses not much more than graffiti created from materials to hand, and in many cases the artist is unknown. Generally created unofficially, it was tolerated, particularly in the USAAF, and often even encouraged because of its importance as a means of building crew morale. Its use was also not lost on the media who widely promoted the medium and the messages sent, at times both literally and metaphorically. Conversely the US Navy prohibited nose art on its aircraft. Other Allied aircraft carried nose art in varying degrees but within the RAF it was normally only on bombers and again those operating directly in a combat zone.

In many instances what was tolerated was down to individual group commanders. Occasionally there were clean-up attempts, particularly in the UK when some of the images became rather risqué. The more scantily-clad female forms sometimes had to be reworked or have some form of garment put on to cover her ample charms! As a general rule though, the closer an aircraft got to a war zone, the more brazen became the artwork. With more pressing issues to concern them, commanders generally turned a blind eye to some of the more outrageous designs.

Some aircraft were merely 'christened' while others became artistically adorned with images of virtually any subject one could think of. Popular were pin-ups, particularly those based on the work of American émigré artist Alberto Vargas. Vargas' work, in particular his 'Varga Girls' illustrations for *Esquire* magazine, were widely used for inspiration. Images based on film stars of the day, lines from popular songs or humorous puns and innuendo, were also popular sources for aircraft names, as well as the obvious patriotic references. Some squadrons painted their aircraft using a common theme.

Phil Brinkman, a pre-war commercial artist serving with the 834th BS 486th BG at Sudbury, with the encouragement of his CO, painted all the squadron's B-24 Liberators with the signs of the zodiac. Cartoon characters of all sorts made appearances in many guises. In fact every group and squadron would have had an official emblem, many of which were based on cartoons officially designed by studio artists in the US, such as those under the direction of Walt Disney and his peers. These images again would appear on jackets, walls and signs around the bases.

All of this work would have been completed outside official work hours, and a good artist would have been in high demand, at times making quite a lucrative living on the side. Some pieces took several days to complete, and some aircraft were never completed as they were lost in action before the job was finished. The majority of artists were ground crew or ground support staff, some with a peacetime background of commercial art or similar. Probably one of the best known of the aircraft artists was Corporal Anthony L. Starcer of the 441st Sub-Depot , attached to the 91st BG at Bassingbourn. Tony Starcer painted many of the early aircraft of the 91st, beginning in the US prior to the group's move to England. Although he continued painting at a prolific rate once in England, he is probably most remembered for his artwork on the *Memphis Belle*.

Because of its close proximity to London in comparison to other stations, as well as the comparative luxury of the base facilities, Bassingbourn and the 91st BG received significantly higher press coverage than other groups. For this reason, among others, much of their wartime artwork was recorded and can therefore be attributed to a known artist. This situation is far more difficult to verify in less well-recorded groups.

Another of the 91st BG artists was Crew Chief Sgt Jack Gaffney of the 401st BS. Jack was not only in charge of keeping his planes in the air, he also spent much downtime working on them:

My career in the 91st in England started as an assistant crew chief under M/Sgt. Robert Dalton on *Invasion 2*. After we lost her, we were assigned another B-17 from the 95th BG. I named it *The Shamrock Special* and painted the nose art with 2 different pictures on the nose section. Later I added a nude on the dorsal fin and I believe it was the only plane in the ETO with 3 different pieces of art work. In the fall of 1943 it was parked outside the 401st. hangar and I was working on some oxygen lines when it was hit in the rear by a plane landing after a mission with the hydraulics' shot up. This plane was *The Careful Virgin* of the 323rd Squadron. It really tore up the tail section and we and the Sub-depot replaced the damaged section with the good rear section of another plane which had the front section tore up. I then was promoted to crew chief as a Sergeant on *Destiny's Child*, then *Sunkist Sue, Los Angeles City Limits*, and *Hot Shot Charlie*. I did the nose art for most of these planes. I did receive the Bronze Star for meritorious engineering achievement on my first plane as a crew chief; it was *Destiny's Child*.

Aircraft names became perceived as such an intrinsic part of group and squadron morale that several high profile naming ceremonies were organised. Important visiting celebrities were, on occasions, invited to perform the task, those around hoping perhaps that they would impart some form of good fortune upon the recipient of their patronage. Perhaps the most publicised of these ceremonies was performed by Princess Elizabeth, the current queen, when she named a B-17 *Rose of York* on 6 July 1944. Unfortunately however, even royal patronage wasn't enough to save an aircraft and *Rose of York* was lost over the North Sea returning from her sixty-third mission while flying with the 306th BG from Thurleigh.

All this artwork on aircraft combined with other markings such as crew position names, mission tallies as well as the official group and squadron insignia on wings, fuselage and tail, made for an extremely colourful air force! When it was decided to stop painting aircraft in camouflage drab and leave them in natural metal 'silver' finish they looked even more vibrant and exotic – small wonder they captured the eye and stayed in the psyche of those who remember. In fact by the end of the war there was very little room left to paint anything more on the average American aircraft!

Technical Site

A side from the operational airfield itself, the technical site was the largest functional area on any station and, as well as aircraft servicing, was the location for most of the technical operations. Although normally actually part of the overall airfield site and not a dispersed location, it was always considered a discrete site for purposes of identification.

Permanent airfields had all their technical functions collected together in one small area, whereas temporary stations often had two technical sites, usually with at least one hangar each. A primary site would be located near the camp main entrance and a secondary, smaller site elsewhere on the airfield, often on the opposite side to the mainsite and close to the firing butts, where test firing of aircraft guns and some live shooting practice was carried out.

The functions of the technical sites can be categorised within four distinct groups:

Engineering Support for aircraft repair. Workshops for all aircraft components and systems, motor transport service and repair and general engineering support for all of the base services.

Supply of technical stores for aircraft, motor transport, support equipment and fuel and lubricants for aircraft and vehicles. Domestic supply for the station, such as rations and consumables. Provision of flying equipment, armament, photographic services and anti-gas equipment.

Training: simulated for aircrew, trade training such as vocational, on the job and continuing skills accumulation and general military training included gas attack drill, shooting and small arms use.

Administration: technical administration for the above facilities, squadron administration and headquarters, and technical inspection of aircraft and associated systems.

Technical Site Organisations

By far the largest unit operating on the technical site would have been the Sub-Depot (or its predecessor or successor organisations the Service Squadrons or Air Service Groups). The Sub-Depot's role was such that it handled many of the above functions, particularly engineering technical supply and the administration thereof. For ease and clarity we will only refer to the Sub-Depot performing the Engineering Support role, even though its predecessors and successors performed a similar role.

The technical site also housed the headquarters and some technical support functions for each of the individual squadrons. Once again in line with the general policy of pooling staff, those squadron specialists not directly involved with aircraft servicing, such as parachute and photographic technicians, worked in areas along with members of other support units. Quartermaster units would also be on the technical site operating the storage and supply of items related to the domestic side of running the camp: food, fuel, domiciliary supplies and so on.

The technical site would also house the motor pool workshops. These were normally operated by the Ordnance Company, providing the necessary skilled motor mechanics. Transportation drivers were normally supplied by the Station Complement unit.

Facilities

The largest buildings on the technical site, the hangars, were often divided between the Sub-Depot and squadrons for longer-term work on aircraft that couldn't quickly be completed outside. On some sites the Sub-Depot operated both hangars as at Horham, and Framlingham, with one used for working on complete aircraft while the other used for sub-assembly work. At other stations one hangar was sometimes used as a store, as was the case at Ridgewell, or even as motor transport workshops. These variations were largely down to how individual base commanders wished their station to operate.

Other buildings that would be found on a technical site included:

Squadron armouries
Free gunnery trainer, normally a small hangar such as a blister type
Crew lockers and drying rooms
Squadron and flight offices
A photographic block
Bulk oil storage facility
A parachute store
A respirator store
Main workshops
A gas chamber
Motor transport sheds
Latrines and blast shelters
A Link trainer building
An Air Ministry Laboratories (AML) bombing teacher building
The main stores building

Aside from those found on permanent stations most of these buildings would be of the temporary type, either of temporary brick construction or Nissen or Romney hutting. Again the list is not exhaustive and many variations existed.

All recyclable material would be collected and the technical site normally had an area for this. Most also ended up with a graveyard for airframes that were salvaged from aircraft too damaged to repair but which provided a valuable spares source.

The following is a look around some of the departments that inhabited the site, again the list is by no means exhaustive, but gives a good indication of the variety of work undertaken.

Sub–Depot

The men of engineering and supply were under constant pressure to complete repairs on damaged aircraft and send them back to the squadrons for another mission as soon as was practically possible. The Sub-Depot's primary role was to provide third echelon service facilities, but in practice they became largely responsible for the repair of combat damage, generally categories A and AC but sometimes category B. This they achieved by supplying the skilled men and equipment for the task and the parts required for repair. Beyond that, they provided support for many other departments present on a heavy bomber base.

The Sub-Depot had two departments – engineering and Air Corps Supply – and also provided its own administration department.

Engineering Department

The engineering department was the larger of the Sub-Depot's two sections. It was they who provided repair facilities for aircraft and their auxiliary equipment which was beyond the scope of the squadron ground crews, therefore avoiding the need to remove the aircraft from the station. This would include fabrication of parts, repair of aircraft and equipment, and the provision of specialised personnel and heavy or non-portable equipment and machines. They were also tasked with the salvage recovery of battle-damaged aircraft.

During the course of their work the Sub-Depot would have been responsible for implementing technical order changes as well as other theatre directives and the keeping of all records pertaining to the execution of these instructions. Included under the engineering section were a number of specialist workshops including:

Aero repair section
This section usually employed between forty and fifty men usually working in two-man teams under the direction of two hangar chiefs. This unit normally controlled at least one hangar, as it was here that damaged aircraft were dismantled and repaired.

Sheet metal section
This was the team that undertook all sheet metal repairs, again working in two-man teams under the direction of a chief. Crews repaired any damaged aluminium part or assembly removed from an aircraft, such as flaps, control surfaces, all types of doors, outer wing panels, wing tips, horizontal and vertical stabilisers, and so on. Richard Creutz remembers the situation at Horham:

> I was assigned to the 457th Sub-Depot, which was the Engineering and repair group of the base. I was assigned to the sheet metal shop; we had about 25 [working] in the shop.

Engineering personnel, probably from the 441st Sub-Depot, repairing the nose section of a 91st BG B-17 at Bassingbourn. (USAAF)

The base was buzzing, lots of activity; our shop was overloaded with work to do. When planes were scrapped, all usable parts were removed and put away to be repaired. There were piles of flaps, rudders wing panels etc. to be repaired. We could not keep up with the battle damage the planes were getting. We had to repair the planes on the hardstands first, to get them ready for the next day. Our shop consisted of a double Quonset, with space in the middle to make it larger. After the hangars were completed, we moved to a new shop between the hangars. Hangar No. 1 was where the badly damaged planes came; hangar No. 2 was used for engine repair and other work.

We did major and minor repair work, sometimes making parts we could not get. As mentioned before, the first year most of the work was out at the hardstands, which was pretty hard in winter.

Working conditions at times were brutal, 12 to 15 hours a day. You just wanted to hit the 'hay' after those days. After the first year things got a lot better, our planes got better protection, and the damage was less and we worked less hours and got more time off.

The following smaller units within the Sub-Depot organisation looked after their own specialist disciplines. Working in various workshops on the technical site they would also provide assistance to the aero repair section as and when their skills were required.

Aircraft battery shop
A small workshop with around three staff members, whose job it was to look after all the batteries used on the site.

Aircraft dope, fabric & paint shop
This small section of around five men dealt with any fabric-covered parts such as ailerons. The crews maintained the paint and dope stores and painted official marking and insignia on aircraft. The shop would have had a fairly efficient heating and ventilation system provided, not only to keep it clear of noxious fumes but also to aid with paint materials drying, particularly in colder weather conditions.

Aircraft electric shop
The ten men of this workshop tested, repaired and recalibrated all electrical components used on an aircraft, as well as testing and repairing all electrically heated flying clothing.

Sheet metal crew re-skinning and repairing a damaged wing tip. Left to right, David Rosner, from Hartford, Con. and right, Sgt Joseph J. Tucker, from Coleman, Texas. (USAAF)

Engine build-up workshop

The personnel of this workshop, usually around twelve men, built up engine assemblies ready for quick changes by squadron crews. New engines would arrive from base air depots (BAD) and require ancillary units to be fitted, such as control cables and engine mounts. They would also salvage all usable ancillary parts from old engines for repair before dispatching worn engines back to the BAD.

Aircraft hydraulic workshop

Three men provided this facility for the testing and repair of all hydraulic components as well as the manufacture of new hydraulic pipelines for aircraft.

Aircraft instrument shop

This small unit tested, repaired, adjusted and recalibrated aircraft flight instruments, engine operation instruments, gun sights, oxygen valves and gauges. The work was normally performed by a team of around eleven men.

Machine shop

The machine shop provided support to all the repair shops and other base departments such as the utilities section, ordnance, Chemical Company, fire fighting and motor pool. It was usually operated by around seven skilled machinists.

Henry G. Johansen was a machinist with the 444th Sub-Depot at Molesworth. He rarely worked on the aircraft and explained that he spent most of his working day in the machine shop making parts such as special bolts and tools. He remembered the one job he did have to do out working on the aircraft was one he particularly disliked: removing broken exhaust manifold studs on the engines. He explained that when the drill was in the confined space, visibility was nil, making it very difficult to see what he was doing.

Parachute workshop

The parachute store was a self-contained stand-alone building usually with its own source of heating. Its distinctive shape is still easily distinguishable. The high 'clerestory'-style roof section enabled parachutes to hang and dry correctly prior to packing. In total there were normally around twelve men running the workshop.

Machine shop of 448th Sub-Depot, 381st BG Ridgewell, showing a quite extensive range of machine tools available, 22 April 1944. (USAAF)

Podington parachute shop, 92nd BG, 29 November 1943. The parachute shop repaired, rigged and repacked all of the parachutes used by the group as well as the parachute harnesses and other canvas repair work. Personnel running the shop were drawn from the parachute riggers in each squadron as well as specialist from the Sub-Depot. (USAAF)

Aircraft propeller workshop

The propeller shop dismantled, cleaned and rebuilt every propeller removed from a worn engine. The ten personnel would then ensure that they were tested and balanced ready for reassembly on new engines.

Welding shop

The welders provided support for many departments of the group doing many and varied tasks. Some units even undertook limited foundry work, casting non-ferrous components. Normally a team of around eight provided this service.

Woodworking shop

The woodwork shop was another facility that provided a lot of support for many other units on the camp. A small team of around four men were kept very busy building all manner of repair stands, fixtures, aircraft support cradles and packing crates.

Engineering office

The engineering office was the hub of all the repair operations being performed by the Sub-Depot personnel. The twelve men of the office managed the entire overhaul, repair and testing activity of the organisation. To them fell the task of maintaining the records of each aircraft repaired. They also oversaw the inspection and certification of each repair for compliance with technical orders.

Supply Department

The second but equally important part of the Sub-Depot was the Air Corps Supply Department. It was they who were responsible for seeing that no aircraft was grounded for need of a new part or fuel.

Air Corps Supply had the responsibility of maintaining control of procurement, storage and distributions of all classes of air force, signal and corps of engineering property. It acted as an intermediate supply point between the depots and the squadrons, controlling supply both to and from, as repairable units were also packaged and returned to the air depots for reconditioning. Normally the department was operated by two officers and around fifty enlisted men.

Air Corps Supply comprised five departments:

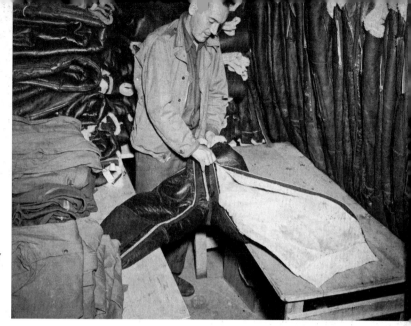

As well as all aircraft components, the Sub-Depot supply department were also responsible for maintaining supply and inventory control of all personal equipment,used by the group's air echelon. Items such as electric flying suits, oxygen masks, headphones and head sets all came under their control. Here Sgt Garvey stores flying suits in an equipment room – 381st BG Ridgewell, 4 August 1944. (USAAF)

The central office section
This department was operated by around twenty personnel. Here they accepted parts requisitions, either from Sub-Depot or squadron ground crew for any part listed in the twenty-odd classes of Air Corps materiel. They also administered the process of returning repairable units back to the relevant BAD for overhaul.

Close co-ordination was maintained with the engineering shops and squadron engineering staff to ensure sufficient items such as engines were available for quick engine changes.

Most groups would have an RAF officer assigned to them for the purposes of accounting lend-lease supplies. Close liaison would be maintained from this office, with the lend-lease officer, as this would prove vital for local procurement of generic hardware and supplies, as well as contracting for the overhaul of certain common accessories.

The main warehouse section
Received serviceable parts and stored them in designated locations. The more frequently used parts and supplies were normally stocked in-house. Parts not available locally were back ordered to the BAD. When a part was back ordered, it was common practice to borrow a serviceable part from an aircraft undergoing repair. Items such as engines and propellers requiring further work before fitting to aircraft would be routed to the appropriate engineering shop for assembly. Normally around fifteen men administered this function.

The warehouse reparable section
This department of four men handled all repairable items, crating them as necessary prior to dispatch to an overhaul facility, usually a BAD.

The transportation section
Although the Sub-Depot had its own transport section, in line with the policy of resource pooling, it operated as part of the base motor pool. It provided transport services for the entire Sub-Depot, moving parts and supplies to and from the overhaul facilities. The twenty men of this section also transported Sub-Depot and other base personnel on official business trips and liberty runs.

92nd BG aircraft supply warehouse at Podington, 29 November 1943. Personnel working here were often on the front-line when frustrations borne out of difficulties of parts supply manifested themselves. (USAAF)

The fuel service section

The fuel service section worked remotely from the main Sub-Depot site, as it was the six men of this section who operated the aviation fuel dumps out on the airfield. It was they who accepted delivery of aircraft fuel and engine oil from the British transport supply system and monitored the pumping of the fuel into the station storage system. They also loaded squadron fuel tank trucks and issued barrels of oil. As well its two functional departments, a Sub-Depot also had its own administration section to oversee its operation and housekeeping. The section administered all of its personnel records, finance matters and correspondence.

The Spare Parts Situation

The provision of spare parts for aircraft and vehicles to the USAAF was always problematic during the war. The general perception is that the US forces arrived in Britain in 1942 along with every piece of equipment and convenience imaginable. The reality, however, was precisely the opposite.

Although administration and control of supply were at fault to a degree, the practicalities of distance from the US and a long sea crossing were far bigger problems. While some small quantities of spares were carried in aircraft being ferried to Britain, regular long-haul cargo flights were still in the future. All shipping crossing the Atlantic was at risk, therefore all cargo space was strictly controlled. Supplies for the USAAF vied with space for supplies to other branches of the army. Clearly structured classes of supply existed for shipping of materiel based on importance of need but some items, due to bureaucracy or misunderstanding, were not handled with the same degree of urgency. This was where the BADs ultimately proved their worth, enabling all the European numbered air forces to 'live off the land'.

However, providing what were essentially aircraft parts, factories would take time, especially as much of the essential machinery required to equip them also had to be brought over from the United States. The first groups to arrive in Britain had an especially difficult time trying to become operational. Air echelons obviously flew to Britain and were only able to carry a limited amount of tools and equipment with them. All other personnel and equipment came by sea and were often slow to catch up.

Fortunately, as the airfields allocated to these early groups were not brand new and had been occupied by RAF units, there was already a certain amount of specialist equipment and vehicles on site. This is where some of the earliest example of 'reverse lend-lease' came in, official and unofficial, with much of the equipment required by these groups being supplied by the RAF and Air Ministry. This was quite a common practice throughout the war and a lot more equipment was supplied to the USAAF by Britain than is commonly thought. It was through trial and error and a lot of local improvisation that these original 'pathfinder' groups of the 8th smoothed the way for the later arrivals.

The 91st BG was typical of the early arrivals in Britain, arriving in October 1942. Some of the means by which it brought itself to operational readiness, 'fair and foul', are explained by Whit Hill:

> When we first arrived at Bassingbourn, not all our equipment had arrived. We were assisted by an RAF unit that was still on the base and worked with the 441st Sub-Depot, until we became fully operational. They provided us with aluminum [sic] sheets, rivets, Pop rivet guns, bucking bars etc. They machined large steel bolts into rivet-sets used in setting rivets by hand with a hammer.
>
> American supplies were stored and issued at the master American depot at Burtonwood AFB, near Manchester. While attending an RAF Airframe School at Burtonwood, my Engineering Officer arrived with a staff car, and he and I were invited to go through the warehouses and point out the tools our squadron was short of. The NCO in charge had a table of authorization, and gave us what we were authorized. For things not authorized like off-set Electric drills & rivet guns, air compressor, British pop rivet guns, curved shears etc, we acquired through a 'mid-night requisition'. The 323rd Squadron was well equipped.
>
> The 441st Sub-Depot, located in Hangar 1 maintained some spare parts such as tyres brakes etc, or ordered for air shipment large items as engines etc., from Burtonwood.

Rudi Steele agrees with the difficulties faced during the early days of the 91st BG in setting up their operations:

> When we moved from Kimbolton to Bassingbourn, things were still fairly primitive out at the hardstands, with no covered accommodation, even though it was a British permanent base. Decent tooling was slow to catch up with us.

Paul Kovitz says that he and the other squadron engineering officers of the 390th BG, at Framlingham, would regularly meet with the Group engineering officer and Sub-Depot Command to sort out operational requirements and problems and parts supply. However, it was often a struggle to meet the squadron's requirements with regard to some of the more difficult items to obtain. When those situations arose crews had to turn to other means.

Paul continued by illustrating other methods of 'moonlight requisitioning': the means of obtaining hard-to-get parts. Ground crews would learn all the group and squadron numbers of those inhabiting neighbouring airfields. Sometimes they would visit other airfields and pass themselves off as members from that group to remove parts from the stores. Unofficial removal of parts from other aircraft within the group was also not uncommon, particularly from aircraft that were temporarily grounded for one reason or another. Paul Kovitz recounts:

> Sometimes, due to parts shortages, 'moonlight requisitioning' would have to be resorted to. Oxygen regulators and oil coolers were a couple of items in short supply. One trip, we

went to Woodbridge, to 'requisition' some oil coolers from the large supply warehouse there. We got onto the base and into the stores and picked up some coolers. We were stopped going out the gate and taken into custody by the MPs. They interrogated us and were going to detain us overnight, not for 'requisitioning' but for what we saw on the base. That was a massive build up of C-47s, gliders and troops etc. We were finally released with the oil coolers after it had been verified who we were, and after we had promised not to relate to anyone what we had seen on the base. The next day was D-Day, and the air was black with C-47s and gliders for the invasion. The whole trip turned out to be an exercise in futility, as when we went to install the coolers, a closer inspection revealed they were for B-24 aircraft, not B-17s. We had to return the coolers and sneak them back into the stores.

Henry G. Johansen recalls the situation at Molesworth, similar to that which occurred at many other bases:

Usable parts are salvaged from a disabled Boeing B-17 of the 390th BG, Framlingham, 28 July 1943. In some extreme cases of 'recycling', whole airframes were reconstructed from scrap aircraft such as this. The 444th Sub-Depot at Molesworth, with the help of Boeing field service representatives, rebuilt at least two B-17s using major parts from other wrecks. One of these was recovered by 'cutting and shutting' a recoverable tail section from aft of the radio room and joining it to a salvaged front fuselage section. (USAAF)

A piece of tooling developed by members of the 535th BS, 381st BG, for safely removing B-17 tyres from their wheels, avoided much potential injury. (USAAF)

I remember how in the first few months of combat when supplies were hard to get, that crew chiefs were reluctant to leave their B-17s in the hangar overnight. Too often there was a 'Moonlight Request' done on them; nobody knew where the parts went but we were sure that it put another plane in combat status. This ceased when supplies became more plentiful.

As well as scrap airframes being cannibalised and stripped of every usable component, Paul Kovitz also recalled racing to the site of air crashes that occurred in the locality, 'like a bunch of vultures', to see if there were reusable parts they could retrieve from the wreckage.

The resourcefulness of engineering personnel didn't end with the spare parts issue. Many special tools and pieces of equipment to speed up processes or to provide the unobtainable were also developed by both the Sub-Depots and squadron crews.

Crash Recovery

Another task that fell at times to crews from the Sub-Depot was crash recovery, particularly that occurring on the home airfield. Air crashes were an all too frequent and tragic occurrence in the Second World War, with Britain's skies crowded with both RAF and USAAF aircraft. Returning from missions, low on fuel, with damaged engines and aircraft structures, crews would battle to make landfall and try not to succumb to a watery end in the North Sea. Having reached the coast of England, however, often the ordeal was not over, and the desperate desire to set a badly damaged aircraft down often became too great a task. Sadly, far too often crews failed at the last hurdle, many within a short distance of 'home'.

Aircraft would often try to land as soon as they crossed the Channel at the first airfield they came to, especially if the crew were aware that they were in a particularly perilous state. To better provide for this situation, three enormous emergency landing strips were constructed on the east coast of England: one at Carnaby in Yorkshire, one at Manston in Kent and the third at Woodbridge in Suffolk, the latter being very close to some of the 8th's 3rd Air Division bomber airfields.

In these situations, aircraft landing away from their home base and requiring repairs or salvage would come under the jurisdiction of the relevant Strategic Air Depots (SAD). SADs operated Mobile Air Depots (MAD) for the purpose of repairing aircraft away from their home station. These were units fully equipped with mobile workshops, lifting equipment and other specialist items to enable them to operate independently.

If aircraft returning from missions were known to have serious damage but weren't in immediate danger, then the normal procedure, if possible, would be to divert and make for the relevant SAD to land as recovery and extensive damage repair was part of the SAD's remit. This practice also went some way to alleviating another potential problem. An aircraft crash landing could easily put an active airfield out of action by blocking a runway, especially if the crash became a more serious incident. As damaged aircraft, particularly those with injured crew on board, were given landing priority, an incident such as this could make it very difficult for the remainder of a group's aircraft to land.

Those that made it made it back to their home station could often run into difficulties at the point of landing. Undercarriage or brake failures, caused by battle damage and rendering control systems inoperable, were often only discovered when an aircraft was on its final approach to the runway – too late to divert by that point. Many times aircraft would have to try and land with wheels up or would carry on rolling off the end of the concrete and into the surrounding countryside. At times like this it fell to the Sub-Depot, with its heavy equipment, to jack aircraft back up onto their wheels or extract an errant aircraft from a hedgerow or ploughed field.

Sub-depot personnel became very adept at this procedure and it could be achieved quite quickly. Rudi Steele recalls more assistance being provided at Bassingbourn in solving these problems:

> I remember we borrowed an ancient WW1 era compressor from some Irish labourers working on the camp. We had no proper lifting kit to raise aircraft with until the RAF provided us with their inflatable airbags, prior to that all we had was wooden blocks.

An example of a typical day's recovery work is well illustrated by this excerpt from the November 1943 logbook of the 448th Sub-Depot, attached to the 381st BG, Ridgewell:

> In the Engineering Section, constant operations and subsequent damage kept the crews operating at top speed, 24 crews being in operation in most shops. The Hangar crews ready at a moment's notice for all sorts of work. So on 18 November, when 42-37721 (534th GD-L *Sugar*) came in on her belly, this crew was 'Johnny on the spot' and removed it to Hangar # 1 for repairs. Twice previously this aircraft has been in for major battle damage and repair. On the same day the crew again dashed forth with their equipment to raise 42-37754 (534th GD-I *Whodat – The Dingbat?*) which also came in wheels up – Hangar # 1 also received this. Stations 4–9 [distinct areas of the aircraft] were severely damaged. This was the third time in the hangar for this aircraft, for major repairs. Twenty six days later however, this plane was out again dropping its eggs on Hitler's domain. It took 2,464 man hours, four new engines, four props, two flaps, landing gear and considerable sheet metal work, to get her into the air'.[1]

B-17s tended to fare better from belly landings than B-24s. The design of the B-17 still allowed for partly exposed main wheels in the inner engine nacelles, even when fully retracted to take some of the load. Provided the ball turret had been withdrawn to its raised position, negating the risk of the aircraft breaking its back on landing, then the damage was usually lessened. It would also normally be the procedure to try to land on the grass field rather than the runway to further soften the blow and decrease the risk of sparks causing fires. B-24s, with their high wing and totally enclosed retracted main wheels, tended to come off worst, as there was less to protect the underside. Both types were, however, repairable, and returned to service after belly landings, which occurred fairly regularly.

Air jacks being used to lift a 91st BG B-17 out of the mud at Bassingbourn. These offered a much better system than conventional hydraulic jacks and wooden blocks, as they minimised any damage to the airframe and could be used on soft ground without heavy reinforcement. (Joe Harlick)

Single-wheel landings were a particularly precarious feat for both types to attempt, but were accomplished on occasions.

Aircraft which couldn't be repaired would be salvaged for spare parts and reusable materials, particularly aluminium, would be collected and sent for recycling. The Ministry of Aircraft Production (MAP) co-ordinated aluminium salvage and operated several scrap collection centres around the country for collecting aircraft wreckage. One such metal and products recovery depot was operated on behalf of MAP by Morris Motors Ltd in Oxford. A number of First Air Division B-17s ended up being salvaged by this unit. According to Whit Hill, these facilities were sometimes used as an unofficial source of spare parts:

> For aircraft structural repairs, some aluminium stringers and pressed angle shaped and circumferential stiffeners may have been available, but parts were more readily available more quickly, in the junk yard located outside of Cambridge, and within a few miles of Bassingbourn.

For air crash sites away from airfields, the procedure was usually for specialist RAF salvage crews to clear them. If it was a USAAF aircraft, the RAF crews were normally assisted by personnel from the relevant SAD.

Motor Transport Section

The US Army and the USAAF in particular was a highly mechanised force. Every airfield had a large array of vehicles for general and specific duties, the four squadrons and the HQ unit alone having around 200 allocated between them. Once again, as with personnel on a base, all motor transport, apart from vehicles with specific functions, would be pooled. When all the groups' vehicles were added together the size of the motor pool rose to around 500 road vehicles and trailers. At times the airfield perimeter tracks could be very busy places. Surrounding villages and roads would also become very crowded and noisy; small wonder that the 'Yanks' left such a lasting impression on rural communities still largely dependent on the horse!

The most common vehicles would be the trucks, the most instantly recognisable being the Jeep or truck, ¼ ton, to give it its correct title. Then there would be a considerable number of Dodge, GMC and Studebaker trucks in the ¾ ton to 2½ ton weight categories, the most numerous being in general cargo-carrying configuration. There would usually be staff cars coming and going carrying senior officers to and from meetings. Many of these cars were American in origin; examples from all of the big three manufacturers, Ford, General Motors and Chrysler, appeared, as well as larger British saloon cars that were provided to USAAF.

More specialised were the trucks operated by the squadrons, Sub-Depot and emergency units, as well as those operated for base defence purposes. Specialist equipment operated by squadron personnel included trucks and trailers for delivering bombs from storage to the waiting aircraft; the US Army provided both the Chevrolet M6 bomb service truck and the M5 bomb trailer for this task. Fuel tankers, particularly the larger articulated units by Federal, Biederman and Reo, must have seemed enormous against British civilian lorries of the day. Probably the most unique vehicle operated by ground support personnel would be the Cletrac. These were small tracked tugs used to manoeuvre aircraft around the airfield. Originally manufactured by the Cleveland Tractor Corporation, hence Cletrac, they were also later produced by two other agricultural machine manufacturers, Oliver and John Deere. Colloquially known as 'bomber nurses', they were often seen towing aircraft, or providing air or electricity from their onboard compressors and generators. Due to their tracked drive they were also very useful for extracting mired aircraft and hauling them back onto hard surfaces.

The Sub-Depot furnished their specialist equipment in the shape of the very specific Model 606 'plane wrecker' crane by Federal, mobile workshops hauled by White or Autocar tractors, as well as dedicated trailers for transporting such things as engines and propellers. Sub-Depots were also sometimes lucky in being allocated another much prized possession: a forklift truck.

Many other vehicles on the stations, however, were of British origin, supplied by the RAF under the reciprocal aid scheme. A considerable number of AEC aircraft refuelling trucks, Austin ambulances and various fire engines were supplied, particularly in the early months of the 8th's establishment, as well as large quantities of RAF C-type bomb trolleys and David Brown airfield tractors.

The motor transport (MT) sheds were normally situated on the technical site, although there do appear to be instances where hangar space was used for the function. Once again MT buildings came in a wide range of types and sizes, but by the time they were being constructed on wartime stations they would normally be of the now familiar temporary brick. The MT shed would comprise multiple vehicle bays, usually eight to ten in number, set alongside the MT yard, a large area of concrete for extra vehicle parking. Facilities would also include a transport office, latrines and sometimes a vehicle-loading ramp.

As one of their official functions, the Ordnance Company assigned to a bomb group normally ran the maintenance section of the station's motor pool, supplying sufficient staff to carry out their duties. The US Army also maintained its vehicles using an echelon system much like that used for aircraft maintenance. First echelon checks would be carried out by the vehicle driver, such as fluid levels and tyre pressures; the satisfactory accomplishment of these tasks was policed with periodic maintenance inspections of both paperwork and the quality of workmanship. All Second World War era vehicles required a lot of regular greasing and oiling and this would have been a regular task for those working in the MT section. There was usually a greasing pit over which vehicles would be driven; the occupant would have been kept very busy!

One bay of the MT shed would be turned over to the tyre-fitting team; given the number of vehicles on site this would have been another busy unit. As well as being very fit, they would also have to have been resourceful, as replacement vehicle tyres were often in very short supply, making repairs essential. The study of period photographs often show vehicles on airbases not to be carrying spare wheels and one assumes that this was a luxury that could not be continued in times of such shortages. However, on Dodge ¾-ton and 1½-ton trucks used around airfields, the spare wheel was often removed by airmen, due to the fact that it was mounted in an awkward position which inhibited the driver's swift entry and exit from the vehicle.

The higher echelons of maintenance, for more extensive servicing and repair, would be handled by the MT section mechanics with spare parts supplied by the Sub-Depot supply section. The Ordnance Company mechanics were usually a well-prepared outfit; their equipment allocation provided them with several special-purpose motor vehicle workshop and welding shop trucks, normally based on GMC 2½-ton chassis. From these mobile machine shops mechanics would often manufacture their own spare parts and specialist tools.

Regular vehicle movements were usually undertaken by a pool of drivers supplied by the transportation section of the Station Complement Squadron, and this unit would have an office near the MT yard. The office would contain a vehicle dispatcher who organised transport for all the departments on the camp. This would have been another very busy office to work in as on average, dispatchers answered a call for transport provision every two minutes, such was the need for their services!

Off-base trips normally averaged thirty a day with the average daily mileage per camp being around 2,000. Off-base runs could be popular with drivers, especially during the summer months with a chance to get to know the locality better, but British rural roads were not built for large American vehicles and so were less pleasant in the depths of winter with only meagre blackout lights to see by. Problems of driving left-hand drive vehicles on what to the servicemen was the 'wrong' side often caused altercations of the minor, and unfortunately on occasions, major, nature. Coupled with the lack of road signs, removed for the duration to avoid aiding an invading enemy, it is hardly surprising that problems did occur.

Drivers from this pool also operated all the air crew transportation around the airfield, to and from their aircraft. Official transportation around the base was normally provided by truck, usually the ubiquitous 2½-ton GMC or ¾-ton Dodge but sometimes commandeered British buses were used. However, the best form of personal transportation, next to having access to a vehicle, was the bicycle. Whether just for getting around the airfield or exploring the local pubs, it was a must-have item. Contemporary photographs show them in the hundreds, all varying styles and makes, from the official RAF or Air Ministry standards to civilian models 'borrowed' from the locals, or purchased second hand in the larger towns. Bicycle maintenance became another necessary off-duty activity!

The other vital facility situated along with the MT yard would be the station MT petrol pumps, drawing fuel from a buried 2,000-gallon tank. Petrol supply, like aviation fuel, would be regularly delivered from a local rail depot. Demands for petrol deliveries were made through the British fuel supply system via the RAF liaison officer. Petrol would be dispensed against a voucher system which had to be authorised by HQ and then passed back through the reciprocal aid channels. A department within the camp quartermaster stores dealt with overseeing the administration of fuel supplies as well as all reciprocal aid returns.

As well as the requirements of all the airfield vehicles, reserve stocks tended to be held in case other military convoys in the area required their tanks to be refilled; the MT section generally ran a 24-hour service to cover such eventualities. On average 25,000 gallons of petrol and 500 gallons of oil would be consumed per month on every airfield. Constant inspections were made to ensure that actual supplies matched those on the returns; in a country with strict petrol rationing, checks had to made to ensure that it wasn't literally being siphoned off in other directions!

Photographic Section

With all the work for mission planning, aerial photography became a vitally important element in the air war against Germany. As Britain already possessed a complex infrastructure established for this task and the USAAF did not, this was yet one more thing they had to learn from the RAF. Initially, USAAF officers joined the RAF Photo Interpretation Unit at Medmenham near Marlow, Buckinghamshire. Some USAAF officers had in fact already been attending courses at the unit from June 1941, prior to the US entry into the Second World War, under the guise of official 'observers' watching Britain's fight against Germany.

The first photo reconnaissance (PR) missions for the USAAF were flown by the RAF until sufficient American aircraft became available. However, even after the USAAF were flying their own missions, all intelligence material was channelled through the RAF. Even then, in yet another example of reverse lend-lease, the RAF supplemented the 8th by supplying some PR aircraft types.

As well as the dedicated PR units, most combat aircraft, fighter and bomber, also carried cameras to record bomb strike detail, and gun cameras to record combat with enemy aircraft for future evaluation of tactics and training. In this way the fast-maturing USAAF intelligence organisation was also able to increase its knowledge base from another primary source.

Photography at Group Level

Among its staffing tables the USAAF provided combat squadrons with photographic specialists and all bases so inhabited would contain photographic laboratory facilities. From here personnel could speedily process strike and combat photos taken from the group's own aircraft, for post-mission assessment and other intelligence gathering purposes. The photo section comprised around twenty-two men. The Group HQ section provided two: the senior photographic officer and an enlisted airman photo technician, and the squadrons were tabled to provide five each, all either photographic interpreters, camera technicians or photo lab technicians. The whole unit operated as part of the S-2 Intelligence department. The photo laboratory would again be housed in either a pair of Nissen huts or a standard temporary brick structure.

Staff from the photographic section not only had to process and evaluate the photographs taken by the group, but they would also have to load and retrieve the cameras fitted in the aircraft. In some instances photographic technicians even flew missions to ensure that equipment functioned correctly. Technicians would have to go out to aircraft and load strike cameras prior to missions and remove the camera and take the film for processing after the return of the aircraft. Once returned and unloaded, cameras would be checked mechanically and then reloaded with film. It would usually be in the very early hours of the morning that photo lab staff would be alerted to the requirements of the day's mission; they would then have to visit the hardstands and refit cameras in aircraft that required them.

This wasn't too bad if it was your home base, but sometimes much travelling was required. Sergeant Joe Harlick, a photo lab technician with the 91st BG at Bassingbourn, remembered well the trouble it was if group aircraft were forced to land at another base, often some distance away due to bad weather:

> We would have to transport cameras, film and other equipment to the next base and prepare the planes for the next mission. The English roads were very narrow and winding (and they drive on the wrong side of the road!) so just to navigate to another base in the dark is a challenge. The one time I remember more than others, was Christmas Eve, December 24, 1944. The mission that day was to bomb German airfields. Our base was completely fogged in, so the B-17's from the 91st were directed to land at a base about 70 miles away.[2]

On their return, photographs would be processed immediately; the complete operation took around three hours. Firstly the film would be developed and then printed, after which the prints would be washed and glazed to give a glossy finish, and finally dried. Once ready they would be checked to ensure the exposure and processing had been completed correctly

Joe Harlick photo loading a K17 bomb strike camera into the camera well of a 91st BG B-17. (Joe Harlick)

before passing to S-2 personnel at the HQ site. All the processing work was carried out within the photographic laboratory with all the facilities and equipment necessary provided within each unit.

As well as handling the cameras and processing photographs, technicians from this section also had to repair, maintain, and at times come up with some quite innovative ideas to advance the science of aerial photography. Due to the chilled air present at the altitudes flown on missions many problems had to be overcome to enable cameras to function correctly. Control equipment had to be modified or developed that would allow strike cameras to automatically operate once ordnance had been salved, so that the results and accuracy could be recorded. Joe Harlick was awarded a certificate of merit for designing a switch that enabled this to happen. His team also developed camera heaters for high-altitude operation by modifying 24V heating muffs supplied for the Norden bombsight. The department would also provide all manner of other photographic support for the group:

> One of the darker sides to our job was photographing group aircraft that had been involved in crashes. One day a call came in that an aircraft of ours had come down and I had to get in a jeep, with my camera, and go and record the scene. Well we drove for hours, but due to secrecy I had know idea where we were going. We got there eventually and I recorded what I could, not nice as the crew had all been killed in the crash.

As Joe says, he had no idea where the scene was and it was only in June 2004 when he was invited back to England that he found out he had been taken to Wincanton in Somerset. Quite a journey from Bassingbourn at the best of times, but in a jeep in pre-motorway days one can only imagine the discomfort.

This incident was the crash of *Old Faithful* B17G 42-37958, which narrowly missed the town of Wincanton while returning from a raid in France on 25 June 1944, and crashed on some farm buildings, killing all on board. Joe recounted this story during the dedication of a memorial to this event.

As the majority of servicemen employed in this role were keen photographers as well, comprehensive photographic records also emerged from some of these departments. As well as official records of events around their own allotted squadron or group, such as official posed crew photos and ceremonial pictures, many pictures of personnel going about their day-to-day tasks were also recorded.

Unfortunately when the Americans pulled out of Britain at the end of the war, a lot of their surplus material was simply disposed of. Many a base's photo record was considered of no more importance than the general rubbish. Happily there were instances of a more enlightened approach. The 390th BG at Framlingham organised the publication of a book to record their exploits and systematically collected together a magnificent photo record that was published just after the war. The 'Blue Book', as it became known, records in great detail their two-year stay in Britain.

It seems that American servicemen were more able to make their own unofficial photographic record. This may have been because of a slightly more relaxed operational attitude but more likely due to a greater availability of cameras and, more importantly, film than to their British counterparts. Hence many American servicemen went home at the end of hostilities with an album or two of their own exploits. Indeed it would appear that later in the war photography was encouraged by airmen as, according to John Sloan, the station post exchange (PX) at Podington started taking in film for developing as a service for personnel based there.[3]

It would appear, from studying the back of period private photographs, that they, like letters, had to understandably pass before an official censor and be stamped as checked.

Domestic Supply – Quartermaster Corps

Whereas the Sub-Depot oversaw all the technical supply necessary for the effective operation of the group's aircraft and equipment, the Quartermaster (QM) Corps unit, another of the group's component organisations, controlled and distributed supplies of a more domestic nature, necessary for the smooth running of all the station's departments.

Although centred on the technical site the quartermaster's operation spread over several other areas of the camp. Ration stores were normally located on communal sites, close to the mess halls. Coal stores were provided on all the dispersed sites with the main compound located close to the utilities compounds. Vehicle petrol supply points would be operated from the motor transport section.

The quartermaster unit normally comprised between forty and fifty personnel, handling around fourteen different areas of supply operations. The unit was usually divided into smaller departments each specialising in one of these supply functions. The following is a breakdown of sections of the 1,207th Quartermaster Company attached to the 381st BG at Ridgewell and can be considered typical of the duties of a quartermaster unit on an 8th AF station. Included in the fourteen sections would be those handling the four primary supply classes that the quartermaster system had identified as essential stores. Class I was the provision of subsistence supplies for the station, classes II and IV were administrational consumables such as stationary and all domestic supplies and consumables. These two classes were normally administered together within the bomb group. Class III was the supply of petrol and oil (POL) for motor transport. Many of the remaining supply departments handled areas of supply and provision of services peculiar to operating in Britain. The departments comprised:

1   The first department administered the unit's operation and contained the company headquarters staff.

2   Handled the subsistence supplies – all the food required by the group on the station.

3   Provided all class II and IV supplies. This department processed all allocations of equipment as established by such appropriate sources such as the T/O&Es. It also dealt with the processing of requisitions of additional equipment from both US and British supply. Equipment required from British sources was requisitioned from the RAF through the liaison officer. Records of all camp and station property were maintained by this department.

    New supply and replacement of damaged personnel equipment was also supplied by this department as well as the retrieval and processing of equipment and the effects of personnel lost in combat.

    All janitorial supplies were issued from this department, as well as stationery, provided to the base S-4 office to administer and distribute to the necessary units and departments.

4   Provided class III supply, the provision of fuel and oil for motor vehicles.

5   Was the solid fuel section. This department handled supplies of all the house coal, steam coal, coke and kindling used on the camp.

6   Handled the salvage and recycling of usable waste materials generated by the station. The staff oversaw the collection and sorting of this material and usually had a compound close to the utilities area. Records were kept by the department for statistical accounting.

7   Dealt with laundry, dry cleaning and shoe repair. These services were provided by the quartermaster for enlisted men, hospital, and Red Cross personnel. Around 1,200 bundles of laundry were normally processed a week.

8   The Railway Traffic Office (RTO). This office arranged all rail transportation for personnel and equipment and provided rail warrants for official business and leave. The department received and distributed baggage of newly assigned personnel and traced and located owners of lost and unclaimed baggage.

9   The space supply and issuing of Special Service equipment. This was equipment for the use of service personnel largely during their off-duty time. The types of items in this class are day room furniture, athletic and recreational equipment, libraries of educational books and other items.

10   British service ration cards, authorised under certain circumstances for personnel – both officers and enlisted men – who were messing away from the station while on pass, or leave, or at a USAAF rest home.

11   The station quartermaster acted as a purchasing and contracts officer, and as such was authorised to make local purchases of items of extreme operational necessity up to the sum of £5. Should the cost of any items have been between £5 and £25, the station commander would have had to approve the purchase. Purchases in excess of £25 had to be approved by higher command. Detailed records of purchase orders, goods received and paid invoices were maintained by this administrator. The volume of local purchases was usually very small due to the fact that higher HQ urged that all possible items be procured through official supply channels in order not to deplete local civilian stocks.

12   All vouchers concerning receipts of supplies and/or services from the British were forwarded from station supply officers to this office where they were recorded in a register and forwarded to higher HQ for processing into reciprocal aid records.

13   This section administered the repair of office machines. In the main these were typewriters; where available, local civilian specialists were often contracted to carry out this work. Invoices were recorded and forwarded to higher HQ for reciprocal aid purposes.

14   The last section in the quartermaster department handled the issuing of officers' clothing ration cards. These cards were authorised for all officers to purchase an annual allowance of clothing. They were only issued once an officer had been in the ETO for a minimum of ninety days. Once again all records of issues and receipts were maintained.[4]

Training

Training within a bomb group was a very wide subject and affected all personnel attached to a unit in one way or another. Training could basically be broken down into three distinct areas: air crew training, standard basic military training, and trade or vocational training. Further to these three, there were also educational programmes introduced towards the end of the war, giving airmen a taste of vocational and non-vocational subjects that they might wish to take further after being released from military service. Each HQ unit contained senior air rated officers whose job it was to establish the flying training requirements of

91st BG personnel entering the gas chamber at Bassingbourn to experience the use of their gas masks, 20 November 1943. (USAAF)

their group. Each squadron would also have an officer in charge of training, and again these personnel would be pooled to form a training unit within each group. To co-ordinate the specific requirements of air crews. Some Special Services staff also became involved with some of the vocational and non-vocational education programmes, dependent on requirements established by other departments. Quite a number of personnel would at any time be heavily involved with training of one sort or another.

Basic military training would have consisted of ongoing programmes based on the elements of the basic training servicemen and women would have encountered when first enlisted. Although USAAF ground support units weren't frontline troops, they were still soldiers first and foremost and were expected to perform as such if called upon to do so. Programmes of gym, or callisthenics, as the army liked to call it, were regularly introduced to keep general fitness levels. Shooting practice would also be held whenever possible to keep skill levels up should they be called upon to defend the base. One form of basic training that all staff would have had to undertake at some point would have been gas mask drills, which enabled them to have a little experience should they need to be used in a real emergency.

Vocational Training

For the most part, personnel engaged in a ground support role, particularly the more skilled trades, would have passed through one of the USAAF's schooling programmes in the US. Operated by the Air Force's Technical Training Command, two of the biggest were at Keesler Field Mississippi and Chanute Field Illinois, where thousands of skilled technicians were trained every year. Paul Kovitz explains the situation at Framlingham:

> Basically the engineering people were trained in their speciality but it continued on the job as pertained to the B-17. The Group training section was concerned mainly with flight crews.

Those lucky enough to have attended good craft training programmes at air force schools and colleges, or to have good civilian engineering skills or qualifications were

An obviously posed photograph of training being undertaken literally in the field! This would appear to be personnel under instruction from a fighter group, judging by the aircraft profile illustrated on the case. (Author's Collection)

swiftly placed into squadron ground crews. Others it seems were placed into the USAAF system with a very rudimentary training and expected to gain the necessary on-the-job experience in their 'chosen' (allotted) speciality. To assist those in this situation, as well as to provide continual updated training on new systems and developments, the USAAF operated programmes of training for ground support staff on all of its airfields.

Other specialists were not quite so fortunate with the scope and breadth of their training. Rod Ryan recounted being drafted in October 1942, having previously worked in a bearing factory. He was given just three days' specialist training for his role in handling bombs and ammunition before embarking for Britain! Leroy Keeping had this to say about his induction into the air force:

> I was called up on 20th April 1942, the call up being deferred until 29th due to me being in a car crash. I had no previous engineering experience, before attending three months training in school, which was all class based, in Denver, Colorado. Facilities at that stage were fairly basic. An elderly couple who lived near where I was billeted, took some buddies and myself 'under their wing', providing us with proper meals etc. Bearing in mind I had been allocated the trade of Power Turret Specialist, I didn't get work on a turret or even see a real one until I got to my allotted bomb group, to work on airplanes for real.

It is a great tribute to the large numbers of engineering personnel that they had the ability to learn quickly the technical nuances of the machines they had to keep in service. The youth of this era had proved themselves extremely adaptable and resourceful; many, having grown up among the privations of the depression, quickly taken to new expanding technologies. Many ground crew members had come from a rural background and were not only very adept at repairing mechanical equipment out of necessity but were able to do so in the most rudimentary of conditions.

Air Crew Training

While flight training in the US for officer members of bomber crews, particularly pilots and navigators, was of a high standard, operational training, once formed into individual air crews or groups, appears to have been variable in quality. This would largely be dependent on when in the war one enlisted or to which group one was assigned. There are many stories of elements of flight training that were skipped, especially in the early rush to get crews to theatre. Many of these shortcomings no doubt contributed to the enormous number of bomber crew losses, particularly in the early stages of the 8th's activity in Britain. The lack of good formation flying skills for instance has been cited as detrimental to survivability. It wasn't until air crews actually started to complete tours in the European theatre and return to the US that good experienced instructors could be engaged on impressing the realities of combat flying upon rookie crews. As a result, it became imperative to impart the experience of combat on new crews before they were committed to it for real. Once deployed, air crews would also have to be instructed in all the necessary elements of transition to flying in Britain.

The problems with the training of air crews new into theatre were largely addressed by the establishment and operation of the CCRCs where new crews were trained in the specifics of flying in the ETO, particularly the need for tight formation flying and the complicated and dangerous processes of formation after take-off and returning to base after a raid, especially in some of the appalling weather that Britain could provide.

Once allocated to a group, training for crews didn't stop. More specific training for gunners and bombardiers was provided on the group's home camp and constant training was provided to try to improve the skill and accuracy of those tasked with these roles. Training was also vital in R/T and wireless communication, to fit with RAF methods, and this was often done once replacement crews had been allocated a group. It would also be vitally important that skills were regularly 'updated', as systems and weaponry developments accelerated as the war progressed.

Training at group level was usually carried out under the direction of a senior officer within HQ tasked with that function. At Framlingham for instance, the 390th BG established a ground school whereby new crews were given an eight-day intensive indoctrination course to instil the group's flying and bombing methodologies into them. Schooling was split between classroom and practical training and crews had to complete the course before flying any missions. Here they would learn new strategies of heavy bombardment and new tactics, all learnt by the group the hard way. When periods of bad weather struck they weren't wasted where experienced crews were concerned, as top-up sessions were given to impart new techniques on subjects such as 'how to keep a damaged bomber flying', 'aerial first aid' and escape and evasion techniques if shot down over enemy territory. Dinghy drill training for air crews was sometimes carried out in the static water tanks on the ground at airfields, and parachute drills and procedures for ditching at sea would be rehearsed in the gymnasium.

One major development of the time was the introduction of synthetic training, or what today would be known as simulators, particularly for gunnery, bomb aiming and 'blind-flying' training. The RAF and Air Ministry had been involved in the development and subsequent use of various systems for some time, as had the USAAF. Most RAF stations had specific training buildings on them and these were taken over by the USAAF on occupation and complemented on occasions by some of their own equipment. The three main synthetic training installations found on bomber stations were the Air Ministry Laboratory (AML) bomb teacher, the Link trainer and the turret/free gunnery trainer.

An early form of flight simulator, the link trainer, enabled the 'pilot', when closed in, to fly with instruments alone. Results of these 'flights' would be recorded on the plotting table. Given the British climate and changeable weather conditions, instrument flying practice such as this would have been vitally important. Some of the early arriving 8th bomber pilots also undertook live 'blind flying' training, from RAF Watchfield in Oxfordshire. (USAAF)

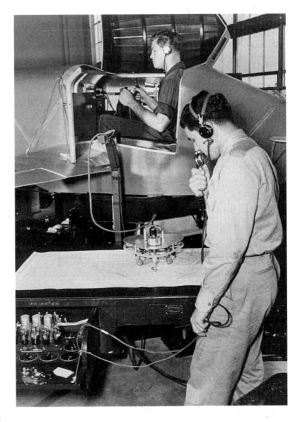

AML Bomb Trainer

Projecting equipment, housed in a 20ft by 20ft two-storey building, 'shone' a slow moving, large-scale landscape image onto the ground floor through a hole in the first floor. Operating from the first floor, bomb aimers and navigators would train to improve their targeting skills on simulated targets. The AML teacher would have been adapted to use the Norden bombsight with which to train. AML buildings appeared in many configurations from single to quadruple examples.

Link Trainer

An American invention by Edwin Link, this was an aircraft simulator used for instrument or blind flying. Although an American device, the RAF had used them from 1937 and a single-storey building in single or double configuration was provided to house the equipment.

Free Gunnery Trainer

This facility was usually housed in a small blister-type hangar. In USAAF usage this often housed a selection of gun positions found on the relevant American bomber type used by the group. Often these gunnery positions were actual examples removed from salvaged aircraft to provide more realism. Guns were modified to provide simulated fire onto a projector screen. The system evolved from the basic USAAF gun-training simulator, the 'Jam Handy' trainer, which used a double projector system that displayed a fighter on the screen while another showed the gun's ring sight. The main technique taught to students involved mastering the art of deflection shooting; in other words, practicing aiming just in front of an enemy fighter at where it will shortly be, as opposed to where it currently was. Another important aspect often instructed was the correct cleaning methods to keep guns firing at high altitude, where any trace of oil and grease could cause a gun to seize.

One group, the 390th BG at Framlingham, although probably not unique in this, even went as far as to set up redundant aircraft tail sections at the shooting butts to enable gunners to gain real practice firing the .50-calibre weapons. Around twenty instructors were often on hand, some still active gunners putting in hours on missions. In one, and no doubt not unusual occurrence, the USAAF provided a trainer for specialities of which there was no need in the European theatre. John Appleby arrived at Lavenham just prior to war's end, in March 1944, as a celestial navigation trainer, having performed this role for a couple of years previously in the US:

> I spent that first morning 'checking in' at my new station, which means I trudged from the hospital to public relations to tech supply, having a slip of paper initialled by anyone I could find.
>
> At the end I had an interview with the personnel officer, who was stumped by the fact I had been a Celestial Navigation Trainer Operator in the States. The 8th Air Force had no celestial navigation trainers, for they are expensive and bulky gadgets, requiring a large silo to house them and air conditioning plant to keep them at exactly the proper temperature and humidity. Furthermore, celestial navigation was not practiced by the 8th Air Force, since all its operations were carried out by day and all its navigation done with radio aids. The RAF however, was reputed to have celestial navigation trainers, and I suggested hopefully that I might be loaned or transferred to the Royal Air Force. This was regarded as a highly frivolous proposition and came to nought. I was assigned to the director of training.[5]

One can only surmise that perhaps there would be a requirement for such with the relocation of crews to the Pacific theatre now that the European war's end was in sight. John Appleby ended up providing support for other training functions, although by this stage it would appear that most things were winding down. With the arrival of VE Day, he was able to spend a lot of his time cycling around Suffolk and Norfolk exploring the villages and countryside, and engaging in his newfound hobby of visiting churches and carrying out brass rubbings. He appeared to enjoy this so much that he managed to get transferred to Thorpe Abbotts with the 100th BG when his initial group, the 487th BG, were returned to the US in July 1945, enabling him to stay for a few more months. He was then mainly engaged in running the Link trainer at Thorpe Abbotts.

Armament

The USAAF's standard weapon in all aircraft for both offensive and defensive purposes was the Browning M2 .50-calibre machine gun. The .30-calibre M2 Browning was fitted as nose defence armament in early B-17 E and F models and in some B-26s, but it was rarely used after the spring of 1943 due to shortcomings in the frontal defence of early aircraft being identified.

Gun maintenance and ammunition supply was undertaken by squadron armament personnel. Having first been removed from aircraft, guns would be taken to the squadron armament facility, which was usually located on the technical site, or near the squadron hardstands on the flight line, for maintenance and cleaning. Once cleaned and oiled, guns would be stored ready to be replaced in the aircraft prior to the next mission.

Squadron personnel would also have to link the belted ammunition. B-17 G models initially had thirteen M2 machine guns, each of which used between 300 and 500 rounds per mission, so a lot of time was spent preparing ammunition. It was a monotonous job but one which also required extreme care to avoid ammunition jamming in the guns.

Testing of guns to check operation and alignment characteristics would be carried out at the shooting butts, located around one hardstand adjacent to the perimeter track out on the flying field.

Linking ammunition at Ridgewell with personnel from the 381st BG. Ammunition belts were assembled depending on the pattern of ammunition type, specified for a particular mission; these would normally comprise tracer, ball and armour piercing rounds, 25 October 1943. (USAAF)

Administration

As has been recorded on previous pages, the various organisations located on the technical site all included their own administrational departments. Other offices that were located on the technical site would include the HQ units for each squadron and the Group Engineering HQ. The squadron HQ offices would have included their own individual administrational departments, handling the day-to-day operation of each squadron as well as facilities such as stores for the squadron's own tool and equipment supplies.

Group engineering would co-ordinate the engineering effort provided by the squadron and Sub-Depot staff and liaise with the Group HQ to provide as many combat ready aircraft as were required, or possible, for each mission.

Working in and with all these units would have been the technical inspectors. Both squadrons and group units had inspection staff and it was their job to ensure repairs and maintenance to all equipment, including complete aircraft, components and systems, as well as vehicles, armament and aircraft control systems, were done in the correct manner and the records administered appropriately. All modifications required by technical directives would also have been administered by this team.

7

The Control Tower

The Signature Building

The control tower has become in some way the identifying structure of an airfield, the symbol of the site's survival. If the tower exists then even if the runways have gone the airfield somehow survives. If the tower has gone then the field has gone. Perhaps the connection has come about because quite a few former towers are now museums. Among others, those at Framlingham, Debach, Rougham, Thorpe Abbotts and Bassingbourn are now all fine examples and act as wonderful memorials to their station's former occupants. Others have survived in different guises but as such are still seen in a similar light. Podington is now a house, Lavenham, Hethel and Attlebridge survive as offices and Rattlesden is a headquarters for a gliding club. When derelict, however, their bulk and gaunt, large, windowless facades seem to echo the mournful fate of an abandoned station.

Virtually every structure on a British Second World War airfield went through some form of evolutionary period of design and development, whether in function or purely constructional method. The control tower was no exception. Initially referred to in its original Air Ministry designation as a watch office, it first appeared on RAF airfields as a separate building around 1926. It was simply a small single-storey office, situated close to the flight line. The building started to evolve a little later with the provision of a shed close by for storing flare path lamps, used to mark out a landing strip during conditions of poor visibility.

The first major development came in 1934, when once again the expansion era heralded many new building types. The watch office grew into a two-storey affair, starting to take on the more familiar form of future designs. The watch office was then absorbed into a larger structure, becoming just one of several rooms with a dedicated purpose. Ultimately this again became a larger single building of two or even three storeys with the option of a further 'glasshouse' structure added to the flat roof. This was available in several design types, providing additional observation capacity.

The designation of the building also started to change. During the Second World War, particularly on airfields occupied by the USAAF, it adopted the American term and became a control tower containing a watch office, and encompassing all the functions necessary for controlling air to ground operations on that airfield. The RAF term 'watch office' continued until after the Second World War, by which time the American 'control tower' had become universally accepted.

The tower's positioning was obviously very important: well away from hangars and other buildings so that the ends of the runways were visible from its upper floors. On early grass airfields it was often found that with the arrival of surfaced runways, the watch office was in the wrong alignment. In those situations a new tower was often built to the current design pattern and the old tower was generally, but not always, demolished. Kimbolton retained both its original and replacement towers right through the war, which were eventually demolished in the mid-1970s, long after the airfield had ceased operations and been closed.

Most of the control towers on 8th heavy bomber fields were situated, along with a small cluster of air traffic control related buildings, slightly away from the main technical site. Bassingbourn and Horsham St Faith differed in that their position was dictated by pre-war planning and they were among the crescent of hangars that bordered the flying field.

Alongside the control tower would be cluster of smaller structures and facilities. These would normally include a pyrotechnic store for keeping a convenient but safe store of flare gun cartridges for signalling to aircraft. A night-flying equipment (NFE) and floodlight trailer store would also be sited in the vicinity of the tower. These two buildings would house flare path equipment and floodlights to illuminate the runways in the event of emergency landings at night. Once improved airfield lighting systems were installed the use of NFE equipment decreased, particularly as the flares were difficult to extinguish in a hurry should the need arise.

Also close to the tower would be a fire engine shed and crash crew facilities. Sufficient concrete hardstanding would be provided close to the tower for parking emergency vehicles,

Ridgewell tower site, showing the control tower, station identification code (RD), emergency vehicles and the signals square. Three of the most common signals can be seen in the square. In the lower right-hand corner the most regularly used is a red square indicating that the airfield was not open to the public. If superimposed by a white diagonal strip, as this is, it meant that temporary obstructions were in place on the airfield. This would be most often used when grass cutting or runway repairs were taking place. Turning the symbol into a white cross indicated a total landing prohibition. The white T, indicates the active runway, and would be moved depending on wind direction. It would be aligned with the active runway, pointing in the direction of landing. The white dumbbell indicates that the airfield was unserviceable except for runways and taxiways, and on wartime airfields was usually used to indicate that no landings on grass were permitted, due to the danger of aircraft becoming mired. (USAAF)

as well as a concrete road normally leading directly to the perimeter track. In front of the tower would be the identification and signals area, normally 40ft by 40ft with a white border. It would contain any ground signals in use; the type used would be changed to suit various circumstances. Although the RAF had firmly entered the age of wireless communications, there were times when such equipment was inoperative and visual methods of air control would be required. A signals mast would also often stand close by and would be available to replicate any ground signals pertaining to the current flying situation at the field. The identity of the airfield would also be laid out by means of a two-letter airfield code near the control tower.

Alongside or nearby would be erected the sleeve streamer mast, more commonly known as a windsock, marked by a 20ft-diameter ring on the ground and would be a visual indicator of the wind direction and condition. Other small structures close by would be provided to house meteorological instruments.

Tower Variations

By the end of the war the USAAF had gained a wide variety of control tower types and styles in their collection. This variety is highly indicative of the regular rethinking of airfield requirements, particularly from the early-war period, and represents the changing role of these particular fields in the frantic reshuffle of allocations once the Americans 'came on board'. Two of the earliest examples were at Bassingbourn and Horsham St Faith. The tower at Bassingbourn was a pre-war 'Fort' type 207/36. Built to a pre-cast concrete design, this type was the RAF's first standardised design. It was used at over forty expansion era airfields. The other operational heavy bomber expansion era station allocated to the 8th AF was Horsham St Faith, near Norwich. It sported a later 5845/39 type. Described as a 'watch office with Met section' it was also available as a pre-cast concrete design under diagram 2328/39. By the outbreak of war, much more consideration was being given to future internal space requirements, resulting in much larger buildings. This type was probably one of the most attractive designs in the Art Deco style, with the ground floor extending forward to support a balcony, and the walls of the upper floors having curved corners.

Like all other airfield structures, once into the war, control tower designs became more utilitarian both in style and construction method, form went out and function became the driver. Yet again there were a wide range of types designed for various station purposes, but externally tending to look alike due to the temporary construction methods utilised, usually cement rendered over brick.

Bassingbourn control tower. Bassingbourn was unusual as although the original tower position was still in a suitable location when the runways were laid, the tower was not of sufficient size. Instead of being replaced, a new control room was built around it, and a new signalling floor added to the top, evolving into a unique design. The tower now houses a museum. (Author's Collection)

Flying Control

Prior to 1937 there was virtually no flying control on a military airfield save for a duty pilot in a watch office during flying hours. He would have little more than a logbook to record flights and a flare pistol to signal with. From early 1938, attempts were made by the Air Ministry to reorganise things along the lines of the existing civilian flying control. With ever more sorties being flown the problem of losses due to failings of co-ordinated air traffic control for military aircraft began to be felt and specialists in this field became an urgent requirement. Due to staffing shortages, early in the Second World War, civilian flying controllers were drafted to form a new regional control school at Brasenose College, Oxford. This unit would form the nucleus of control on six airfields considered of strategic importance in various parts of the country. Late in 1941, the new organisation moved to the appropriately named RAF Watchfield in West Oxfordshire, to form the renamed Flying Control School. Many of the 8th's control tower staff attended courses at this school. Normally of around six week's duration, it was here that they were fully integrated into the British methods of flying control, learning the rules from AP3024, the flying control bible! This was one of the earliest and most important areas of RAF and USAAF liaison, as there was no room in the crowded skies of Britain for dual systems of flying control! The groundwork for establishing and integrating these vital elements of air force co-operation, owed a lot to the hard work performed during Eaker and his team's initial meetings with RAF and Air Ministry officials in early 1942.

The control tower would have been the nerve centre of the airfield, certainly as far as any aspect of flying was concerned, and no aircraft could take off or land without permission from flying control. For all movement of aircraft, even if only on the ground, the tower would normally be informed. While missions were in operation the tower would have crash and ambulance crews as well as flare path crews ready on standby in case of fog or poor light, providing more assistance to pilots trying to land. Also contained within was accommodation for the signals and weather units. The flat roof of the building was often used for weather observation and placement of specialist monitoring equipment.

Staff in the tower would normally be the first to get word on a returning mission, through the signals unit. Obviously radio silence was important unless vitally necessary while over enemy territory. Mission accomplishment was usually indicated via a coded message transmitted on return from the target. If a mission was aborted after take-off then the signals staff would call the aircraft back, using the correct code of the day. While in the vicinity all aircraft, particularly those landing or visiting, would remain in radio and very often, visual, contact. The tower would also be in constant contact with other airfields in the area as they maintained control of their piece of airspace.

Air traffic control staff were normally provided from another of the component supporting units of the bomb group, the Station Complement Squadron. In addition, many that came to be senior control officers were pilots who had been grounded through health issues or injury. When the first USAAF groups started flying from England, control towers were initially operated by RAF personnel. As training increased, more US flying controllers became available and were able to take over most of the duties. Most airfields, however, still retained an RAF control officer in a senior position. The tower would have been manned around the clock, with flying control personnel operating a three-shift system. The most important position was the airman-of-the-watch, an RAF term taken on by the USAAF, much like a lot of the equipment they used. To this individual fell the task of constantly knowing the current status of the airfield as well as keeping a record of every aircraft movement in the station logbook.

The normal procedure would require two flying control officers (FCOs) to be on duty during landings: one to control aircraft on approach and the other to control aircraft in the circuit. The FCO controlling aircraft on approach would operate from a flying control caravan near the touchdown point of the active runway.

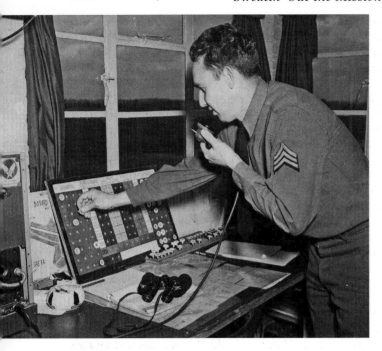

The officer in charge of
flying control would have a
diagrammatic map of the airfield
in the tower and kept track of all
the aircraft with coloured pins.
A rudimentary system, but it
worked. Sgt R. A. Chamberland
of Taunton, Massachusetts,
324th BS, 91st BG, checks
in aircraft as they land at
Bassingbourn, 24 June 1943.
(USAAF)

A senior officer would be in charge of ensuring daily changes in operational procedure
were enforced. These could be due to such things as runway maintenance or grass cutting.
He would also ensure that daily checks of runways for damage or obstructions had been
completed.

Runways were identified by a number utilising their angular alignment and reciprocal
bearing based on the compass points. Numbering started from the runway end nearest
north, continuing in a clockwise direction. As there were three runways, this resulted in six
numbers. The main runway would normally be aligned as close to SW/NE as possible to take
advantage of the natural prevailing wind. This would be used most of the time, unless it was
unserviceable or peculiarities of wind direction dictated otherwise. It would be very unlikely
that a mission would be launched from any runway other than the main as even this was
only just long enough to allow fully laden bombers to take off from for much of the time.

As challenging as co-ordinating the safe departure and return of thirty or forty
aircraft could be, at times the British weather tended to complicate the issue even further,
particularly with fog. When guiding in a damaged or lost aircraft or preparing for a forced
landing, the job became more challenging. The worse the conditions, the more problems
were caused.

Operating in Poor Visibility

Flying controllers and air crews did, however, have a number of systems available to assist
them in conditions of poor visibility. Previous mention has been made of the flare path
equipment but there were a number of other somewhat more sophisticated systems either
in use or under development. The first and possibly most important piece of equipment all
Allied aircraft were fitted with, although not a navigational aid, was an electronic device
known as Identification Friend or Foe (IFF). This constantly sent out a signal to identify the
aircraft as being 'friendly' and warn Allied air defences not to fire upon it.

Various systems using radio beams to guide aircraft in to land were put into use during
the Second World War; early versions were based on the German Lorenz system, first

installed in Britain at Heston Aerodrome in 1936. The original RAF adaptation, known as Standard Beam Approach (SBA), was first introduced at the six regional control airfields along with an early form of airfield runway lighting. SBA allowed a pilot to hear when he was on the correct approach, as radio transmitters on the ground would project a signal that apparatus in the cockpit would pick up and convert into sound in the pilot's headphones. A single note meant correct alignment, any deviation to the correct the path turned the signal into dots or dashes dependent on which side of the alignment the pilot had strayed. The system could be heard up to 15 miles away and the approach began 12 miles out from the airfield. The final glide path started when the aircraft picked up the outer marker beacon on the ground, about 2 miles from the airfield, this then aligning the aircraft with the inner marker, usually at the end of the runway. The system, however, was only suitable for larger aircraft that had room for equipment in the cockpit.

Blind-approach training, as it became known, was originally carried out at RAF Mildenhall (later the aforementioned RAF Watchfield was also used for the purpose) using Airspeed Oxford aircraft. The system was adopted by the 8th AF and was fitted to their aircraft.

A later development by the Americans was the SCS-51 Instrument Landing System, but wasn't completely introduced until almost the end of the war in Europe. SCS-51 equipment was normally mounted in mobile units that could be moved around the airfield as required which obviated the need for fixed systems to provide for each runway.

In clear conditions at night, pilots were also able to use 'pundit' lights to establish their location. All military airfields had identification beacons code named 'pundits', flashing in red Morse code the two-letter station code. However as this beam could also be seen by enemy aircraft the beacon was usually positioned a few miles from the airfield and occasionally moved. Air crews were normally notified of the beacon location in relation to the airfield during briefings. Another system developed by the RAF, known as 'Darky', provided a means of homing in at night on radio bearings to get a positional check. Introduced in 1942, selected centres maintained a 24-hour service watching for aircraft in distress and provided a direction finding fix to airfields clear of bad weather. From February 1943, all US bombers arriving in Britain were modified to 'Darky' requirements.

One slightly less high tech, but at times nonetheless effective method of assisting a 'lost' aircraft, was the use of another British system known as 'Sandra', a relic of the First World War. Used by the RAF early in the war, although later overtaken by more sophisticated systems, it involved the use of searchlights to 'cone' the errant aircraft and then provide a flight path across country to a suitable airfield, by the use of a chain of further searchlights. Of more use was FIDO. Previous mention has been made of the three emergency landing strips constructed on the English east coast. These three plus an additional fourteen RAF airfields had FIDO (Fog Investigation & Dispersal Operations) installed. A system of pressurised fuel lines were laid parallel and either side to the runway, which had burner jets mounted regularly along the full length of pipe. In times of emergency, these were quickly lit, usually manually, by driving or cycling along the length of the pipe with a burning torch. The resulting rise in air temperature was sufficient to disperse fog in the immediate area of the runway, allowing aircraft to make a visual landing.

USAAF crews would receive instruction on these systems, often while at the CCRCs prior to being allocated to a bomb group. However, as the technology behind radio communications and navigational aids improved many of the more primitive methods soon became obsolete.

Airfield Lighting

Possibly one of the most important airfield flight control systems that saw rapid development during the Second World War was airfield lighting. The RAF's need to mount night operations, requiring take-off and landing in the dark, gave a major impetus

FIDO fog dispersal system being demonstrated at RAF Woodbridge, on one of the three emergency landing grounds. In this instance a B-17 of the 493rd BG from nearby Debach makes a successful landing on 16 November 1944. As can be appreciated from this photograph, the system's main drawback was that it was incredibly fuel hungry, using around 100,000 gallons of petrol per hour on class A airfields and double that amount at the emergency airfields. It did, however, prove its worth on many occasions, saving many lives. (USAAF)

to the provision of workable designs. Later, although the USAAF requirement was less important as they generally flew daylight missions, it nevertheless became an important tool in their continued flying in Britain's variable weather conditions and winter months.

Pre-war, most airfield runways were rarely lit at night and only then with paraffin burning flares. The only type of electric runway lighting was used at civilian airfields, known as 'contact' lighting. This was unshielded and therefore didn't meet blackout requirements.

All the wartime airfield lighting programmes became known as 'Drem' systems, from the airfield in Scotland where initial developments were carried out. The Drem Mark 1 system provided remotely controlled hooded lighting which could only be seen by pilots once they had been guided into the correct approach pattern. Illuminated landing circuits were provided to guide aircraft onto their approach and these were particularly necessary where airfields were close together and their patterns overlapped. The system as it developed was constructed in a very rudimentary way, often using any materials to hand to manufacture such things as light housings. However, components did develop into standardised designs and the system was approved for use by the Air Ministry War Department, and ninety-seven airfields were thus provided by the end of 1941.

With the introduction of newer, heavier aircraft types, the Mark 1 system was rendered obsolete almost immediately as more robust components became necessary. An improved Mark 2 system was developed using smaller components and consequently using less materials. The new system also now incorporated a system of taxiway lighting. Operation of the system from the control tower became easier and a mimic panel was provided in the tower to replicate the system on the ground.

A later development was the Mark 3 system, which included such enhancements as more illuminated signage on the ground to improve taxiing, and modifications to the indication of outer circle lights, again particularly where airfields overlapped. In all, between 1939 and 1945, 421 airfields had one of the three versions of Drem lighting installed. Although the systems were expensive, it was estimated that the loss of one single aircraft would cost more than the lighting installation cost at a single airfield.

In addition to the Drem systems, the USAAF introduced a semi-portable form of airfield illumination called High Intensity Low Visibility Lighting (HILVL). This was used on many USAAF and RAF stations. These were quite large lights, about 18in tall, so, unlike the British types, they were not flush fitting with the runway surface. One of their major effects was to prompt a standard colour coding for all airfield lighting systems that were introduced.

Lt Thomas Palmer of the 91st BG demonstrates airfield lighting on the mimic panel in the tower at Bassingbourn. On the panel can be seen the airfield plan as well as the illuminated outer circuit lighting. (USAAF)

Communications

As we have seen, the control tower was the hub of all communications, both on base and with aircraft in flight. An aircraft was officially recorded and identified by its six- or seven-figure serial number, normally painted on the vertical tail. This was usually shortened to the last three digits for local reference purposes. The three letters on the fuselage side comprised its two-letter squadron code and radio call sign.

Although direct communication with the aircraft was via the flight control personnel, the actual infrastructure to support this essential service would normally be placed some distance from the airfield. In the main there were two systems in operation, in two very separate facilities. Placement away from the airfield provided both of them with space away from other structures, allowing 'sterile' zones around them to keep spurious radio interference to a minimum.

Very High Frequency radio (VHF) was used for radio communication between aircraft and base – the transmitter site could be located up to a mile distant from the airfield. Normally housed in a temporary brick building, as a metal Nissen hut was of little use, the site would also be the location for the transmitter aerials. The second major system in use would be High Frequency Direction Finding (HFDF), often referred to as 'hufduf'! The system was used in association with the assembly and homing beacons, known as 'splasher' and 'buncher' beacons, and linked to the radio compasses of aircraft. This system allowed an aircraft to be navigated by high frequency radio waves, particularly at the critical assembly and return phases of a mission. The HFDF equipment would operate from another separate building, although this one was often located within the airfield perimeter but away from sources of interference, and was often of timber construction. Staff operating this equipment would again have been trained in methods that corresponded with those in use by British authorities.

Many other early types of avionics appeared on aircraft of the period; developments in radar for navigation and target location were used. The most common of these was H2X, a US development of the British H2S system. Popularly known as 'Mickey', it was the main blind bombing system utilised by the 8th AF later in the war. Different types of radio direction finding equipment and radio countermeasures were trialled by different groups at various times during the war and were often developments by both British and American scientists.

All of this equipment had to be maintained, and several workshops operated on the technical site for this purpose. A bomb group would also operate a ground radio school within its training section to further familiarise operators with the technicalities of each system. Another group of important personnel would be the radio and telecommunications linesmen, who kept all the site communications working. An average airfield would have over 250 telephones, seven teletype machines and thousands of feet of wiring for these personnel to look after.

Some of the equipment, particularly the teleprinters, would be housed in the tower, with most towers containing two: one for meteorological reports and one for communications. The system in operation had originally been developed by the GPO, using telephone lines as a means to link all RAF sites. The system was based around a coded seven-hole ticker tape to relay messages. The communications machines had to be started manually with the passing of identification codes between the broadcasting and receiving ends, whereas the meteorological office machines were constantly set to broadcast, which meant that once a code was sent from the broadcast end only, they would automatically start disgorging data. Repairs and maintenance of the system was usually under the direction of the GPO, with assistance from some RAF specialists. As American units became more widely established they started to replace elements of the system with their own equipment, as it was considered more reliable.

The control tower was also a major hub of the station public address system – the tannoy. It would contain address equipment linked to many parts of the station, in particular the aircraft dispersals, to allow messages such as taxiing instructions to be relayed. The broadcasting equipment was housed in a special-purpose building, normally located on the HQ site.

Flying Control Caravan

Although air traffic control was administered from the control tower, the actual control was operated in very much a hands-on way, from the end of the active runway. The Flying Control Officer (FCO) orchestrated mission dispatch and return, as a remote 'outreach', from the chequerboard-painted flying control caravan normally parked to the left of the

The mobile flying control caravan of the 379th BG at Kimbolton, 7 February 1944. The airman next to the jeep is using the on-board radio to communicate with the incoming aircraft. The airman in the foreground is holding a signalling lamp used to give a visual landing signals to aircraft. The jeep is painted in a similar checkerboard paint scheme to the caravan. Normally in black and white, they were commonly known as 'follow-me' vehicles, as another of their functions was to meet visiting aircraft upon landing and lead them to a suitable hardstand. (USAAF)

touchdown point of the runway in use. There were often small sections of hardstanding provided at the ends of runways for this purpose, to prevent it becoming mired in poor weather. The use of a caravan or some form of vehicle meant that it could easily be relocated. Being this close gave the FCO a much better view of the operation than in the tower. The caravan would often have been fitted with an observation dome, many of which were converted from redundant plexi-glass nose cones from B-17s or similar aircraft.

The FCO was responsible for aircraft taxiing from the marshalling point onto the runway for takeoff, and for aircraft approaching from the downwind leg onto final approach for landing clearance. Essential tools of the job were binoculars, a map of the airfield, the colours of the day, red and green Aldis lamp and a Very (flare) pistol with red cartridges. The caravan would be linked to the tower by a field telephone line and wireless R/T would be available to communicate with aircraft. Other requirements would be a decisive and organised personality and, at times, nerves of steel!

Crews would be provided with details of take-off time and order at briefing. This would not only avoid confusion when marshalling prior to takeoff but also lessened radio traffic in case it alerted the enemy to a pending mission too soon. At the allotted time a coded message from the tower would instruct the lead aircraft to start taxiing, followed by a short message to alert each aircraft to pull into their slot in the queue. Once positioned at the end of the runway, ready for takeoff, the FCO would flash green to go with an Aldis lamp from the observation dome of the caravan. Sometimes, depending on conditions, start was given by flare pistol at the established time and each aircraft would follow its leader at a set time, usually at around 60 second intervals.

The FCO would also control the movement of road traffic around the intersection with the perimeter track and the runways, particularly at mission departure and return times. Prior to the return of aircraft the FCO would place the landing tee, one of several landing signals available at the end of the active runway to indicate its use from the air, if radio communication was unavailable. As well as radio communication, the FCO would use his variety of visual communication methods and again these would be vital if an aircraft had lost its communications system due to enemy action or failure of some kind. Once an aircraft was on a landing approach the FCO would check that wheels were down and if all was okay, give a green light to land. Many times, however, he would have to hold aircraft off from landing, particularly if others had wounded on board; these would generally signal the fact by firing red flares as they approached the airfield and would be given landing priority. Other situations that would be prioritised included aircraft with serious damage and those with landing gear malfunctions. These, and many other challenges, would all be in a day's work for the FCO.

Meteorological Office

The changeable weather, with a predisposition towards rain, left a lasting mark on those Americans stationed in Britain. It became a hugely important factor in the planning of missions over northern Europe and a constant source of frustration. In fact the intervention of adverse weather conditions probably had the single largest effect on minimising the bomb damage to the infrastructure of Nazi-held territory by regularly causing missions to be 'scrubbed' or postponed.

The USAAF had established their precision daylight bombing theories from training and development in the clear skies of the western United States; very different from the climate in northern Europe. Forecasting the latter's weather patterns came to gain an enormous importance in the fight against Nazi Germany and precise weather forecasting came to be one the most important tools in the arsenal of the war planners.

Local weather conditions in England were also of vital importance. The 'forming up' period for a mission could often take well over an hour of flying time. Aircraft had to gain sufficient altitude and assemble in the correct aerial formation prior to clearing the coast and heading out over the North Sea. With hundreds, sometimes thousands of aircraft all trying to climb to their prearranged position, this time period could prove extremely dangerous, even fatal. As aircraft were often trying to climb through conditions of minimal visibility, the sooner they could find clear space above clouds the better the chance of assembling successfully. These same conditions could also cause enormous problems in trying to land this vast aerial armada on their return.

By the time the US entered the war, Britain already possessed an extensive meteorological service, gleaning weather information from all over the world and in particular areas vital to pursuing active campaigns in Europe. With the US now involved the process was expanded further. Northern hemisphere weather charts, extending from the eastern United States across the Atlantic and Europe to central Siberia, and from virtually the North Pole to the northern Sahara, could be updated twice a day. The European charts covering the area from the central Atlantic to the Urals and from north-east Greenland and Spitzbergen to the Azores and Tunisia, would be updated four times a day. In addition, upper air charts and graphs over the British Isles would also have been regularly updated and completed.

The data would come partly from the British Isles, the United States, Canada, the USSR, and 'neutral' Sweden and Spain. The British data was transmitted on closed lines to which only the British had access. The North American and Soviet data was transmitted by radio in secret code and had to be decoded in England before being forwarded over classified lines to the bomb division central weather offices. The Swedish and Spanish reports were broadcast uncoded, as the two countries were neutral and transmitted their data openly to anyone who wanted it.

The Allies also drew observations from the vast area of the Atlantic from a couple of weather ships located in the centre, between Iceland and the Azores. There were also weather observation flights from south-west England to the Azores and from Wick, in northern Scotland, across the Norwegian Sea. The Germans also flew a weather reconnaissance flight in about the same path, from Bergen almost to the northern tip of Scotland. Rumour had it that British and Nazi weather planes over the Norwegian Sea would often see each other passing, but each was unarmed and respectful of the other's work.

As well as these reports from all across the northern hemisphere, the teletypes at Bomber Command and Division HQ would be continuously printing out half-hourly reports from several hundred stations in the British Isles; allowing the meteorological staff to keep a virtually continuous track of changes in local conditions for take-off, assembly, and landing.

Despite the fact that the use of the RAF's forecasting facilities were extended to the USAAF, planners at 8th AF HQ decided that as their mission was somewhat different to the RAF, they required their own service. It was felt that as they flew daylight missions, requiring good visibility over the target, it was essential to develop their own forecasting service for their own particular needs and to provide information to air crews specific to their daylight role.

This service came to be operated by the USAAF 18th Weather Squadron, whose headquarters unit arrived in Britain in June 1942. After establishing itself at 8th AF HQ, the 18th Weather Squadron created remote detachments to operate at every operational 8th AF station. Initially these detachments were organised under the group weather officer, but gradually they were expanded to form a small unit of around three officers and eight men, comprising observers, forecasters and clerks. John Borchert served with the 18th Weather Squadron on detached service with several groups:

> I served overseas with the U.S. Army Air Corps from May, 1943, until September, 1945. I was a meteorologist – trained in the Air Corps Aviation Cadet program at the Massachusetts Institute of Technology, then assigned to forecast weather for air corps

operations. After leaving MIT, I spent five months as base weather officer at Brookley Field, Mobile, Alabama. Then I was transferred overseas.

My overseas duty was in England. The first five months were at 8th Air Force heavy bomber bases – about six weeks at a B-17 'Flying Fortress' base, the rest of the time at the bases of two B-24 'Liberator' groups. For the next year and one-half I was stationed at the headquarters of the B-24 division of the 8th Air Force at Ketteringham Hall, in rural East Anglia a few miles from the city of Norwich.

I experienced the war in Europe from the margin; yet I was never far from the nerve centers. I certainly have no first-hand accounts of high-level strategy, intrigue, danger, romance, or misery that are the stuff of the central stories of the War. Instead, my work was specialized, technical. I did not make big, strategic decisions; yet my forecasts went into briefing material for the generals, and I sometimes discussed my weather maps with them. I was never in combat; yet I shared personally with bomber crews the nerve-wracking preparation for missions and the exhilaration and tragedy of return.

Staff of the weather detachment normally worked a three-shift, 24-hour rota so that the unit was always manned. Four personnel would normally be on duty at a time, usually two observers and two forecasters. The meteorological offices were normally located on the ground floor of the control tower or, at pre-war permanent stations, had their operations centred on the HQ block.

Enlisted weather specialists would assume the roles of weather observer and forecaster. Their tasks would include analysing weather conditions locally by monitoring the recording instruments. They would record wind velocities, cloud amount, changes in temperature, humidity and barometric pressure, as well as the amount of rainfall and other conditions. They also had to assist in the preparation of weather maps and reports. Once prepared, they would then relay that information back to forecasters at Division HQ, to begin to build up the bigger picture. Every effort was made to ensure that operation planners had an as accurate picture of weather over Europe and Britain as was possible.

Monitoring equipment would comprise a small shelter housing instruments for recording maximum and minimum temperatures and humidity. A weather observer read and recorded the temperatures and humidity every hour, night and day. Nearby would be a theodolite position used when releasing hydrogen balloons to obtain data for plotting wind direction and velocity. On the control tower roof would be a weather vane and an anemometer connected electrically to wind indicators in the flight control room and the weather office. These constantly displayed the direction and strength of the wind. Sometimes these instruments would be connected to a recorder in the weather office, which produced a chart of the wind directions for the 24 hours. Wind speed and direction was critical for aircraft landings and take-offs. The majority of the equipment within the control tower would have been of British supply or manufacture.

Another vital task of the weather office staff would be the preparation of materials for the briefing of aircrew prior to flying a mission. This would not only cover the weather situation along flight routes over Europe but the conditions at take-off and the expected weather conditions at the group's estimated time of return. These factors would include expected cloud cover at the target, estimated wind speeds to calculate fuel usage as well as wind data to enable the bombardier to set up his bomb sighting equipment correctly.

Although the group weather officer would be the most senior in the group, mission briefings were normally undertaken by the most senior member of the weather detachment. Senior weather officers would also take part in the de-briefing process and analyse feedback on actual weather conditions encountered during missions. John Borchert continued:

A truck from the base met the train and took me and my baggage to the base at Thurleigh. It was Saturday, May 22, 1943. This was my first assignment – a B-17 Flying Fortress base, 306th BG. Night was chill and rainy; I had little idea of what the place was like, save

A meteorological officer of the 379th BG, Kimbolton, launches a weather balloon to measure wind velocity, 20 April 1944. (USAAF)

that everyone was very friendly, uniforms were rather varied and sometimes sloppy, and food was good.

I had a look about the next day. This is what is called a dispersed airdrome — the establishment is scattered all over the countryside so as to make it less conspicuous. It is one of the many bases from which the 'Forts' are bombing Germany. I feel nearer the war now for the first time.

I began to get acquainted with the weather station, the weather officer and enlisted observers, the maps, and the patterns of fronts, highs, and lows over the British Isles. May 28 I had my first experience with a briefing for a mission. Tense, sharp men – rough looking gunners, young kids; the officers, some keen, fine looking men, some smoking nervously, yet also seem very much composed; all very intent on every word. Some amazing detail of routes, targets, weather, and timing.

Several days later a mission to Kiel was messed up because of pre-warm-frontal cloud. Average cloud cover in this theater is 7-8/10 – which really means 70%–80% of the time overcast, one of many weather limitations and hazards.

Around the middle of 1943, the USAAF started to operate weather reconnaissance flights. Initially these were operated in conjunction with the RAF. Ultimately they developed what they termed heavy and light weather squadrons for operations dependent on the distances that required to be flown. Although the information collected would be fed into the rest of the data, there appeared to be a more urgent requirement for immediate weather flights to be flown prior to missions to establish local conditions prior to formation. These flights were organised on a fairly informal level, with one aircraft normally making a flight to full altitude at the assembly point, and taking off about an hour before mission departure time. Although the 18th Weather Squadron had no official flying requirement, its personnel were often called on to accompany these flights as observers to report on cloud ceiling, wind speed, temperature and visibility. These flights later became operated on a more regular basis as it was realised fairly early in their operation that due to their random nature they were giving the enemy advance warning of an impending mission. The normal procedure was for the operation to be rotated through several groups within a division.

Lastly, one of the most important weather forecasting functions provided by the weather staff, certainly as far as ground-based personnel were concerned, was ensuring that a cycle ride out to a pub in the locality could be accomplished in dry conditions! Personnel embarking on such missions would often call the station meteorological office before setting out.

Fire & Rescue

Adequate fire and rescue cover is closely allied to flying control, for if and when operations go seriously wrong it is important to have well-trained specialists capable of swift intervention on hand.

On USAAF airfields in Britain during the Second World War, provision by the RAF of fire and rescue services was probably one of the most extensive and visible examples of reverse lend-lease. Fortunately the RAF fire service was able to expand at a sufficient rate to cope early on with the influx of USAAF groups.

The first training course to provide the RAF with specialised personnel for fire support was instigated at Cranwell in 1922. Prior to this, fire and rescue provision for the RAF had been fairly limited. These first courses were operated under the auspices of the London Fire Brigade, as it was they who provided the instructors and designed the syllabus. A new trade of aircraft handler/fire fighter was established for those who graduated from the scheme. The Second World War heralded a series of moves for the Fire Training Unit, ultimately in 1943 establishing a longer-term home at RAF Sutton-on-Hull and being in the process a change of name to the RAF School of Fire Fighting.

The USAAF, on the other hand, didn't really start any serious programme of unified training schemes for aviation fire fighters until just prior to the Second World War. Previous to this, both through a lack of funding and traditionally relying on the army to control such issues, individual base fire fighting provision tended to be organised at a local level.

After Pearl Harbor, a huge expansion of the AAF fire service took place. A specialist training school was opened in Hartford, Connecticut, during the summer of 1943, moving to Camp Pontchartrain, Louisiana later that year. The first graduates of this school went straight to Europe to fill the void being identified by commanders there. Later more AAF fire fighting schools were established to further swell the ranks.

These new units were designated Engineer Aviation Fire Fighting Platoons (EAFFP). They were to be considered distinct from the army's existing Engineer Fire Fighting Platoons (EFFP) as they had equipment tabled for the specific use on aviation fires and crash rescue. Existing EFFPs were only equipped with general fire fighting equipment. Earlier in 1943 some of the EFFPs were transferred, during a restructure, to the EAFFP role and these units formed the basis of the first personnel trained in aviation-specific methods at the new schools.

The first units to pass through the system comprised one officer, a 1st or 2nd lieutenant fire marshal, and twenty-eight fire fighters. However, once deployed to theatre, that number often decreased, especially during the early build-up, as sometimes a platoon would be split between two groups. Like other support units, a fire fighting platoon would be self sufficient, comprising drivers, mechanics and administration staff among its personnel complement.

Once arriving in Britain, it was usual for USAAF fire fighters to train with the RAF on the specifics of British equipment. Much of this was performed at individual stations, but some classes were operated for USAAF personnel at the RAF School of Fire Fighting.

Development of Equipment

Globally, developments in the means of tackling aviation-related fires and crash rescue equipment continued fairly universally, in line with the evolution of aircraft design. The nature of early aircraft construction would have generally permitted water jets from hoses or hand-held extinguishers to be sufficient to extinguish most fires. The earliest purpose-built 'crash tenders' would have been trucks designed to just carry this simple equipment. As aircraft designs started to evolve, potential fires from larger quantities of oil and fuel, as well as flammable elements of their construction, became more of an issue.

Major developments in the field of specialist aviation fire and rescue vehicles was only implemented as a result of improvements in fire fighting technology, the most important of which was in fire-suppressant foam. Although forms of chemical foam, created by mixing various agents together, had been in existence since the late nineteenth century, it wasn't until the introduction of mechanical foam production methods were introduced that aircraft fire fighting vehicle development progressed.

Mechanical foam was created on a vehicle by mixing air, water and a foam agent together in a rotary type pump, the product of which was discharged through hoses. The first foam agents used for this process were soap derivatives known as saponines. The development of these new agents led to improvements in vehicle and equipment designs, particularly delivery pumps, enabling higher rates of foam discharge to be achieved. In the early 1940s a further development came with a new protein foam agent developed from soya extract. This was considered a better agent due to its improved expansion rate over its predecessors as well as its ease of handling. Aerofoam, as it became known, was used extensively during the Second World War and the post-war era on aviation fires.

The second major fire fighting product to be developed and added to the Second World War era fire fighter's arsenal was carbon dioxide, CO_2 systems were developed to complement existing foam supplies as well as to be a fire suppressant source in its own right. The idea was very sound: spray CO_2 into the heart of a fire and it immediately neutralised the oxygen, thereby extinguishing the fire. However, there were several limitations, including the provision of sufficient CO_2 to fight the fire, and the ability to physically spray the CO_2 in sufficient quantities from a safe distance to enable it to work. Safe spraying of CO_2 required the development of booms and probes to get the substance to the required point, which was often inside an aircraft structure at a considerable distance from the fire truck. It was also recognised that it couldn't be used where casualties may still be present, as spraying CO_2 in the vicinity would asphyxiate them before any rescue could be achieved. Neither could it be discharged close to the rescue vehicle, as again removal of oxygen would cause the engine to stop, therefore rendering the machinery vulnerable to the very fire it was fighting! In the main, fire fighting on USAAF bases largely depended on a combination of both early forms of mechanical foam production and high-pressure water mist.

From the early 1930s, the RAF continuously developed airfield crash tenders in order to match the increasing quantity of military air traffic as well as the evolving size of aircraft

The USAAF developed a specific CO_2 fire truck, the class 150 'Cardox' machines, and deployed them to Britain; however, their use was limited. Supply of sufficient quantities of CO_2 gas to replenish them was a problem as the necessary gas production equipment was lacking in many areas. A Cardox appliance is seen here, in use in a training exercise with the 91st BG, at Bassingbourn. The boom can be seen discharging CO_2 onto a burning engine, a safe distance from the vehicle's engine. (USAAF)

designs. Pre-war civilian vehicle types were often adapted for use; both Ford and Morris commercial models were converted to six-wheel chassis for the purpose. A favourite supplier of vehicles to the RAF during its early years was Crossley. With the re-armament of British forces increasing from the mid-1930s, Crossley again became heavily involved with its former customer.

As the result of a War Office specification for a 3-ton, four-wheel-drive truck in 1940, Crossley began supplying its 'FWD' or 'Four Wheel Drive' model truck, a basic utilitarian design with an open cab and canvas roof. Nearly 800 were delivered, over 200 of which were crash tenders, with the foam fire-fighting equipment supplied by the Pyrene Company.

The War Office also developed a specification for a larger crash tender on a six-wheel chassis, normally in a 6x4 arrangement. The tenders were built on various chassis, the most common being the Fordson WOT1 and the Austin K6. They all carried the same fixed fire fighting system, which consisted of a water tank that held around 200 gallons, a saponine foam agent tank that held 25 gallons and a PTO-driven water pump. Until the mid-1940s, the RAF tenders also carried four carbon dioxide extinguishing cylinders that discharged in pairs and were completely independent of the water-foam system.

Developments in the US followed similar lines to those in Britain but with the Air Corps still being the poor relation of the army, they were restricted initially by the army dictating the pace and requirements of development. Prior to the Second World War responsibility for the US Army's fire-fighting needs were under the control of the QM Corps. Camp Holabird, in Baltimore, Maryland, a QM facility, was the main testing and development centre for the US Army's motor vehicles. It became synonymous with US Army fire equipment developments in the inter-war period.

In a move to rid itself of many obsolete types, in 1925 the army decided to standardise on fire-fighting equipment and plans were put in place to design and build a bespoke appliance for this purpose. The project was given to the Holabird engineers. The resulting designs evolved through the 1930s into a set of standard classes of army fire-fighting trucks. In the early 1930s the Air Corps too finally started to be able to develop a specific fire and crash rescue vehicle for its needs. However, early designs were developed with civilian manufacturers such as Mack, who by now were working on designs for the

An interesting comparison shot of American and British crash tenders, belonging to the 2095th EFFP at Deenthorpe, home of the 401st BG. On the left a USAAF class 110 or derivative crash tender and the right its RAF counterpart, a Fordson WOT1. The fire fighter pictured is being prepared in his asbestos protective suit. These could provide around 4 minutes' protection to the wearer, should they be required to enter a burning aircraft. (USAAF)

civilian aviation market. In 1937 the first Air Corps fire/crash truck was demonstrated at Eglin Air Force Base; its combination of equipment proved so effective that it became the blueprint for all systems used by the Air Corps/Force throughout the Second World War.

In the late 1930s Holabird became involved in these Air Corps designs, and ultimately crash rescue trucks became incorporated into the army's standard series of fire-fighting vehicles. In 1939, Holabird upgraded the previous Air Corps machine on a bigger, specially designed chassis in a 6x4 configuration with a 130hp engine. This new design was the first to have an effective foam and CO_2 mixing system for use on fuel and oil fires. In 1941 the basic crash truck was again redesigned and now designated the class 110. The new design was mounted on a Chevrolet 4x4 chassis. Holabird built 337 vehicles to this design. Later improvements followed, designated classes 125 and 135, although the format of the class 110 effectively became the standard for all medium-duty airfield crash trucks during the Second World War for the USAAF.

With the looming war clouds of the early 1940s the US Army decided that Holabird, probably due in part to its commitment to crash truck production for the Air Corps, would be unable to supply the quantities of fire trucks it required. Therefore it had no option but to return to the commercial manufacturers to supply its needs, but utilising staff at Holabird to oversee the design and development role and continuing with its policy of standardised designs. Over 8,500 fire trucks of all types were supplied to the US Army before the end of the war by the commercial sector.

Even with these production figures, insufficient quantities were supplied and many fire fighting units supplemented their equipment with modified standard army trucks, notably of the Dodge WC series, both the ¾-ton 4x4 and 1½-ton 6x6 types. Some GMC CCKW-type 6x6 trucks were adapted as crash trucks and carried CO_2 equipment. A range of smaller fire-fighting pump trailers was also supplied to provide additional equipment; these could be towed by any of the trucks available to the fire department.

In the Second World War, USAAF fire trucks were painted olive green after the Pearl Harbor attack, as it was realised that red was not the best colour! In contrast, RAF fire-fighting vehicles were generally finished in their standard vehicle paint scheme of dark blue.

Fire Fighting in Britain

From the outset, fire fighting was an area in which Britain agreed to supply the necessary men and machines to bridge the gap until the US could support itself. In the event, the US never could provide enough machines to fully equip all the bases it inhabited in Britain and RAF appliances supplemented US types until the end of the Second World War.

From the outset, fire and crash rescue services were provided at all the bases occupied by the USAAF. As American units began to arrive, some station complement personnel were assigned to assist RAF fire fighters. Once fully trained EAFFPs became available the existing arrangement could be curtailed and the RAF units removed, though not before training the Americans on the use of British equipment, and often leaving their appliances behind.

Fire personnel would often be based in at least two locations on the airfield. The main fire party headquarters, as mentioned previously, would often be near the camp main gate, with accommodation in the Guardhouse or a separate fire station close by. A second fire engine shelter would on some stations be provided close to the control tower, to provide fire and crash rescue crews with their own more convenient accommodation. The main fire station on the camp would often include workshop facilities for the maintenance of fire fighting equipment as well as of vehicles, normally undertaken as part of the fire fighters' day-to-day activities. Buildings again were either Nissen huts or of temporary brick constructions on most stations.

USAAF fire crews attend a blazing B-17 at an unknown airbase, possibly during a training exercise. Interestingly they are being assisted by members of the National Fire Service (NFS), the British civilian fire brigade. The NFS gave considerable amounts of assistance to American fire fighters during the Second World War particularly where off-base fire and rescue services were required. (USAAF)

As well as being prepared for any type of fire on a station, fire-fighting personnel undertook a number of other tasks. Fortunately the number of major incidents were generally few and, for the most part, far between. For the majority of the time they would be engaged in routine duties involving fire prevention, conducting safety inspections, enforcing fire rules and codes, inspecting and maintaining extinguishers and training and contingency planning.

As an example of the workload falling on a fire fighting platoon, during the time the 2034th EAFFP was stationed at Framlingham as part of the 390th BG, a total of sixty-two fires were attended; of these twenty-five were domestic and thirty-seven aircraft related. Of the domestic fires, all but a few were minor and three were trees that had somehow caught fire. One was a large fire in the propeller shop and another a large fire in the old briefing room, which involved a loss of life. The aircraft fires included a number of crashes off base; most of the aircraft fires on base were engine fires.

Although at times the day-to-day work could be routine, it wasn't without its risks. The 2033rd EAFFP attached to the 44th BG at Shipdham lost two of its members while attempting to put out the fire at the site of a Liberator crash near Gerveston, Norfolk, in which all the air crew were killed. Unfortunately, shortly after the arrival of the fire fighters, part of the bomb load exploded with devastating results, killing the two platoon members. Both were posthumously awarded the Soldier's Medal for heroism.

Return of a Mission

Having earlier documented the events leading up to the departure of a mission, within this section concerned with flying control its time to reverse the procedure. Art Watson:

> When the ship taxied to position for take off, most of us stayed until the group was airborne, then we went for breakfast or to the barracks for a nap or played cards, some exercised by throwing a baseball and playing catch – each did what he inclined to do at the time and waited for the return of the mission. We had a time that was their ETA and so all the men went out to their responsibilities and sweat the ships in.

Most personnel would get to know the estimated time of arrival (ETA) back from a mission, and many would often start to congregate in groups awaiting the arrival of aircraft back to base around the time they were expected. Others, like Rod Ryan, would still be working but couldn't fail to miss the return and be curious about the outcome.

> Out at the bomb dump we were too distant from flight crews so never really got to know any. We didn't really have much to do with returning missions as we weren't directly involved with the aircraft, but I do remember the first Schweinfurt mission (17 Aug 1943). We dispatched 16 aircraft from the group; everyone knew it was a big one. Well when they were due to return, only one came back, there were all these ground crews not knowing what to do as their aircraft hadn't returned. Not all were shot down, a couple crash landed at other fields, but it was the only one to come back that day, it was a shock to us all, I will never forget that one.

The control tower was often the focal point for waiting as it was there that news would be heard first. Those that were working would often stop, with everyone on the base hoping that all the aircraft would make a safe return. However, it is probably fair to say that no group wished it more than the squadron ground crews who had the closest association with the aircraft personnel, having invested enormous quantities of energy, both physical and emotional, into caring for their charges. Jack Gaffney remembered the emotions well:

> Ground crews literally prayed for the safe return of every plane and crew & 'sweated' until the end of every mission. They knew when a mission went off there would be planes downed over Europe, men would be in POW camps, lives lost. When chaplains came out to the hardstands to give their blessing the ground crews knelt with them to give spiritual support. After the missions they would be fascinated by the stories especially the vivid descriptions of flak and fighters accompanied by appropriate hand gestures.

If the weather conditions were good, aircraft would be spotted, often in large formations flying much lower across the countryside than at their departure. These formations would

Officers and men of the 303rd BG, Molesworth scan the skies for returning aircraft, 28 September 1944. In the centre of the picture is a Dodge 4 x 4 ambulance and to its left, a Crossley FWD crash tender. (USAAF)

Ground-crew members of the 91st BG at Bassingbourn 'sweat out' the return of their aircraft.
Date unknown. (USAAF)

often comprise aircraft of other groups making for their bases in the vicinity as well. Those
aircraft of the home group would then start to peel away from these main bodies and
start to circle the base in their circuit patterns, awaiting their turn to land. Firstly though,
the FCO working at the end of the runway would have to sort the priority cases. These
included those in the worst predicaments, either with battle damage, fuel shortage or, as
the red flares issuing from some aircraft would indicate, those with injured crewmen on
board. The FCO may already have been aware of particularly severe cases, as once over
the English coast those requiring a swift landing may have already indicated so if their
communications equipment was still functioning.

Fire crews would have been alerted some time before the ETA and would be manning
their vehicles either close to the control tower or within easy reach of the active runway.
The base hospital services would also be on standby and ambulances would already be
lined up waiting, especially if it was already known to have been a particularly difficult
operation.

Once in the circuit, air crews would go through their landing sequence checks and all
crew other than the pilot and co-pilot would be making for their appropriate positions in
the aircraft for landing. The landing gear would now be lowered. It was sometimes at this
point that an otherwise fault-free approach might indicate a problem. Undercarriage may
not lower fully or at all due to a previously unknown fault. These situations provided the
FCO with an additional aircraft in difficulty to deal with.

Generally the landing order would be dictated by the FCO, who would have to be ready
to orchestrate changes to accommodate any emergencies, which he would do either by
radio or using the visual signalling methods at his disposal. After being given permission
to land, the aircraft would turn in on its approach path, and once over the runway
threshold the pilot would touch down. The normal procedure once on the ground would
be to allow the aircraft to roll the length of the runway to avoid burning out the brakes.
Engine cowl flaps would also be opened to fully cool the engines; this also had a secondary
function of adding additional drag and thereby assisted in slowing the aircraft. On a B-17,
the tail wheel lock would be released to enable the aircraft to be controlled around the
taxiway to its designated hardstand. The inboard engines would be shut down allowing
the two outboard engines to be used for final manoeuvring.

If the aircraft was severely damaged or had landed wheels-up it would normally have
been directed onto the grass field. If it had ended up obstructing the runway, the FCO

would have to hastily arrange for any other returning group planes to use another runway, even if wind conditions were less favourable. This is why damaged aircraft were often advised to fly directly to the relevant SAD or other suitable airfields to land. Aircraft with wounded on board would often taxi as quickly as possible to a convenient point to meet the ambulances and medical personnel. Ambulances were sometimes to be seen chasing behind aircraft in these situations, ready to be on hand once the plane had stopped. Chaplain James Brown recalled the return of aircraft to Ridgewell:

> The scene is one of anguish as we stand out on the airfield awaiting the return of our fliers from combat. We gaze and we gaze. We look for the tiniest speck in the sky. Someone exclaims 'I see a plane' Another says, 'There they are! They are ours! They are coming toward us!'
>
> But then we look and worry, for one plane is ahead of the rest. If he comes straight to the field before the entire formation he probably has a wounded man (or men) aboard. So we look – does he flash his lights, the sign that wounded men are aboard? And when he lands does he keep his flaps down, another sign of wounded men? If so, the ambulance will hurry to the place where the plane comes to a stop.[1]

For those returning without problems, once taxiing to the hardstand had been completed the aircraft would be turned through 180 degrees to face the taxiway; the crew chief would be ready with wheel chocks and the pilot would shut down the remaining engines. He and the co-pilot would go through their post-flight procedures, ensuring that all control locks were in place.

Once out of the aircraft the crew chief would hand the pilot forms 1 and 1A to complete, which would indicate anything that required urgent attention. Art Watson again:

> When they returned, the pilot and the crew chief discussed the flight and whether or not there was anything that needed adjustment or fixing and whether there was any flak damage, etc.
>
> We went out to reclaim the bombsights and check all the equipment for which we were responsible.

In some groups the air crew would remove their guns, otherwise this would be done by the ground crew before dispatching them back to the armoury for maintenance. The air crew would then be picked up and taken to the briefing room for post-mission interrogation. The cycle of maintenance on the aircraft would begin again in preparation for the next mission, with relief on the faces of its crew that it had made it back from another one. For ground crew whose aircraft hadn't returned or was overdue this would be an extremely difficult period of waiting to discover its fate. Some may have landed at another field and would return at a later time, but for many this was an emotional time as severe as any bereavement.

8

Communal Site

The majority of airfields were, and still are, compact communities in their own right, not unlike small towns. As well as all the facilities that support their reason for being, an airfield provides many other services to sustain those who operate them.

On pre-war RAF stations, domestic services such as mess facilities were laid out around the periphery of the main camp area. Once the move to disperse came, those elements were again located further away. Many of the functions needed to support personnel, aside from living accommodation, would be grouped together and placed on what became known as the communal site. A variety of buildings were to be found, including mess halls, ablutions blocks, recreational facilities and the chapel, as well as utility functions such as the standby generator house, sometimes the station water supply, and fuel stores. Occasionally, living accommodation was constructed on the site if space constraints dictated, but normally separate domestic sites existed for that purpose. If living accommodation was to be found, then it would often be provided for the CO and senior officers or enlisted men engaged in operating the site's facilities, for instance – such as mess hall staff. The main communal site at Framlingham included accommodation for some of the Station Complement Squadron, presumably for this purpose.

On some camps the site contained an area suitable for use as a parade ground or exercise yard for PT, and on some older airfields, sports facilities such as squash and tennis courts. Lastly the station post office, Post Exchange (PX), ration stores and ration breakdown building would be found on the communal site, as well as workrooms for the station tailor and barber. Every airfield had at least one communal site; some had two, a main site and a secondary smaller one. Some sites which had been laid out early in the war for RAF occupancy would also have had a small combined living and communal site allocated for women: the WAAFS.

Much effort was expended in providing facilities, by various military and civilian organisations, to make the conditions for resident servicemen as bearable as possible. Due to the longer tenure that the USAAF had on its camps, as opposed to many of the regular army units, there was time to provide some relatively sophisticated amenities.

The provision of arrangements for rest and relaxation for all ranks was considered of paramount importance to maintain good morale, as it was realised early on that the job entrusted to the groups and the air force as a whole wasn't going to be achieved overnight, and as personnel were deployed for the duration, they could be stationed in Britain for some time. What must be remembered, contrary to the popular stereotype, was that not all US servicemen were loud and colourful; many had arrived from quiet country communities from all across the United States; far from home in a strange land, bustle and raucousness were as alien to them as to the local British population. They had to settle in and find their way around, and for this they would need a little help.

The two component units of the bomb group that would have had the most impact upon the communal site would have been the members of the Special Services unit and the Station Complement Squadron. Other units would also be represented due, once again to the pooling of personnel. Civilians could also be found working at the communal site.

Left: The main communal site at Ridgewell, site No. 3. Ridgewell had two large communal sites, this one contained three mess halls; and a large institute building, and site No.4, two further mess halls and another institute block, as well as a WAAF communal site with another dining hall and institute building. In the centre of the picture is the main dining hall, to its left the institute building and on its right the sergeants' mess. In the lower centre is the officers' mess and bathhouse and on the extreme left of the picture the long building is the gymnasium with the chapel annex on its right-hand end. Other structures to be seen include ablutions blocks, ration stores and blast shelters. (USAAF)

Right: All US service personnel deployed to Britain were given a copy of this booklet to enable them to become accustomed with such things as British currency, customs and culture. (Author)

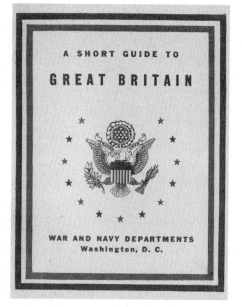

The largest organised civilian group was from the ARC, who would run the clubs set up on camps. Many workers were American women but quite a number were British recruits as well.

Civilians would also often hold a number of other posts; in particular British workers would often be employed as stokers for the many boilers required for cooking and for hot water on the communal site. Many of these would be local residents employed to run these essential services. Civilians would sometimes be recruited to run some of the smaller camp services, such as the tailor's and the shoemaker's, as well as unofficial individual arrangements providing laundry services.

Generally, the largest buildings on communal sites were the dining halls. According to official AM plans for each RAF Class A airfield, every communal site would have a dining hall, a sergeants' mess, an institute building and an officers' mess. If there were two communal sites then obviously this number would double. In addition, if a WAAF site was included at a particular airfield then up to three more communal buildings for the various ranks may have become available.

The USAAF combat units tended to put the buildings supplied to slightly different use, or at least the terminology was changed. In every case, bomb groups had a requirement for a minimum of two dining halls, one for enlisted men and the other for combat crews. Officers were provided with a mess that had facilities for dining. Non-commissioned officers (NCOs) usually adopted the former RAF sergeants' mess as a club and the institute buildings allocated for RAF use would often be taken over by the ARC to provide club facilities for enlisted men.

The Dining Hall

Most dining halls were created from groupings of Nissen-type buildings, although some were of temporary brick construction, normally laid out in a double 'H' pattern, with the kitchen in the middle and a dining hall on either side. Serving hatches on both sides of the kitchen enabled both halls to operate simultaneously. The consolidated mess would provide meals for the enlisted men of the ground echelon and tended to operate broad bands of meal times to try and cater to all personnel no matter what shift pattern they were working. A separate dining hall was provided for combat crews due to their differing work schedule, as well as providing for special dietary requirements.

The layout of the combat crew facility enabled one dining hall to be used solely by combat officers, while the other was allocated to the enlisted combat crewmen, with one kitchen catering for both halls. This dining hall probably contained the hardest worked kitchen, due to the high numbers of fliers who had to be fed in a short space of time, and often the simulation became even more difficult after increases in squadron strength. Separate dining arrangements also normally existed for ground echelon officers as part of the mess facilities within the officers' clubs.

Although food supply and ration allocation were controlled by the QM Corps, overall operational responsibility for dining arrangements, certainly as far as the enlisted men were concerned, was administered by S-1, the personnel department. Standards of cleanliness and efficiency were monitored by the administrational inspection team. Any

Combat crew dining hall, 93rd BG Hardwick. Combat crew ate separately due to specialised dietary requirements. Most groups followed variations in operating procedure but all quickly began to feed air crew fairly bland food for breakfast. Anything that would cause gas in the human digestive system was avoided. At high altitude, with the lower air pressure, gas in the body formed much more easily, causing discomfort, if not outright pain. (USAAF)

breaches of cleanliness leading to health or hygiene problems, which did occasionally occur, fell to the group medical team for investigation.

Once again, many of the mess hall staff would be from the group's individual component units; as they were all self-supporting, they would have cooks among their tabled allocations. For instance, according to T/O&E, each bomb squadron provided twenty-one catering personnel, while the HQ unit provided four. Other catering staff would have been drawn from specialists within the Station Complement Squadron.

Catering staff would also often be supplemented by personnel who for one reason or another, whether it be due to some form of misdemeanour or punishment or official duty, had to spend time doing KP, 'kitchen police/patrol', or in British vernacular, 'spud bashing'. Their duties, under the title 'cook's helpers', would usually be the less pleasant ones such as scrubbing pans, disposing of kitchen waste, peeling potatoes and cleaning floors and surfaces.

Kitchen Facilities

Little or no use was made of electricity at this time in kitchens for cooking; this was performed by steam heat. An annex to the central kitchen area would have housed a coal or coke-fired boiler. On pre-war sites, central boiler houses powered and heated the station; once sites were dispersed, each facility requiring hot water would have a small boiler house attached. Civilian stokers were generally employed to keep this equipment in operation. Large steam kettles were provided for boiling vegetables and cooking soups and stews. Ovens would be provided for roasting and baking, again heated by steam, with hot plates or griddles on oven tops, in the traditional fashion.

Nearly all the kitchen equipment was of British supply and would have been provided by the Air Ministry during the construction of the camp. One additional luxury, however, which the USAAF brought to the kitchens on many of its camps, was the dishwashing machine, again operated with locally produced hot water. They weren't always the great boon they were intended to be, as the hot water supply had never been calculated for this type of equipment – the RAF usually relied on manual washing up – and it was sometimes difficult to keep them supplied with sufficient quantities to enable them to be truly effective.

The kitchens were sub-divided to provide separate food preparation areas as well as the aforementioned serving counters. Most dining halls were designed and constructed to provide meals for between 500 and 1,000 personnel at each sitting, but many were often providing for far more than these numbers at any one time.

Cooks at Bassingbourn prepare pancakes on oven-top hotplates, 1944. (USAAF)

As well as being better fed, it has to be said that in not having to survive under the strict wartime food rationing that the British population did, American service personnel were somewhat more wasteful with food. This became quite a big concern to higher command, both from a supply perspective as well as a potential PR problem. The high quality of kitchen waste became so well known in some localities that bins were often raided by local children looking for extra sustenance. A big emphasis was placed on keeping waste to a minimum, with poster campaigns encouraging personnel to eat all the food they took and not to be greedy, as the following statement from the chief quartermaster's office illustrates:

> Our ration in the European Theatre of Operations is excellent. With a minimum of shipping we have a ration equal, if not superior, to that of any other place in the world. This demands good cooking, attractive serving, and the complete elimination of waste; i.e., loss of food via the garbage-can route.[1]

Loss of food via the garbage-can route was still not always wasted, however, as it was often eagerly collected by local farmers to supplement their allocation of pig feed, thereby finding its way back into the food chain.

Food Supply

Meals fed to American servicemen serving in England were always considered a subject of contempt by personnel, if one believes the cliché portrayed by films. Nonetheless a great deal of effort was expended on providing a good balance of nutrition dependent on the role that particular individuals were engaged in. Certainly to the British population by comparison, already suffering under several years of severe rationing, the average American was supplied foodstuffs that could only be imagined. The British diet was considered bland by comparison, but different peoples have differing dietary tastes and so it was for the visiting Americans. There were those who, when given access to American rations after years of austere living, found the diet difficult to digest. My own paternal grandfather for instance, LAC Charles Holland, an RAF radio engineer who was stationed at Andrews Field (Great Saling) with the 322nd BG, 9th AF, remembered suffering severe stomach disorders due to an over rich diet.

American servicemen in general were not too keen on the British habit of drinking tea, preferring coffee, as well as having little liking for brown bread, potatoes or mutton. They were also little impressed with the poor variety of fruit and vegetables in British rations, as well as preferring a greater variety of meat in their diet. Top of the list of universal dislikes, however, has to have gone to the much-maligned Brussels sprout! It was said among air crews that if they had to make an emergency landing over British soil, they should aim to put their aircraft down in a field of sprouts, so as to remove as many from source of supply as possible.

For a few months after establishing the ETO, the first American troops had to live on a straight British ration. This was later modified to the so-called 'British-American ration', which included items more palatable to the American soldier and eliminated more of those for which they had no particular fondness. By the end of 1942 all American personnel were being fed the standard American ration. This did, however, comprise much in the way of locally sourced foods, particularly fresh goods that went into American staple meals. Much research was carried out by the QM Corps into providing good wholesome meals with the 'taste of home' without the need to ship all the constituent ingredients from the US. Much effort was put into avoidance of wastage both through spoiling and also serving up meals that did not agree with the American palette.

Every month the office of the chief quartermaster, ETOUSA, assisted by the chief surgeon's office, prepared a standard menu. The menu was based upon stocks on hand or obtainable locally, variety to avoid monotony, and general nutritional requirements. Despite this, it was sometimes still difficult to prepare a menu conforming to all three conditions. The optimum ration composition took most of the first year in Britain to discover but ultimately succeeded in reducing the calorific value from around 4,500 calories to 4,000 per person per day. Paul Kovitz's opinion of the catering at Framlingham was very positive:

> The food was pretty good, they had Enlisted Men's mess halls and Officers messes and I thought they took pretty good care of us over there.

The average USAAF base in Britain during the Second World War handled over 50 tons of food every week, much of it butter, tinned goods and coffee shipped in from the United States. Meat, for the most part, was frozen and also shipped from America. This would then be held in British cold storage plants until issued to the stations. Large quantities of tinned meat would have also been shipped over, such as Argentinean corned beef, pork sausage, Vienna sausage and bacon. Fresh vegetables, potatoes and bread were usually supplied from British sources.

Some attempts were made to grow vegetables on individual camps at times, as in this example at Podington, described by John Sloan:

> The Group Agricultural Officer, Lt Stanley Loupus of the 32nd Station Complement, at month's end had slightly over nine acres under cultivation, of which seven acres were potatoes. Lt Loupus, appointed in February, had in cooperation with the Air Ministry and with the assistance of the Bedford War Agricultural Committee, planted the majority of the acreage in May. One-fifth of an acre was experimentally and optimistically devoted to sweet corn, to the dubious interest of neighbouring farmers. Almost two acres were allotted to garden vegetables. Land Army girls were supplied by the Bedford organization to assist with the planting of the potatoes.[2]

With regard to British bread supplies, attempts were made by the US Army caterers to make it more palatable to American tastes, which generally preferred much lighter varieties. British flour was mixed with flour produced from Canadian wheat that had made it across the Atlantic, which they learned to use to produce lighter bakery items more to the general liking of American service personnel. Coffee supplies were also partly from both British and American sources, with the US Army via the QM Corps running its own roasting and grinding plants.

At higher levels, the chief quartermaster's office conducted tests and competitions to 'secure the keen interest of the company cook' and to get the maximum food value from some of the items, which, for military reasons, had to be supplied to Britain. Items such as dehydrated eggs and dehydrated vegetables, it was said, properly cooked, could be most palatable. Whether or not these initiatives actually filtered down to the level of the individual airbase however, is rather doubtful![1]

The quartermaster operated a system that involved several types of food and ration arrangements to suit the various operational situations that arose at each USAAF camp; these comprised the following six types:

Regular rations which were based on the master menu, published every month by the chief quartermaster. Rations were received on an automatic issue from the central depot, based upon the 'present for duty' total of the unit's morning reports. This figure would be phoned to the depot, in code, once a week for dry stores, and daily for perishables.

The system of ordering in use was devised so as to prevent any station accumulating any excess, and to ensure a constant turnover of current stocks. The class I section from the QM department periodically checked the mess hall storage rooms to ensure that the system was being adhered to.

Perishables, such as frozen meats, butter and fresh vegetables were delivered to the site daily. Vegetables were delivered daily, except on Sundays, by British hauliers who were contracted by the British NAAFI organisation.

Supplies arriving on camp would be placed in ration stores before being broken down into the day's requirements, often in a building provided for this purpose. The day's ration would then be delivered to the relevant mess hall for processing.

Combat rations comprised items that were variations on the regular ration, considered important to furnish combat crews with the necessary dietary requirements for operating at high altitude. As with regular rations they were ordered weekly from the central depot, on the basis of combat strength. Generally the whole week's issue would be delivered to the combat mess hall in one delivery, instead of making a daily breakdown.

High carbohydrate rations were made up of sweets and gum, to provide combat crews with some extra 'comfort food' while in flight. The extra allocation proved highly successful, furnishing just enough nourishment to provide a 'good lift' for crews during their return from missions

Augmented rations were made up to provide extra lunch meals served from around midnight until the early morning, due to the nature of work for some personnel, particularly ground crews, who needed to work odd hours or shifts. The extra ration was also used for those times when missions returned late or at irregular hours when the crews needed to be fed. The extra items of this ration included canned meat, fruit juices, canned fruit, coffee, evaporated milk, bread, butter and sugar.

Emergency rations were normally one day's supply of army-standard C and K rations that were kept in stock in case of emergencies. Issue was generally small and infrequent and was normally only issued to personnel travelling longer distances on orders.

10 in 1 ration was a later war expansion of the system. A reserve stock of this ration was authorised for operational use. Normally one 10 in 1 ration would be issued to each crew for use in the event of the aircraft being diverted away from its home station on return from a mission. If the ration was not used it was to be returned to the store.

Clubs & Institutes

USAAF personnel on the whole tended to be well provided for in terms of places to spend off-duty time while still on camp. Generally three types of club appeared on USAAF airfields, catering to the needs of three groupings of rank. As stated earlier, the RAF requirements were provided for with an officers' mess, a sergeants' mess and an institute building. The first two are self explanatory, but the institute was a multi-function building for the lower ranks, airmen, in RAF terminology. The building title comes from the fact though it was provided not only as a place to go to when off duty but it would provide facilities of an educational nature for self improvement, but it wasn't normally operated as a club like those that higher ranks were provided with. No matter who they were provided for, all these facilities filled a similar role: that of being somewhere on camp to relax.

The clubs were normally administered by their own team or committee, much the same as in 'civvy street', and were permitted to levy a subscription for members. This usually went to pay for additional luxuries over and above those initially supplied, as well as for remodelling work or refurbishment. Officers' clubs would provide dining facilities with waiter service, bars and lounge areas, with barbershop and laundry facilities also often available. NCO clubs would also have a bar or lounge where drinks and snacks could be purchased, as well as having quieter areas for reading and writing. Often the clubs would also contain a games room with pool and table tennis tables. Membership of the 'Rocker Club' for NCOs of the 390th BG at Framlingham, for instance, cost an initial 11s to join and 5s in monthly dues. Again this money was reinvested in the club for improvements and entertainment.

When the USAAF first took over British airfields, club provision was often only available for officers and NCOs. However, enlisted men started to push for better facilities. Although institutes were available they usually only had limited catering arrangements; those that existed were often provided by the British NAAFI. On many camps, such as Podington, enlisted men's bars became established. Podington's bar was opened for the men of the 92nd BG on 13 March 1944 by movie star James Cagney while on a whirlwind tour of the ETO. This venue was obviously well patronised; for example, according to John Sloan, on 13 April 1944, thirsty GIs consumed thirteen barrels of beer in one evening![2] Other bomb groups provided facilities in different ways. Leroy Keeping explains the arrangement at Framlingham:

> In mid 1944 they put a large tent up for the enlisted men to buy beer. Staff sergeants and above could buy spirits as well at the Rocker Club. There was a Red Cross club on base staffed by two Red Cross girls. It stayed open all day for lower ranks to have doughnuts and coffee when required.

No matter which type of club on the camp, they would all close early on the nights before missions. Some would use illuminated signs in a similar manner to the red flags flown elsewhere on site, to indicate that it was back to business.

Improvements came for enlisted men when the ARC started introducing its Aeroclub programme. It had become apparent that there was a need for some sort of support infrastructure for those people either stationed away from the main centres or, because

NCOs of 401st BG relax in their club lounge at Deenthorpe, 16 May 1944. (USAAF)

of their duties were unable to easily get away from their jobs. The USAAF approached the ARC with a view to providing facilities, as many of those that fell into this category were its own personnel. For groups or stations with more than 500 personnel, the ARC agreed to set up Aeroclubs on airfields. A Red Cross field director and two Red Cross girls, plus British paid and volunteer workers, ran each club and virtually all USAAF airfields were provided for by the end of the war.

Aeroclubs were generally sited in one of the former RAF institute buildings set up on the camp. These buildings were normally either a temporary brick structure, or larger Nissen huts. The Red Cross girls transformed these drab austere huts and made them extraordinarily homely, warm and welcoming. Great resourcefulness was demonstrated in the decorating, and all sorts of material was begged, borrowed or 'requisitioned' to help furnish them, and airmen often gave their time freely to assist in the tasks required. According to some contemporary photographs some very elaborate decorating appeared, brick-built fireplaces were understandably very popular! Aeroclubs served as an entertainment centre for GIs while off duty, with the facilities offered very similar to those previously established for NCOs and officers, although it did not serve alcohol.

Another important programme established by the ARC for service personnel, particularly those stationed oversees, was Home Service. This operated as a link for servicemen and their families if problems occurred at home or vice versa. All ARC chapters provided Home Service for the benefit of families of service members. The ARC director at each Aeroclub would have access to these sorts of services and they would be available to all US service personnel stationed on the camp.

Katherine Kay Hutchins of West Palm Beach, Florida, worked in the Aeroclub programme in the Second World War. She volunteered for overseas duty with the American Red Cross in October 1944. She went to Washington DC for training in November, but the effects of the German counter-offensive over Christmas 1944 delayed the *Queen Mary* sailing to the ETO until 23 January 1945. Kay's first assignment was as staff assistant at the Aeroclub at Sudbury, Suffolk, home of the 486th BG. The club, with three American girls serving as hostesses, was open from 9 a.m. to 10 p.m. They 'met the mission' with coffee and sandwiches until VE Day. The girls maintained a snack bar with the help of a dedicated English staff, and provided varied entertainment for the GIs. Kay served there until the end of August 1945, and was the one who closed down the club after the war.[3]

The décor and interior adornments of these club buildings were often quite elaborate and it was here that many of the extensive works of wall art were to be found. The NCOs club for the 95th BG at Horham is one example. It is still extant and in use as a museum; known as the 'Red Feather Club', it still contains some incredible artwork from the period. The officers' club and the NCO's 'Rocker Club' at Framlingham were two more examples. The murals in the Rocker Club were painted by Sgt. Stanley Komocki, of the 458th Sub-Depot. Although both have since been demolished, contemporary photos show that they also contained features such as cocktail lounge furniture, imported from the US, and modern bars with elaborate lighting effects. These facilities were often utilised for social events such as dances, film shows or concerts, particularly at holiday times when special programmes of events would be provided. The clubs at Horham provided a very important service according to Art Watson:

My memory of Christmas is not to full. Christmas 1943, we had bad weather and we were not flying. Most of the guys went to the Red Feather Club (non-com's club) or to the Red Cross building and drank beer or had coffee, or stayed in the barracks and played cards.

Christmas 1944, we had a mission and it was just another busy day. On Easter, me and some of my buddies went to the little church in Horsham.

Clubs would also contain areas for quieter pastimes, such as reading or letter writing. Educational programmes were also organised, particularly later in the war. It was realised that returning demobbed GIs were going to have to make changes regarding their futures and the US government was offering the means to return to study and education. There would also be a well-stocked library as well as the latest in papers and periodicals. It was considered vitally important to keep everyone up to date and informed on how the war was going. Great emphasis was applied to the supply of information in publications. Generally, there was a good supply of quality printed matter available to the serviceman. Newspapers and magazines from home were an important morale booster, and most of the big name publications kept working throughout the war.

In addition to the ARC, the US Army also had specialist units assigned to assist in maintaining morale among its troops, operating as part of the Special Service Branch. Their purpose was to advise on moral matters, welfare and recreation of enlisted men. Headed by Special Service officers, these specialists were provided to bring personnel trained and experienced in many forms of sport and recreation to all combat units. As they also operated with ground troops on or near the front line, Special Service personnel were still combat soldiers first and foremost. Those assigned to USAAF units in Britain must have appreciated the greater degrees of comfort that they were afforded compared to their colleagues assigned to elements of the regular army.

A Special Service unit normally had two officers and around twenty-five men. Those assigned to bomb groups were smaller, often with only one officer and seven or eight men, suggesting again that units were divided into detachments operating between a number of groups. Special Service personnel had talents that were many and varied

The Special Service library at Bassingbourn. Enlisted men of the 91st BG enjoy its facilities. (USAAF)

Sporting competitions and fixtures have always been an important element of life within a military unit and the 8th AF were well catered for with various events organised on a regular basis. The winner of a bike race crosses the finish line, 303rd BG Molesworth, 11 March 1945. (USAAF)

but often comprised such things as PT instructors, theatrical artists and directors, film projectionists, radio presenters, musicians and sports professionals.

Most of the equipment available on base for entertainment and relaxation was provided and administered by the Special Services Branch. During the winter they ran film shows and staged theatrical events and concerts. During the summer months a lot of sporting competitions and fixtures were arranged between various groups within the air divisions. Tennis, volleyball, table tennis, softball, baseball, football, and cycling were all popular among the groups with many teams participating. Special Services also ran other field and track events and PT sessions, as well as quiz competitions which all helped foster team spirit and kept the mind and body fit. For the less active, they supplied much of the reading material available on camps and acted as unofficial 'tourist advisers' on places to visit while on leave.

Another important function was to act as liaison between all other organisations which offered some form of pastoral care, such as the ARC and other volunteer groups, as well as base retail outlets such as the Post Exchange. They provided education programmes and lectures and oversaw the United States Armed Forces Institute (USFI) educational programmes, which allowed many servicemen to receive credits towards college degrees through their studies.

Some stations even went as far as having their own music broadcasting service. The 390th BG at Framlingham, for example, were served by a base radio service known by the tongue-in-cheek handle of 'DNIF', which was an air force term for 'Duty Not Involving Flying'. This was available to many areas of the station, and offered news and music with records requested by station personnel. The hardware for these systems was often assembled by communications staff in their spare time under the guidance of Special Services.

Special Services also had the duty of organising the 'liberty' runs to local towns, and organised the truck convoys for such, as well as those to pick up local girls for dances and parties on the station. One of the most sought after jobs would have been bringing in local girls and, it is said, was the one time that drivers from the station motor pool volunteered for overtime! The 300th mission party for the 390th BG at Framlingham, for instance, entailed the conveyance of over 1,000 guests from their home towns to the base and back home again afterwards.

Dances, concerts and social events were organised on camps at every opportunity. Most messes would organise a dance or party at least once a month. Although many of these events would feature the popular music of the day, other genres of music and arts would also appear on club programmes. Artists performing many of the American regional sounds would appear. Spiritual choral music would be popular, especially among coloured units, as well as early forms of American folk or country music as it has become known, such as western-swing and bluegrass. Concerts were occasionally performed in the communities surrounding the camps; this was often the first time that British people became aware of the variety of musical culture the US could offer and often had a profound effect on many of those who were introduced in this way.

The holiday seasons would also bring large numbers of revellers to the airfields: Christmas and Easter as well as significant holidays in the US calendar, such as American Independence Day on 4 July and Thanksgiving in November. Paul Kovitz has even more reason to remember these social events:

> The Red Cross girls would go out and get women – girls and invite them into the Officers clubs or the Enlisted Men's clubs for dances. We'd have a dance about once a month. When this one particular girl walked in one night, I said I'm gonna marry that girl and I did. But first she was goin' with another guy, but as things turned out he went back to the States on R&R and I got acquainted with her. While he was gone I got together with her and when I proposed she accepted, we got married and we've been together over sixty years!

Many groups had their own bands and they would be kept busy entertaining personnel at their station as well as others in the area. Often comprising former professional and semi-

Parties were organised to commemorate special occasions, such as the anniversaries of a group's arrival in Britain, or significant notable numbers of missions, and, of course, VE Day. In this picture, the 401st BG at Deenthorpe hold a 100th mission party, within seven months of coming to England, 28 June 1944. (USAAF)

The 91st BG band, the 'Airmen' perform at a concert for group members at Bassingbourn. The singer on the right is Jack Gaffney. (USAAF)

professional musicians from the ranks of the group, using instruments often supplied by Special Services, many of these bands were very popular. Many had catchy air force related names, such as the 'Bombcats' of the 390th BG, the 'Rockets' from the 381st BG and the 379th BG's 'Toggleers'. Jack Gaffney performed with the 91st BG band at Bassingbourn:

> I was the vocalist for the 'Airmen' dance band of our group and we played at home and also other bases. One nice thing was that we got to wear the Eisenhower jackets (which were very sharp looking). We also put on our version of 'Red Hot and Blue' which was a stage show. When I was in High School, I danced professionally and was on the Orpheum circuit, playing four shows a day at the Hippodrome Theatre in Los Angeles for $8 a day!

There were also bigger concerts held on the bases, often in a hangar or outdoors if weather permitted. Probably the most famous of these were the concert tours performed by Major Glenn Miller and the American Expeditionary Force (AEF) band. These ran from July 1944 at many air force bases, hospitals and other establishments, up until the band leader's disappearance in December 1944. The band continued operating on the continent afterwards, fulfilling their obligation to entertain troops across Europe until the end of the war. Rich Creutz remembered the event held at Horham, which occurred on the evening of 10 September 1944. His recollections are a little out of step, however, as this was over three months before Miller's disappearance:

A big surprise came to us when the base had a 200 mission party. They brought in Glen Millers big band, we cleared out hangar no. 1 (and) built a band stand. Glen was already missing at that time. Lots of wonderful girls were invited from the surrounding area. It was a party! I think it was a big boost to our moral.

Many other stars came and performed at airfields, or visited service personnel. The majority of these tours were arranged by the United Services Organisation (USO), a private non-profit organisation started in 1941 to bring entertainment, morale and recreational services to the American troops. Celebrities such as Bing Crosby, Marlene Dietrich and Bob Hope, among many others, worked tirelessly performing routines for the USO. Others too, such as First World War ace Captain Eddie Rickenbacker, and Edward G. Robinson came and talked to air force personnel about their various experiences. Some of the London shows also went on the road and visited stations to provide more entertainment to airmen.

One particular type of event at which the Americans excelled, and are fondly remembered to this day by those who attended, were the Christmas parties thrown for the children of the locality. Station personnel would save sweets and treats from their Post Exchange rations and even make or collect toys for children attending. The 1944 Christmas party at Ridgewell was just one of many; Chaplain James Brown wrote of the event:

> The Christmas party was the wildest one I have ever seen. It was a sight to behold and one to be remembered. This was the second annual Christmas party to be held on Ridgewell aerodrome for the English children. Last year, 1943, I sponsored the party, sanctioned by the commanding officer. This year it was not the baby of any one department; rather, it had the support of many elements on the base. All got a kick out of it.
>
> One might think that in a year's time something would have been learned, but such was not the case. Quite the contrary. Last year we had a party well-organized. This year it appeared to be run according to one principle: chaos and general confusion. This did not make it a worse party but it surely was one wild mess!

The very same party described by Chaplain Brown. Confusion reigns at Ridgewell as Santa of the 381st BG distributes presents to English children, 23 December 1944. (USAAF)

Picture 400 and more children pouring onto the base. The trucks drove to one school in a certain designated community with the instructions to pick up 24 children. Sixty piled on the truck. They came from here, there and everywhere. During the year since the 1943 Christmas party, the news had gotten around to villages and towns over a wider area.'[4]

Christmas trees and decorations were put up and Santa Claus would make an appearance. Children were then treated to a Christmas dinner in the dining hall. Once again many of these things were completely alien to many children, especially the younger ones whose only memories were of a Britain at war, with all the privations that it had brought. Once known about, these events were eagerly anticipated and it must have been a great disappointment that the war ended so soon for those who had had the privilege to be so entertained!

The PX – The Post Exchange

We all take it for granted that in the current global 'village' we live in, wherever you go in the world you will be able to obtain familiar goods or products. It is much the same for the military personnel serving their country overseas. In the past, though, this wasn't so. Based on a desire during the First World War to provide a modicum of comfort to troops, in often desperate conditions, the origins of an organisation which later developed into the British NAAFI were formed. The Navy, Army, Air Force Institute is still providing support and services to British military personnel and their families stationed around the world today. Although other organisations have also provided similar services to the British forces, such as church groups like the Salvation Army and Church Army, as well as the Air Force Malcolm Clubs, it is still the NAAFI that is the best remembered of all.

The American armed forces had already operated a similar service dating from the late nineteenth century. Its origins went back to 1895, when the US War department issued directions that all post or base commanders should set up an exchange or trading post on their camps. The Post Exchange, or to give it its correct name, the Army Exchange Service (now the Army and Air Force Exchange Service) was and is an organisation similar to the NAFFI. Its motto 'We go were you go' epitomises its function. It provides US service personnel with services and merchandise to make their lives more comfortable wherever they are serving in the world.

The PX system had its first major combat test in the First World War and although it came through having proven the potential of the concept to be of great merit, it still had many shortcomings and would need the involvement in another global conflict to work through and refine its operation.

By the 1930s most military camps in the US had a PX, often carrying a wide range of goods for day-to-day needs, as well as the beginnings of a move into the supply of more luxury goods. The majority of exchanges, however, were still run as independent operations; some camps in the US had several on a single camp, all running concurrently without any overall controlling body. It wasn't until the threat of war in Europe galvanised the US military into restructuring many of its departments and systems in readiness for conflict that the exchange service came under the spotlight. In early 1941 it re-emerged, re-branded as the Army Exchange Service (AES).

When the US entered the war the AES was only six months old and was still going through major organisational upheavals. Until the Second World War the AES had primarily only operated within the US borders, but now it faced an even greater challenge of operating not only over greater inter-continental distances, but also alongside or within the economic structures of Allied host nations. The only existing army organisation with the ability to deal and control with such logistical complications was the QM Corps, and so for the opening stages of the Second World War, the AES found its operations entwined with this corps. The QM Corps had been to war before, but the AES, certainly in its new guise, had not. It was going to have to learn from its older brother fast, which it did, enabling the organisation by the end of the Second World War to spread its means of supply to virtually every point on the globe where a US serviceman was stationed.

Lt Gen. Brehon B. Somervell, Commanding General, Army Service Forces, had this to say about the service in March 1943:

> And everywhere we have men, I have found post exchanges, the little military stores where a soldier may buy chewing gum or cigarettes or chocolate or a toothbrush or his favourite shaving cream. You can well imagine the job it is to move these stores, with there wide assortment of merchandise, from place to place as the fluid battle fronts role back and forth. But they are worth the trouble – the American likes to be able to buy what he needs, even if it's only a package of spearmint gum. They are not perfect yet – they probably never will be – but they are becoming more adequate every day.[5]

Post Exchanges on overseas camps tended to be far more modest affairs than those that operated in the US. In the case of those established on most USAAF airfields in Britain, they tended to be housed in one of the ever-present Nissen or temporary brick huts. Sometimes they were just run from the back of a truck that toured a given area, in the same way as the Red Cross Clubmobiles were organised. The rolling PX was an idea developed at Holabird Quartermaster Depot and was used extensively at home and overseas. From mid-June 1943 the mobile service was expanded in Britain and trialled to gauge its potential use once mainland Europe was opened up to PX operations. In Britain these units tended to be used more for ground army troops billeted in more remote areas during the build up to D-Day, although at times they did visit USAAF units.

The first exchange operated under ETO control was actually established temporarily at the embarkation point in New York in the summer of 1942 to provide a supply of PX items for troops leaving for Britain. Earlier arrivals of troops in Ireland, from February to June 1942, had had to rely on limited supplies made available to them via the British NAAFI system. In fact as Americans started to inhabit bases given up by British forces, the NAAFI provided overlap supply of services until sufficient US staff and facilities were available. For a time the NAAFI supplied facilities to 75 per cent of all US installations in the British Isles. By the end of March 1942 two exchange systems were up and running in the UK, one covering Northern Ireland and one for mainland Britain.

Due to limited shipping capacity at this time, a serious approach had to be applied to shipping priorities, which resulted in a twelve point system of supply priority being established. PX supply items were considered priority five, except beer and Coca-Cola, which was priority ten. Priority one items were rations, considered the most important, with ammunition second and aircraft and spare parts third. One of the major problems faced by the AES in the opening stages of supply was that of undercover storage: much of the stockpile had to be stored in the open or under canvas, with the resultant losses from spoilage by damage from the elements and from pilfering. There were also the added problems of keeping up supplies in the early stages, with at least one ship laden with PX supplies being sunk by U-boat activity.

The first theatre exchange officer had arrived in England in March 1942 to supervise all exchanges that would ultimately be established in the ETO. The first ration was set at three small candy bars, three packets of cigarettes and one pack of chewing gum a week, additionally one bar of soap and one package (twelve boxes) of matches were permitted each month. Obviously this ration expanded fairly swiftly as supplies started to arrive in ever increasing numbers.

Things were not well with the new service, however. A series of problems of supply, inter-departmental meddling and staffing shortages ultimately caused the operations of the AES in the ETO to be suspended, with all of its assets transferred to the quartermaster. It wasn't long though before the same problems that plagued the AES started to trouble the QM Corps, particularly as shipping space was still as much a problem for them as it was for the AES. It also had a problem with staffing stores, and had no funds allocated with which to hire civilians, which would have been a logical option. Obviously due to the nature of PX stores, pilfering was also still a major problem, especially with many items being of a luxury nature, long unavailable in Britain.

At the beginning of 1943, following an investigation into the AES affairs and finances, auditors found that their operations were actually sound. The inference was that the primary reason for discontinuation of the AES activities had been based less on problems of logistics and more on the suspicion of some form of financial wrongdoing.

In early January the War Department approved an application by the Service of Supply to reactivate the AES in Europe, probably on the basis that the QM Corps was fairing no better. On 1 May 1943, the AES was reactivated in Europe under the control of the commanding general of the Service of Supply. All of its sales stores were once again branded Post Exchanges. However, it was not until February 1944 that an effective plan was established for the operation of the Exchange Service. This plan established a role for both the QM Corps as the wholesaler, procuring, shipping and distributing stores, and the AES as the outlet provider. The AES no longer had to argue for shipping space as the QM provided this. Nevertheless, AES requests for PX supplies were often cut especially in preference for more urgent items, particularly during the build-up required for operation OVERLORD. Despite its various problems, the exchange system continued to expand at a vast rate, reaching its peak in April 1944, when 1,504 outlets had been established. The following month, it started a similarly rapid, but downward trend, as outlets started to close in preparation for the upcoming invasion of Europe.

Given the situation at the time, of course, overseas exchanges could never hope to offer the range of services and goods available in the US. The AES, however, was not short on ambition and proceeded to put together plans to meet the need in areas in which it felt that there were shortcomings in provision of luxuries to British-based customers.

Due to extreme shortages of some items to the British population because of rationing, US servicemen were not allowed to obtain certain items from British sources. Included in these items were any luxury foods such as ice cream. In October 1943 the AES sought to overcome some of these deficiencies and ordered from US manufacturers a quantity of 'soda fountains', ice-cream counter freezers and other associated equipment necessary for the provision of such delights. In January 1944, orders were cancelled after a decree from General Eisenhower, the theatre commander. He felt the provision of such luxuries was not in keeping with US policy. Shortly afterwards, the decree was rescinded and orders reinstated, as apparently technicians had already arrived from the US to install all of this equipment.

It had been deemed acceptable that provided this equipment was installed in outlets that were out of the sight of most British citizens then the operation could go ahead. Therefore the prime locations for such indulgencies would be US Army hospitals and, much to the pleasure of the GI airmen, USAAF stations. This, it was hoped, would minimise any controversy, although whether any did specifically arise due to the provision of these facilities has probably been lost to history! The 92nd BG at Podington were one group who eagerly embraced the new facilities:

On July 5th the long awaited soda fountain opened in the PX, and although Coca Cola was its only drink, queues of thirsty GI's were immediately in evidence. Decoratively the fountain featured a South Seas motif, complete with thatched roof and bamboo. Receipts from the fountain alone were £264 in 18 days, roughly over 21000 glasses of real coca cola sold. Total PX receipts for the month were £3689, highest of the year ...[2]

Funding for units to establish exchanges at their individual camps came from one of several means. Sometimes units were able to fund their own exchanges, but more often either the QM Corps or the AES loaned the funds. Whichever method was used once an exchange was set up, the finances were administered by the central office controlling all exchanges in that particular theatre. Day-to-day operation of the PX, however, came under the control of the Special Services. Although they didn't provide the actual infrastructure, they provided the trained staff to run the outlets.

The AES tried in many ways to meet the additional needs of the soldier above his basic ration allocation. Further attempts were made to use profits to provide better welfare and recreational facilities. Gift and war bond programmes were initiated through the exchanges, a special ordering service was implemented for obtaining one-off articles from the US, and attempts were made to procure surprise items to supplement the standard ration. Sales of books, magazines and newspapers were introduced or increased and always popular were lines such as toiletries, smaller luxury goods and souvenirs.

Another initiative implemented by the AES in the autumn of 1942, in preparation for its first Christmas, was the 'Individual Gift Service'. It provided a catalogue system whereby a serviceman could choose and order gifts through the PX and have them dispatched from a central warehouse in the US to the recipient. Following its success, the system was soon expanded to include overseas exchanges for other major holiday seasons.

Not all these services were available at the smaller camp; PXs and servicemen instead had to visit the larger stores, set up in towns and cities to obtain the more exotic offerings. The PXs established on USAAF bases seem to have been the ones that enjoyed the greatest longevity of operation, that stability possibly being one reason why they were able to provide a plentiful supply of goods over and above the basic ration.

Once areas of Europe became liberated, facilities were sought out for local manufacture of goods and services. Beer and soft drink production was redirected or re-established on the continent for supply to the AES. This not only helped to ease the supply situation, but also enabled manufacturing facilities to transfer back to civilian production, therefore providing employment and putting real money back into local economies.

An example of an elaborate station PX, supplying the needs of the 401st BG at Deenthorpe. As well as a retail outlet at one end it has a beverage counter with 'soda fountain' and seating areas. (USAAF)

The gymnasium and chapel building at Ridgewell in 2009, still just about standing, where James G. Brown ministered to his wartime flock. (Author)

Spiritual Support

The importance of provision for practising religious beliefs has long been considered of importance by many military forces, the RAF being no different. All airfields ,as originally designed, would have been provided with some form of building that could be used for religious services. Station church was often a grand name for a Nissen or temporary brick hut, but this was often all that was provided.

Many stations had this provision with a diagram 14604/40: a combined gymnasium and chapel. The chapel was a smaller annex at one end of the main building, closed off by a set of sliding doors. These could be opened to enable larger congregations to be accommodated in the gymnasium section. The building would also include an office for the station chaplain, some of whom also used this for their own domestic accommodation. Hethel's chapel was of this type and still exists, having now been restored as a memorial museum to the 389th BG, the camp's former occupants.

Chaplaincy

The service of chaplains in the US Army has a long history going back to the wars of independence, but like many organisations, it was the First World War and its aftermath that was to have a profound effect on the position of the chaplaincy within the army. The huge reduction in numbers of men in the US services consequently led to an equally large drop in the numbers of chaplains required to administer to their spiritual care.

Public and Church attitudes after the First World War led to the very role of chaplains within the armed forces being questioned. The rising voice of the pacifist movement harshly argued the need or indeed the ethical position of chaplains, claiming that the Church and military service could not in any way work side by side, as the two were utterly incompatible. These views took hold, pushing forward a sense of national or corporate guilt over the war to end all wars and that 'men of God' should no longer support those involved with conflict. It was only later, once the scale of suppression of free thought and spiritual belief within future enemies' regimes became known, that Church and public opinion changed. It was once again realised that war could have a just cause and that fighting would be the lesser of two evils.

Due to the work of the CCC in the 1930s, the chaplaincy started to regain its status within the US Army. Although primarily a non-military undertaking because of the nature and size of the task, it still needed a disciplined approach. It was here that organisations such as the army chaplaincy started to gain new purpose and experience, ministering to people's spiritual and emotional welfare in a situation of working towards the common good. So it was that the US Army chaplaincy, having assisted in getting the American people to regain a sense of self-respect, found itself far more accepted and prepared to address the requirements of the coming conflict. With the creation of the new post of chief of chaplains in the late 1930s, a number of other issues that had plagued the organisation were also finally clarified.

One man, William R. Arnold, (not to be confused with General H. Arnold of whom he was well acquainted but not related) was to serve as chief of chaplains through the whole of the Second World War. His leadership had a profound effect on the change of status of the chaplaincy within the US Army. One of Arnold's greatest qualities was a sense of absolute fairness and concern for soldiers of all religious persuasions to have the opportunity to worship his or her particular god. His big mission was to push for the chaplaincy to be freed from its previous undefined position, often as camp dogsbody, and be released from secular duties so that it may devote its time to providing the support that its function was established for. Arnold also insisted that all army religious programmes should be wholly under the direction of the Chaplain Corps, without external interference from external civilian agencies as had been the case during the First World War.

By 1945 the ratio of chaplains to soldiers was approximately one to every thousand, a figure Arnold had regularly recommended as his target throughout the war. Recruits to the chaplaincy had to fulfil four requirements to be accepted into the corps. They had to be male US citizens within the age range of twenty-three to thirty-four for the regular army and twenty-four to forty-two for the officer reserve, although the upper age range for both was raised to fifty-five during the war due to a pressing need for more chaplains. They had to be regularly ordained, duly accredited and in good standing with the religious denomination under which they applied. They needed to be a graduate of four years of college and three years of theological seminary. Finally, they had to be actively engaged in ministry as a principal occupation with at least three years of experience, although again this figure was reduced to one year.

To convert these men of the cloth to military life, chaplain school was reactivated at Fort Benjamin Harrison in 1942 to provide a four-week course. In August of the same year, the school moved to Harvard University.

USAAF Chaplaincy

With the huge increase in the numbers of men and women joining the army it was decided that each branch of the service would require specific chaplains and the growing air force was no different. In February 1941 General H. Arnold recommended various existing chaplains to become head chaplains of each of the US-based air forces, as well as for all other divisions of the air force such as Service and Training Command. HAP Arnold was determined that the chaplaincy should be a vital component of the air force. This may have had something to do with his hard-line Baptist preacher grandfather, but he also knew that tough fighting would take place and combat soldiers needed a reassuring presence in times of difficulty. By April 1945 there were 1,861 air force chaplains, 995 of whom were operating overseas.

Chaplain Maurice W. Reynolds was the first staff or supervisory chaplain to be assigned to the 8th AF and began his work in July 1942. On his arrival in Britain he had twelve chaplains under him; by August 1944, 138 chaplains were serving in England at a ratio of 1 to 1,412 airmen. Reynolds returned to the US after ten months to be replaced by Chaplain Arthur S. Dodgeson, who served until 30 January 1945, when Chaplain Charles Carpenter arrived to oversee the 8th AF's chaplains in England.

Due to the nature and growth of the air force chaplaincy many chaplains were rotated around the groups stationed in England; this was particularly the case with Jewish chaplains as there were far fewer of them than their Catholic or Protestant brothers. Many chaplains were shipped oversees to the detriment of units left in the United States as it was desired that those in combat had priority access to religious support. Even so, there was always a shortage of chaplains in Britain for both the 8th and 9th AF. It had been hoped for at least a Protestant and Catholic chaplain to be available to all groups but this was soon seen to be unrealistic and most groups were lucky to get one chaplain of any denomination. Chaplain James G. Brown was fairly unusual in that he stayed with one group, the 381st, for his whole wartime service, from joining the group at Pyote Texas through its deployment to England and its return to America.

Allocation of a particular denomination of chaplain was to a degree based on numbers of servicemen under that denomination. However, in the case of Jewish servicemen it was suggested at the time that there were more than records suggested. The numbers attending Jewish services were always higher than anticipated. The inference being that many Jewish servicemen, particularly air crew serving in England kept their real religion secret in case of falling into German hands. Generally a Jewish chaplain would attend a base for service once a fortnight. However, due the ecumenical way in which the chaplaincy operated, all denominations were able to attend services with the regular chaplain if they so wished.

The job of an air force chaplain was very varied, but the primary task still involved providing for the spiritual needs of the group. The big difference came having to deal day in day out with strain that combat put on air crew members and the continuing loss of crewmen that any good chaplain had made it his business to get to know. For this there was little in the way of protection and only strong faith pulled them through. The provision of further training for chaplains was often achieved by the use of conferences. These were held at all levels within the service and were considered a very effective method of support.

Chaplains did have a series of War Department directives on which to base their work, while instruction in the correct military protocol for many other potential duties would be covered within their initial training. All chaplains were tabled to have an assistant for their duties who was normally drawn from personnel with the military speciality of clerk/typist. However, he would take on many other roles such as that of driver as well as having to be an unofficial 'facilitator' of other supplies and services.

Chaplains were also no different to other commanders in that they still had to send monthly reports on all their activities back to higher command and War Department from No. 3 was provided for this purpose. Examples of some of the suggested reporting categories give a good indication of the wide-ranging duties a chaplain would be expected to encounter:

1. Chaplain's Personal Activities at Station.

Religious: preaching services, prayer meetings, Sunday schools, Bible classes, masses, sacraments, catechism special devotions, hospital and Guardhouse services. This division was subdivided into sections for Sunday activities and those on weekdays.

Joint or participating services, those conducted with other chaplains.

Services visited.

Pastoral, educational, recreational, miscellaneous. Included addresses of moral or educational nature, group discussions, disciplinary cases, welfare cases, celebrations of a

Church service for members of the 401st BG at Deenthorpe, 1 May 1944. The small annex can be seen with the sliding doors drawn back to allow the congregation to sit in the larger gymnasium building. (USAAF)

65532A

patriotic or anniversary nature, dramatics, athletics, sightseeing tours, hospital visits, scout activities.

2. Activities in civilian communities: religious services, welfare work, celebrations, conventions, conferences, official calls... [6]

Although some of these tasks may seem irrelevant in a combat situation, according to Chaplain Brown, many of these eventualities seem to have been encountered.

The last category on the form concerned officiating over religious rites and indicated a duty that was needed all too frequently: the conducting of funerals. This category also rather more happily included marriage. Chaplains spent a great deal of time counselling the many marriages that took place between servicemen and English women. Paul Kovitz required assistance to cut through a considerable amount of red tape:

> I recall having contact with the base chaplain when I was in the process of marrying an English girl. Being Catholic I had to get dispensation from the Pope and get a letter from my wife-to-be's vicar saying she was good enough to marry a Yank!

The Issue of Flying

Chaplains were, of course, non-combatants in accordance with international rules of war. For air force chaplains this posed some degree of difficulty when attempting to support their flock under the most extreme of situations. For chaplains assigned to ground units they could remain as close to the men they ministered to as they wished. For chaplains supporting airmen, particularly air crew, it was different. Although they could fly with them during test flights and the like, they couldn't be close to them in the heat of battle when it really mattered and some felt that this was wrong.

Chaplains like James Brown of the 381st BG and Chaplain Merritt O. Slawson of the 303rd BG were two among a number who felt strongly that it was impossible to counsel disturbed airmen about situations of which they had no personal experience. Giving crews their blessing prior to a mission was simply not good enough.

Chaplain James G. Brown, of Lee, Mass. congratulates 1st Lt William D. Butler, of Flagler Co. one of the original 381st BG pilots after completing his tour of twenty-five missions, 19 February 1944. The morale boost to air crew of the 381st from Chaplain Brown flying several missions with them, must have been incalculable. His experiences fortunately caused him no lasting harm, as he lived to be 107. (USAAF)

Chaplain Brown, after much pressurising of higher command, flew several combat missions over Germany, giving him a much deeper insight into those whose spiritual welfare he oversaw and was always a popular passenger with the crews he flew with. Chaplain Slawson, however, was a little more circumspect about his experiences, although there is little doubt about the fact that he too flew combat missions.

This situation must have manifested itself many times over during the course of the Second World War, and the actions of these two chaplains were surely not unique. Art Watson expressed his view on the role of the chaplain:

> With regards to Chaplains, I wasn't too familiar with them. My life style and philosophy kept me away from them. But they were certainly very valuable and were always available to fill the needs of many. They were always available for those who needed help. With 'dear John' letters from home, wanting to be with their family, fear of the possibility of not returning, etc they were always there to give spiritual strength when needed.

This last section covers some of the smaller facilities that would have existed on a communal site.

Domestic Services

A selection of services were available for personnel on camp to cover general domestic or housekeeping arrangements. These were often located on the communal site. Generally these existed for enlisted personnel, as officers would have their own similar services available through their mess.

Laundry

Official laundry services were available to enlisted personnel through the quartermaster on each camp. However, many personnel, especially those who due to their work pattern were unable to get to the quartermaster regularly, such as squadron ground crews, often set up their own arrangements with local civilians, who took in laundry to make a little extra money.

When US laundry units were not available the quartermaster also used civilian contractors, but these were obviously of a more industrialised nature. According to QM records for the 381st BG, a maximum of nine pieces of laundry could be sent each week by each enlisted man and a charge of 25¢ per bundle was made and deducted on the payroll. The service was also available to hospital and Red Cross staff.

The QM would also organise the dry cleaning of heavier uniform items. Dry cleaning for enlisted men was limited to three pieces per month from the following: a blouse, overcoat, trousers or field jacket. The monthly payroll deduction was 35¢. The QM also arranged for all dry cleaning of flying clothing. All invoices concerning services rendered were processed by the reciprocal aid records department.

Tailor

Another sought-after individual was the base tailor. Sometimes this service would be provided by USAAF personnel from the station complement unit. On other stations the service was operated as part of the PX. In many instances, however, where there were shortages of skilled personnel, the base tailor may have been a local civilian. Again some personnel would also make their own arrangements.

The US Army prided itself in providing well-fitting items of uniform from time of issue, although looking at colour photographs of the period, uniform is not quite the correct term judging by the vast variations in colour of the material supplied! The majority of work undertaken by the base tailor would probably have been repairs and addition of insignia to uniforms.

Some enterprising servicemen went to lengths to obtain steam pressing equipment and base tailors were sometimes able to provide this as an additional service to keep personnel looking smart. Officers provided their own uniforms with an allowance, which would require complete tailoring services. While stationed in England many took advantage of London's top tailors while on leave, although local services were also utilised in towns and cities across Britain.

In general, an airman received an initial issue of two pairs of shoes. Each pair would be resoled twice before being replaced with a new or rebuilt pair. Shoe repair services

S/Sgt Robert T. Mitchell, a valet with five years' experience before the war, invested £15 16s for a presser. Now he has more work than he can handle and has an assistant to help him. Between them they do 150 items a week. He and the station barber set up a tailor shop off one of the showers and the squadron cook assists them in his spare time. Sgt Frederick T. 'Huey' Long waits for his pants to be pressed. Mitchell averaged $100 a month pressing clothes. Station unknown. (USAAF)

were normally under the control of the QM department, and the work often undertaken though by outside civilian contractors.

Barber

Another important member of the base community, and one who would be kept very busy making sure hair was kept to regulation length, was the station barber. Once again the post was not always filled officially and the service was often provided by a member of station complement or another unit. Those with the talent and an enterprising nature could often find customers for their work in virtually any area of the camp. Officers' barber services would once again be provided within the officers' mess.

Station Post Office

Regular mail from home was considered a vital component in creating good morale when units were stationed overseas. Initially base postal services were often operated from offices remote from the camps. As the US Army expanded, more postal units were created, enabling camps to have post offices established on them, although many postal units were divided over two or three camps on detached service.

A postal unit normally comprised around ten men under one officer. It was divided into three sections: directory, distribution and finance. The directory section dispatched mail and redirected that which was wrongly addressed. The distribution section cancelled postage, and sorted, bagged and dispatched incoming and outgoing mail. The finance section sold money orders, stamps and handled registered mail and parcel post.

The average station post office handled 300 pouches of first class mail a month as well as 100 sacks of parcel post. During the run up to Christmas this rose to 2,000 pouches and sacks. The finance section had an average monthly sale of 40,000 dollars of money orders and 3,000 dollars worth of stamps. Mail would be picked up from the nearest rail station and brought to camp. Once sorted it would be picked up from the base post office by individual unit orderly staff and taken to the relevant unit HQ or orderly room for distribution to personnel at morning 'mail call'.

Christmas packages start to arrive for personnel of the 493rd BG at Debach, 24 November 1944. (USAAF)

Domestic Site

hereas communal sites provided facilities for day-to-day living, the actual living or, more importantly, sleeping accommodation was provided on the domestic site. As with many of the other dispersed sites, the number of domestic sites per station again varied, but there were generally around eight. Great Ashfield for instance had ten domestic sites, whereas Molesworth appears to have had only five. This number often included one or two WAAF, or female only, sites. WAAF sites were slightly different to regular domestic sites in that they would often include one or two buildings of a communal nature in an attempt to make them self-contained. This followed a practice, certainly in evidence early in the war, to keep men and women segregated as much as possible. From 1942 however, the situation was largely relaxed due to a further need to conserve materials. Once the US took over RAF stations the provision of separate all-female sites was largely academic and due to the need to accommodate a larger number of men they were put to the latter purpose. From then on, the WAAF site designation tended to fall from use, even though a small number of women, both RAF WAAFs and US WACs, were employed and accommodated on a station.

Just like the airfields, the location, shape and orientation of every domestic site was unique: there was no single standard. Layout of sites usually often only occurred once surveyors and construction workers were on the ground and starting to build. Once again, all of these factors would have been largely dependent on the prevailing topography. Obviously the ideal situation would have been to employ a lot of natural cover in which hutted camps could be concealed. Unfortunately this was not always possible, especially in areas of flat, open farmland, the terrain best suited to building airfields. Layout of buildings on all dispersed sites was made to appear as random as possible, fitting in with existing field boundaries and hedgerows, and using any natural cover to the best advantage. However, although this layout provided the best form of concealment, it was considered a hindrance at times to the efficient operation of the base.

Provision of sanitary arrangements was also made more difficult by the haphazard nature of site dispersal. The ideal provision was for one WC block per three huts, but this often didn't happen due to a need to simplify sewerage pipe runs. The number of huts on each site also varied considerably. Sites ranged from those containing only a dozen or so buildings, including half a dozen barrack huts, to those such as Snetterton Heath, which had some large domestic sites with thirty or more buildings on them. Each barrack hut, depending on type and construction, could accommodate, according to the original scales, up to twenty-four people. However, according to first-hand accounts, this number could increase considerably from time to time. There were standards laid down by the Air Ministry for the space allocations per person. At the outbreak of war it was 120ft^2 for officers, 70ft^2 for sergeants and 45ft^2 for airmen. In 1942 hut space was recalculated and reduced to 96ft^2 for officers, 58ft^2 for sergeants and 38ft^2 for airmen. A further space reduction occurred for corporals and airmen in July 1943 to 32ft^2 per person. These figures were used as a basis for US requirements but again were not always

A typical domestic site Ridgewell site No.10. Note irregular shape of site, the random location of the structures and use of hedgerow to align huts against. From high altitude the alignment would be difficult to spot. A variety of building and structure types can be seen, mainly Nissen huts. The long narrow building in the centre is the EM ablutions and latrine block and beside it an emergency water tank. The group on the far left are officers' quarters and above them the picket post at the entrance to the site. Note the volleyball court laid out in the foreground. (USAAF)

followed, especially when camps were under construction and accommodation space was at a premium.

Under early airfield planning, accommodation was provided for the RAF under a two-tier system for officers and airmen. With the expansion of RAF Bomber Command prior to the beginning of the Second World War, the large increase in aircraft numbers led to a corresponding sharp rise in NCO aircrew, particularly the introduction of sergeant pilots. This then made it necessary to provide an additional tier of specific accommodation, to cater for their new standing within the RAF hierarchy. Facilities for sergeants and other NCOs therefore started to appear in greater quantities as airfield numbers increased.

During USAAF inhabitation, accommodation on a domestic site was generally, but not always, mixed between both officers and enlisted men, though not necessarily in the same building. bomb groups tended to be allocated domestic sites by their component organisation; for example, a separate site would be allocated to each of the four squadrons. The smaller units, however, had to fit in where space allowed.

Structures

Aside from the accommodation buildings, the usual set of utility facilities would once again appear on the domestic site. The site would be guarded from a picket post at the main entrance; then there would be ablutions and latrine blocks, normally allocated by rank. Lastly the smaller structures would include an M&E plinth for the electrical transformer, a solid fuel compound for coal storage, a static water tank and air raid, or blast, shelters.

WAAF sites would be slightly better provided for. On these could be found such provision as ablution blocks with laundry facilities, bath houses, hairdressing facilities, institutes, messes and often separate decontamination units.

Extremes of Accommodation

Although the vast majority of USAAF personnel assigned to Britain had to live in one of the many types of temporary hutting, there were those who were rather more fortunate than most.

Accommodation for airmen provided on the pre-war permanent sites tended to be not only of a somewhat more robust construction, but by contrast of a rather more salubrious nature. The USAAF were allocated several of these airfields, but the two most associated with the 8th's heavy bomb groups were Bassingbourn and Horsham St Faith. Accommodation on these two stations ranged from basic (but still more sumptuous than on temporary stations) two-storey heated barrack blocks for airmen, to married quarters on small housing estates near the camps.

Rudi Steel of the 91st BG at Bassingbourn remembered how his unit were billeted in the permanent airman's housing, probably some of the best quality accommodation available to enlisted men of the 8th AF:

> Heating in the houses was by a solid fuel back boiler. I took pride in always being able to keep boiler alight and heating, while the guys in the other houses could never get theirs to work. Well I guess they got a little tired of me telling them how good I was and telling them how it should be done. I returned back to the house this one day to find the boiler had been removed, the rest of the guys living there got so sick of having no heat and me being so smug about it, they felt if they didn't have heating, me and the guys in my house shouldn't either!

These forms of accommodation would have afforded the most privacy for their occupants, as rather than share a barrack block with up to twenty or thirty others, each room in a house would have been home to only two or three individuals. Coupled with this, their traditional construction would also have provided the warmest and least draughty of accommodation. That is, of course, assuming that someone hadn't removed your source of heating!

Many large country houses and stately homes in Britain were also requisitioned for the duration of the Second World War for military service. They were utilised for a variety of

A row of pre-war married quarters at Horsham St Faith as used for accommodation, by members of the 458th BG. These were the luxury end of accommodation for the lucky few. The disruptive camouflage paint scheme was still visible on the walls when this was taken on 14 April 2010. (Author)

tasks, some top secret, by various government agencies and branches of the service. Some of these properties were provided to the USAAF, though mainly for divisional headquarters. Some groups were also lucky enough to be provided with such accommodation, but of course only for officers. The 92nd BG, while stationed at Alconbury were one such group, having the use of Stukeley Hall for their needs.

Types of Hutting

There were many types of hutting employed in Britain for military use during the Second World War, all utilised in an attempt to conserve more and more vital materials. Generally each new type introduced would herald another evolutionary step along the path of austerity and as the war continued the more temporary these designs became. Having said this, considering their design life was of a very short duration, surprising numbers are still standing sixty and seventy years later, which is particularly remarkable, as many have seen little or no maintenance during the intervening years. Those that have survived tend to be the early rather than later temporary types and best adapted to industrial or agricultural use. Of these types, the most common buildings on wartime airfields were either the Nissen hut or the Air Ministry standard, temporary brick building. Of these, the former was by far the most common accommodation building.

Nissen Huts

The humble Nissen hut dates back to 1916, when a design for a multi-purpose prefabricated hut was developed by Major Peter Norman Nissen of the 29th Company Royal Engineers. Economy of material content and shipping space, as well portability and ease of assembly were all factors driving Nissen's design and in all of these it succeeded enabling a hut to be packed in a standard army wagon and erected by six men in four hours. After the First World War, sales understandably waned; however in 1939 production was once again revived.

Huts of a similar shape were also developed by several other companies. In Britain the Romney hut, usually a much larger variation to the Nissen, was widely used, particularly for stores and workshop buildings on airfields. In the USA the Quonset hut, another design very similar to the Nissen, came onto the market. All of these types were mass produced in vast quantities throughout the war and utilised for a wide range of functions all over the world.

Nissen huts were produced in three standard internal sizes, 16ft, 24ft or 30ft. The longitudinal bays came in multiples of 6ft. Once the steel angle and corrugated shells were assembled the ends were closed in with walls of either brick or wood. Usually only the larger spans had windows in the sides, the 16ft span only had windows, if at all, provided in the end walls.

Another hut type that fell into the corrugated category, although different from the Nissen design was the Jane hut, in both the early Plyfelt and later Richmond types. These were used at Great Ashfield, Podington, Molesworth and Glatton, among others. The design comprised lightweight timber frames clad with flat corrugated sheeting in 3ft-wide wall sections and with a corrugated sheet pitched roof.

Temporary Brick Hutting

Temporary brick structures were introduced early in the war as means of reducing the amount of timber in use at the time. Extensively used on all airfields, this construction

A Nissen hut on one of the dispersed domestic sites, just clinging to existence at Thorpe Abbotts, wartime home of the 100th BG, photographed in 2006. The rudimentary construction method of light steel sections and corrugated steel panels can be clearly seen. (Author)

method, however, was used more for communal buildings and workshops, rather than accommodation blocks. Its main usage on domestic sites was for the construction of ablution and latrine buildings.

Construction was by means of single-skin walls built from poorer quality bricks, rendered with cement on the outside and painted on the inside. Brick piers constructed at 10ft centres supported lightweight steel fabricated roof trusses. Roofs were either pitched or canted and roofing material was corrugated asbestos sheeting. Buildings were constructed with either 18ft or 28ft spans, with three standard wall heights ranging from 7ft to 13ft 6in.

Other types of hutting used on airfields during the Second World War can be broken down into the following groups. Within these groups are a number of different types. Most of these types appeared in varying quantities on camps occupied by the USAAF.

Timber huts

Timber hutting was introduced by the Air Ministry from 1935 to supplement existing barracks. These were high quality temporary buildings, but from 1939 they were gradually superseded by designs using lighter methods of construction. Initially still of all-timber construction, eventually felt covered plasterboard was introduced as a preferred cladding method, with asbestos as a roofing material.

Finally timber was removed altogether and replaced with plywood. Several of these designs appeared, utilising standard constructional sections, supporting flat-felted roofs.

Asbestos huts

As an alternative to steel, used in the Nissen hut design, several manufacturers came up with designs made from asbestos. These had the advantage over the traditional Nissen type in that they could be frameless, as once bolted together the curved asbestos sections had enough strength and rigidity to be self-supporting. The ends were normally finished either with felted timber or brick.

Orlit prefabricated concrete hut at Horham, still in use as light industrial unit, July 2006. (Author)

Concrete huts

In an attempt to move away from using wood, the idea of using concrete for temporary buildings had been developing for many years prior to the Second World War. The first design used extensively on airfields was the Air Ministry standard concrete hut, a First World War design, although this had been largely superseded by the Second World War. A number of new designs came into production from the early 1940s, such as the Maycrete, although this still used timber for roof construction. Wall infill was completed with moulded panels made from a mixture of concrete and sawdust.

From 1942 the British Concrete Federation (BCF) developed a number of all-concrete designs for manufacture by federation members. Both flat and slightly pitched roof types were available. Like most temporary hutting, they were designed to be assembled on light concrete bases with concrete posts supporting the roof. Concrete panels were used to infill, with windows every other bay if desired. BCF designs were tested to have a degree of blast protection. Roofs were either pre-cast concrete panels with felt cover, or asbestos on timber purlins. Interiors were plasterboard lined. The Orlit hut was a similar to the BCF designs, with wall panels which slotted into pillars that supported roof trusses, which again supported a panel felted roof; all of the components were made from concrete.

Many of these types are indicative of much cheaper and more short-lived designs that came into use later the airfield construction programme. However, much experience was gained from the manufacture of these building types that was to serve post-war society well for many years. Many designs and methods were incorporated into much of the temporary housing provided after the Second World War and, indeed, some of the design methods can still be seen on domestic concrete buildings in use to this day.

Living in a Hut

Aside from the previously mentioned lucky few who found themselves living in permanent accommodation, the vast majority of servicemen of all Allied nations stationed in Britain during the Second World War found themselves allotted living space in one of the temporary hut types, most commonly a Nissen. Few of these buildings were designed to have the slightest allowance for insulation, so although one may argue that to live in them would have been better than the conditions afforded the infantry, both winter and summer months proved an exercise in endurance.

Accommodation in each hut varied considerably, depending on the size and type, as well as the rank of those living within, with higher ranks afforded a little more living space. Rich Creutz recalls his living accommodation at Horham:

> Our barracks were around a wooded area and our barracks were long rather narrow, a door on each end with a pot bellied stove in the middle. There were 8 double along each side [room] for 36 men. I believe I am right on this. Most of the guys were from our sheet metal shop where I worked. I spent 21 months in the same bunk. It was a long time.

Living conditions were spartan; the only furniture provided were metal-framed beds, sometimes double bunks or even army camp beds on which to sleep. The only other concession to comfort was a single cast-iron coal-fired stove, placed either at one end or halfway along the hut, but with the meagre fuel ration, it was never able to warm much more than the air immediately surrounding it. This was wartime Britain after all, and shortages of fuel were commonplace.

Fuel was, however, supplemented in other ways. The following taken from the records of the medical section of the 381st BG at Ridgewell illustrates the concern of some in authority about the unhealthy living conditions, but also a certain amount of embarrassment about the lengths some would go to improve their situation:

> An inspection of combat crew's living sites was made this date and they were found to be in a deplorable condition. They are dirty, crowded, inadequately blacked out, damp, inadequately heated, and seem inadequate for the care of this type of personnel.

Life inside an unknown 8th BC hut; an airman keeps watch on the unpredictable coal stove. (USAAF)

The matter of stoves was taken up with the utility officer, Lt Gray, and the Ground Executive, Col Reed, states that sixty American stoves were due to arrive shortly and would be used where necessary on combat sites. It is Col Reed's opinion that much of the grief of the combat crews is brought about by their laziness, lack of discipline, etc., and he feels disinclined to 'baby' them, as he expressed it. The coke is distributed to the site daily in inadequate quantities and is appropriated by the first come, first served method; as a consequence the combat crews have been chopping down trees in the surrounding territory, but the green weed will not burn and the barracks are still cold and damp.

Many of them spend a great deal of their times as scavengers looking for fuel. Just the other night, a clear moonlight night, a 1st Lt. and first pilot, were seen running at full speed across a ploughed field with a sack of coke over his shoulders and an Englishman behind him. He made it but the condition is obviously a rather sad one, and certainly does not contribute to the health and happiness of the troops. Some of the officers have been sleeping in their flying clothes to keep warm.

Col. Reed states that everything that can be done has been done to obtain fuel and that it would serve no useful purpose for the medical department to write through command channels complaining of inadequate housing. Regardless of what measures are necessary (that is to do the work for them, or see that they are severely disciplined to do it for themselves) I feel that it is mandatory for the physical efficiency and morale that their lot be bettered.

Another thing that has come to my attention about the fuel shortage is that such notables as Capt. Murray, the ex-professor of anatomy, and Capt. Bland, Flight Surgeon of the 535th BS, have been visiting the ash piles behind the enlisted men's barracks and are quite enthusiastic about the 'big pieces' of coke they had salvaged. Some ingenious members of the organization have found that a six pence can of shoe polish is a good substitute for kindling wood and that the shoe impregnate supposed to protect against noxious gases is also a highly inflammable item. Praise the Lord! At last we have found a useful use for this material we have been toting across the world for the past six months.[1]

Beds provided little in the way of comfort either, usually having only thin mattresses to lie on. Air Ministry mattresses were nicknamed 'biscuits', and it would often require two or three to fully cover a bed; a similar number of blankets were provided to finish making a bed up. There would be just enough room beside a bed to place a footlocker and hang clothes up. Huts would have been dimly lit, with normally only a couple of often unshielded electric lights provided.

Inhabitants, where possible, especially the longer-term residents, begged, borrowed or otherwise obtained items of furniture, particularly chairs and tables, to improve on the overall comfort levels. However, as all personnel were still subject to regular inspections, huts and equipment had to maintain a degree of tidiness and order. Art Watson also has memories of his living arrangements at Horham:

As to the domestic site, the barracks were there for our domicile. A place for sleep and rest and a gathering place for the men with whom you worked. When we were in from the airfield, we were generally sleeping, reading, playing a lot of cards or just having a bull session.

There was room enough between barracks for the men to play touch football, volley ball and other physical activity.

Ken Blakebrough, a 457th BG B-17 co-pilot based at Glatton, recalls his experiences of living in a Nissen hut:

To me, a Nissen hut during the winter of 1944–45 was a man-made cave. The interior was always gloomy, damp and cold. The windows were covered by thick blackout curtains, the overhead light bulbs, two to a hut, gave scant lighting. The scarcity of coal for the potbelly stove was another reason for avoiding your hut. As a result, the time spent in the hut was mostly for sleeping. Off duty time was largely spent at the officers club where there was a huge fireplace which gave off some warmth, if you stood close enough.

A hut provided quarters for up to 12 men but my hut usually housed 10. There were no chairs, no table. Men in lower bunks could sit down, but men in upper bunks were disadvantaged.[2]

For air crews life was slightly different to the majority of other inhabitants, as they were often left alone after missions, little troubled by military niceties, so their accommodation would often appear less than tidy. Whereas the majority of ground personnel lived in the same quarter for the duration of their time in Britain and thereby formed strong bonds with fellow inhabitants, air crew came and went, often tragically far too regularly. If aircraft were shot down on a mission, surviving crews would be reminded of the constant dangers of the job by returning to huts with rows of empty bunks. For this reason, base commanders would clear personal effects rapidly and attempt to fill empty bunks with new crews as soon as possible.

For those who needed to wake up very early, particularly air crew, a charge of quarters (CQ) was appointed. It was his job to be the personal alarm clock for all those who needed an early call. At the allotted hour prior to a mission, the CQ would take his mission roster

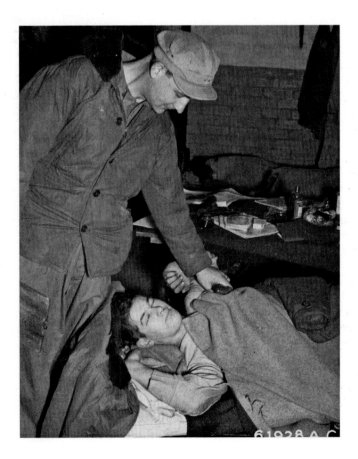

The CQ wakes a crew member for a mission, 303rd BG Molesworth, 9 December 1944. (USAAF)

list and drive around to all the relevant sites and wake up those crews required that day. It is not recorded who woke the CQ up, but one would imagine that, as an important part of mission planning, he would have been one of those who had a distinctive shift pattern, only sleeping once his job had been completed!

There were many others who worked odd hours. We have seen how engineering teams of the Sub-Depot worked a shift system and those involved in mission planning worked overnight. They all had to sleep when they could and some personnel would be heading to bed just as many were starting a day shift. John Borchert continues with his domestic arrangements while stationed at Wendling:

> Then there was Major Stonesifer, an old (age 50?) curmudgeon from Texas, WWI reserve veteran who had volunteered for WWII duty. He was the base station complement commander (i.e. cooks, janitors, guards, etc.). He fumed because the enlisted men in my weather station were on detached service from 18th Weather Squadron headquarters at European Theatre Command, hence completely free of his authority. He fumed at me because I made it clear to him that my men were exempt from KP and all other duties in which he wanted them to grovel; and reminded him that the colonel knew that. He even exploded at me one time because he found my bed unmade in mid-morning. With a smile, I told him I had been up since 4:00 a.m. preparing the forecast and briefing the mission, had just gotten a bite of breakfast, and was now going to get a little sleep as soon he got out of my quarters. What made it worse for him: I was a mere 2nd lieutenant.

Ablutions Facilities

The unheated and draughty latrine and ablutions blocks were another misery with which station personnel had to contend, particularly in winter. Simple temporary brick buildings depending on their function contained either rows of toilets, showers or washbasins. Normally centrally placed on domestic sites, they would nevertheless often be a distance from some of the barrack huts. The more substantial facilities, such as bath houses for the officers and shower blocks for the other ranks, would have been located on the communal site. These buildings can still often be identified by the small water tank tower constructed at one end. Once again water would be heated, if the site occupants were lucky, by a coal- or coke-fired boiler located within the building's boiler house.

Thomas A. Nelson of the 467th Sub-Depot attached to the 453rd BG, Old Buckenham, has the following memories of the toiletry arrangements during his time in England:

> Nearby in separate buildings are the unheated sanitary facilities. In a failed effort to avoid the dreaded trek from a warm bed into the frigid winter night for relief from the 'G.I.'s' (diarrhoea) which does occur occasionally, one suffers the misery of holding on as long as possible.
>
> The unheated ablutions building, furnished with a row of showerheads, is quite distant from our hut. After several days while everyone grows riper, three or four of us decide to brave the cold room to take a warm shower. On the way back to the hut, congratulating ourselves on our cleanliness, one of our party had the misfortune to slip and tumble into a mud puddle, to no little amusement of the others.[3]

By contrast, senior officers when billeted on station were often assigned single rooms in officers' accommodation buildings and although facilities were still primitive, there was at least the provision for a little more in the way of furniture as well as a single stove for the small room.

Interior of a typical ablutions block, this probably being at Upotery, Devon, with enlisted men of the 9th AF, 439th Troop Carrier Group enjoying the facilities! 28 June 1944. (USAAF)

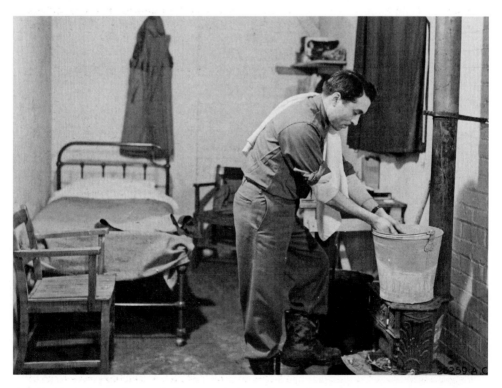

An officer's room, seen here with the occupant heating water for washing or shaving on the coal-fired stove. (USAAF)

After the war, many domestic sites on airfields across Britain continued in their intended role for a number of years once military occupation had ceased. Many sites were utilised to temporarily re-home displaced people, many from mainland Europe, particularly Polish citizens who found themselves homeless after the end of the conflict.

Off-duty Recreation

In the early days of the 8th's operations in Britain, particularly for those involved in aircraft maintenance, there was often little time to escape the routine of work and camp life. When in the evenings a little time could be found, the first task would be to start to explore the locality. One of the first major discoveries for newly arrived Americans was the uniquely English institution: the pub. There was at times some animosity towards the newcomers, particularly as they had a habit of rapidly reducing beer stocks! Generally however, many lasting friendships were formed and the 'Yanks' became part of everyday life. Once groups became established in their new homes, then the opportunity would be taken to organise 'Liberty runs' for larger numbers of personnel into local towns. John S. Sloan makes the following observation from the time that the 92nd BG were based at Bovingdon:

> After a time the press of activity involved in settling the troops in the new station subsided. Then the surrounding towns were full of soldiers every night. 'GI Joe' found that the English pub supplied a unique contribution to Western civilisation, that the Englishman was not nearly so reserved as he had been portrayed, and that there were still some young women not yet called up for the services. A liberty run was established to transport soldiers to Hemel Hempstead every evening and return them to base, late the same night. When this system was found to result in certain saturation, many soldiers obtained bicycles. After that no area within a radius of 15 miles was immune from the 'American Invasion'.[4]

Arthur Ferwerda has similar memories from his time at Hardwick:

> On rare occasions if there was a stand down for the following day and we were caught up on most of our work, we would make a 'pub run'. Our airbase as were all the airbases were carved out of what land had previously been a farm. We were out in the country and outside of the bases there were small villages consisting of just a few homes and a pub. We all had bikes and it was only about a ten minute ride to the local pub. However if there was no moon it was a little tricky manoeuvring in the blackout. It was worth the trip though, because on some of the cool evenings it was nice to be inside where it was warm.

Once leave periods became available, airmen would start to travel further in their explorations. Most personnel were provided with a three-day pass once a month, depending on the workload at the time. One of the first things many GIs stationed in Britain tried to do was visit one of the larger cities, with London being at the top of the list. C.J. Leleux recalls taking advantage of his passes to see something of Britain:

> Days off the base were spent travelling around England. The reverse lend-lease program was on at the time and this meant with a pass one could travel anywhere in England on public transportation without cost. I took advantage of this and travelled most of England and Scotland via rail. I got three days off per month and took advantage of this to site [sic] see. I went to London frequently. I also went to Norwich frequently. I met some really fine people while I was there.

The Woodman Inn at Nuthampstead, a popular watering hole for members of the 398th BG. Although much extended since the war, it still maintains strong links with the former airfield. The memorials to the former inhabitants stand outside the pub, to the left of the photo, and many pictures and artefacts adorn the walls inside the building. This photograph was taken in April 2009. (Author)

With so many visitors, not only American and British, but those from all the other Allied nations, the cities became a melting pot of nationalities and uniforms. Finding accommodation often became a significant problem.

Prior to US troops arriving in Britain in early 1942, the US Army had established its policies for leave while its soldiers were posted overseas. However, it was soon realised that it would be to the overcrowded major cities that off-duty soldiers would flock. A requirement for good basic accommodation was identified and a suggestion was passed to the ARC that this was an area where their experience could be put to good use. This potentially daunting task was the first major undertaking for ARC Commissioner Gibson and his staff after arriving in Britain, and led to the establishment of a chain of clubs throughout the country for the purpose of accommodating US soldiers while on leave.

The first two clubs were formally opened on 6 May 1942. One was the Eagle Club in London, which had already been used by British and US servicemen stationed in Britain prior to Pearl Harbor. The other was located in Londonderry in Northern Ireland. A third was opened in Glasgow in June 1942 and a fourth was opened in London in time for US servicemen to celebrate Independence Day. This latter one was the Washington Club, formerly the Washington Hotel, which was modernised and adapted to specific club needs and formed the blueprint for all future service clubs.

The ARC also opened a number of specific clubs catering to various types of US military personnel. There were officers' clubs as well as those for enlisted men; there were women's clubs for WACs, nurses and ferry pilots, and even clubs for off-duty ARC staff. Due to the US military's policy on segregation, separate clubs were provided for coloured US troops. These clubs were staffed by coloured ARC workers. At its peak there were around 400 clubs in Britain, assisted by 13,000 British volunteers and 10,000 paid employees. British volunteers came from all walks of society, and all too often that work had to be fitted in with running a home. The British Red Cross also helped out at times, along with St John Ambulance nursing services. As in many other areas, long-term firm friendships were forged during those years.

On 11 November 1942 the ARC opened what was probably its most famous club, the Rainbow Corner Club off Piccadilly Circus in London. Open 24 hours a day, it apparently

The American Red Cross Club in Glasgow. (Author's Collection)

never shut its doors until it closed finally on 9 January 1946. The core idea for the clubs was to provide quality, cheap accommodation that resembled a slice of life back home. To that end meals served tended to be fare that reminded service personnel of 'mom's home cooking', and despite the rationing situation, the Red Cross worked hard to fulfil this remit, both in the food available and in training staff unfamiliar with US cuisine to prepare it. The clubs provided much in the way of creature comforts: a cafeteria, snack bars, hot and cold showers, a barber shop, a tailor shop, games rooms and reading and writing areas. There were facilities available for meeting people from your hometown, enabled by the provision of a large map of the United States upon which you could add your details. This facility led to many happy reunions during its time of operation. The clubs also ran tourist information centres, and some Red Cross volunteers even provided unofficial guided tour services.

As with the ARC clubs on the actual camps, the town clubs also put great effort into running dances, film shows, concerts and theatrical performances. Red Cross staff were always on hand to provide a friendly face and often needed to provide an ear for homesick and troubled servicemen a long way from home.

Service clubs ranged from large facilities in major cities, often in requisitioned hotels, to small facilities in towns and villages. The large clubs offered meals, recreational activities and overnight accommodations, but the smaller clubs could usually only provide food and light recreation and were usually located in outlying areas close to American military camps. Many of these were known as 'Donut Dugouts'. Leroy Keeping recalls the one in his locality:

There was a Red Cross club set up in a building in Framlingham to use when they were in town. We went to London four times by train, intending to see the sights but never got much further than the first pub we came to!

As the club idea spread, many buildings were converted in towns and cities around the country. Some were nowhere near as busy or close to offering the range of services that the London clubs did, but were still nonetheless welcome as a bolthole from the ravages of work. For some, like Rod Ryan, a visit could be a life-changing event:

> To start with we would go into Bedford on liberty runs, then we started going to Kettering and finally they used to run us into Northampton. We used to go to the pubs or the Red Cross clubs in town. One day I went into the Red Cross club in Northampton, I ordered a coffee from one of the English girls working there. It was terrible, made from chicory, I took it back and ordered a cup of tea, I went and sat down to write to my girlfriend back home. The girl who served me came over and asked if she could sit and chat. Well needless to say, after a while the girl back home was no longer my girlfriend as I had now met my future wife, and we've been married over 60 years!

In compliance with a request by the British War Department, to keep in line with the practice of British service clubs charging for accommodation, ARC clubs were asked to make a charge for staying in them. This contentious issue has led to accusations in the years since the war of the ARC being out to make a profit from servicemen. This unfortunate situation was not of their making and the ARC tried unsuccessfully not to levy the charge, but the cost of bed and breakfast was 2s 6d, or around 50¢ a night. The charges were well below cost, with the deficit made up from ARC funds. Finally the enormous work done by the ARC club system in fostering and supporting the great task of building and maintaining Anglo-American relations has to be noted, at a time when the situation could have been much more difficult.

There were also those for whom the bright lights of the city had less of a draw. Some would spend their off-duty hours on base, and for them the various clubs and leisure facilities provided there were very important. Men would entertain themselves in many and varied pursuits. A number of airmen took up new, or pursued previous pastimes, some of which were major challenges. The following excerpt from HQ 448th Sub-Depot at Ridgewell reports:

> M/Sgt Grose, foreman of the shop is making himself a 12 gauge shotgun in his spare time while T/Sgt Peloquin is building an English train in a ¾ inch scale, both men are turning out some very fine work.[5]

Others spent off-duty time still working, as illustrated by those engineering personnel who took it upon themselves to rebuild aircraft that had otherwise been written off as too damaged for economic repair. Some also expended a lot of time in developing and manufacturing tools and fixtures to ease the many tasks that they had to complete while working on aircraft systems or components.

For those who chose to leave the camps during their off-duty hours, some pursued aspects of British history or continued with academic study or some other cultural interest. Many bases were close to the historic cities of Norwich and Cambridge, and these towns provided much for those interested in additional study. Robert Grilley, a navigator with the 401st BG at Deenthorpe, spent much of his off-duty time drawing and painting scenes around his station. His time was well spent as after the war he pursued a career in this field, ending as professor of art at the University of Wisconsin. The previously mentioned John T. Appleby spent the 'happiest summer of his life', as he puts it, exploring the cultural and ecclesiastical delights of Suffolk while based both at Lavenham and Thorpe Abbotts at the end of the Second World War.

Sporting activities, both casual games and organised inter-unit events, took up the time of those participants, while others were more concerned with more lucrative competitions: playing cards or other forms of gambling. Of course, many were happy just to spend time with the locals they had befriended, particularly the girls, and some had to fit in time with those they had married! Paul Kovitz married an English girl from Ipswich, but explained it still wasn't easy to get time to spend with her, even though they were man and wife, so every bit of spare time he had, which wasn't much, they would try to meet.

Pets

To finish this story of life on the base, mention must be made of the vast numbers of pets that found homes with USAAF personnel in Britain. The majority were dogs, often the squadron or group's unofficial mascot, some smuggled across from the United States with crews in their aircraft. Many, however, were obtained locally, finding the living good, with a plentiful supply of food. On their return from temporary detachment to North Africa, some of the B-24 groups of the Second Air Division brought donkeys back with them, transported in the aircraft with the crew. Unfortunately it is believed that none enjoyed particularly long lives once arriving in Britain. At least one example of a bear cub appeared in Britain with the 390th BG at Framlingham, although it sadly had to be put down, as once it had started to grow it began terrorising local farms!

The US Army possessed veterinary units and some came to Britain with the USAAF, ostensibly to inspect food supplies. The 10th Veterinary Unit was one such example; based at Framlingham, it served this purpose for fifteen other stations in the area. Although not part of their official duties, the services of the vet were often called upon to keep many of these pets in 'good running order'. There is no doubt, however, that many pets provided much comfort to personnel during their time in Britain and quite a number returned home unofficially with crews at the end of the war.

S/Sgt Victor B. Klonowsky, Apollo, Pennsylvania, a hydraulic and engine expert with a service group (predecessor to Sub-Depot) writes out a report on the work he has just finished on a plane, while Bob, the group mascot, watches. (USAAF)

10

Sick Quarters

At the outset of the Second World War, the USAAF, still part of the army, had to rely on its 'parent' for medical service provision. By the end of the war it had developed its own specialist medical branch able to fully cope with its own specific medical requirements.

Although much of the work performed in establishing medical services for the USAAF was focused on greater improvements in medical care for all air force personnel, an equally large effort was expended in development work on air crew flight equipment. One of the best examples was the production and introduction, during the Second World War, of the 'G' suit. Developed to prevent fighter pilots passing out due to increased 'G' forces during engagement with enemy aircraft, it not only saved lives, but also provided a competitive edge during combat.

The development of a specific medical service was another of General 'Hap' Arnold's requirements for his expansion of the air force. The establishment of this service and its network of infrastructure led to the saving of many lives that otherwise would have been lost. The man behind this expansion was Air Surgeon Major General David N.W. Grant, who had been sent to Britain early in the war and had been able to study first hand many of the specific medical problems faced by the RAF and its air crews. Yet again many lessons were learned which proved to be vital once America became embroiled in the conflict. By the end of the war Grant had created a largely autonomous air medical service, albeit still subject to the authority of the army.

Most British military airfields, particular those constructed to Class A standard, were supplied with a base sick quarters. Once again this was established on its own dispersed site, normally a little distant from the airfield but still within easy reach. These facilities not only provided enough general medical support for the day-to-day illness and ailments affecting base personnel, they were also able to provide fairly comprehensive triage cover for more serious injuries, particularly those sustained during the course of missions or in accidents. The system had been established by the RAF, who backed up these front-line medical units with a number of hospitals dealing specifically with the needs of its military personnel, such as those located at Wroughton in Wiltshire and Halton in Buckinghamshire.

Once US service personnel started arriving in Britain they initially used British hospitals, both military and civilian, but overcrowding soon became a problem. The US Army Service of Supply, tasked with providing medical cover as part of its supply mission for the US forces, wanted hospitals of its own. As at the time it was unable to supply any more personnel or equipment to build them, the job was undertaken by the British. Royal Engineers oversaw a lot of the initial hospital construction and despite a slow start, by the close of 1943 fifty-eight fixed (as opposed to mobile) US Army hospitals were operating.

The US Army operated several differing types of hospital for various purposes, such as general, station, surgical, field, evacuation and convalescent hospitals. Of these fifty-eight hospitals, seventeen were general hospitals, thirty-four were station hospitals,

Oblique view of the station sick quarters at Ridgewell, Essex. The Nissen huts in the centre form the main hospital block, while the ambulance shed/mortuary is at the top, a little distant from the main block. An Orlit-type hut at the front of the site forms some of the staff accommodation. Dodge ambulances can be seen parked in several places. Part of the main ward block now forms a museum to the 381st BG and Ridgewell Airfield, with the station memorial located alongside the access road. (USAAF)

three evacuation hospitals and four field hospitals. General hospitals, functioning exactly as the name implies, provided general medical care, normally providing in the order of 1,000 to 1,500 beds. Station hospitals were smaller establishments serving a group of military camps, usually of around 750 beds in size. This type of hospital has often been confused as being attributed to a single airfield or 'station'. This they were not: the airfield sick quarters provided the latter function.

Evacuation and field hospitals were essentially mobile units whose task was to follow combat elements into battle to provide front-line medical care. However, during the early establishment of US forces in Britain, as there was no ground front, these units became established for longer than was originally intended at fixed locations.

The hospital construction programme continued, providing facilities for all the Allied nations during the build up to D-Day, to deal with expected casualty numbers. Many were built in the south and west of England, often close to good air and rail links, providing swift medical evacuation from the continent. Some of these hospitals are still in use today, albeit in much redeveloped form, having been taken over by the British National Health Service after its establishment in 1948; the Churchill in Oxford, Odstock near Salisbury and Frenchay outside Bristol are typical examples.

Medical support for airmen had been developed by the USAAF along a four-echelon system similar to that of aircraft maintenance. The first echelon was day-to-day care within each unit, provided by its own doctor, usually a flight surgeon. Second echelon was that which could be provided by a base medical centre or dispensary, third was at a station hospital and the fourth by a general hospital or similar specific establishment depending on the care or treatment required. The 8th AF's position to provide such care was hampered, however, particularly during their first year in Britain, by a shortage of their own medically trained personnel. This then led to an interim solution, which ultimately became a more permanent arrangement.

During the planning for air support for the North Africa campaign, which siphoned off a considerable amount of the early 8th units from Britain, consideration was given to the creation of a satisfactory means of medical support for assigned personnel. A new organisation, a Group Clearing Station, was created. This was a small twenty-four-bed mobile medical unit that operated within each air group. It was realised from this that by utilising the existing medical facilities on each RAF camp, a similar unit could easily be created. By pooling all the medical staff from each supporting unit of a bomb group, some of the urgent requirement for second-echelon medical care could be provided. This the USAAF did at each of its station sick quarters. Once the organisations specifically tasked with this function, USAAF Medical Dispensary units, could be created and deployed to Britain in sufficiently large numbers, then they started to assist in the medical care function at each airfield. This relieved the workload of those previously pooled medical personnel and allowed them to return to administering to the needs of their own units, in particular the individual squadrons.

Service of Supply medical operating procedures dictated that any patient requiring hospitalisation for more than four days should be sent from a base medical centre or sick quarters to an army hospital. Because of this ruling, the USAAF medical service argued that they should have their own hospitals as they would be able to serve better the particular conditions affecting injured air crew. They were concerned that airmen admitted into general army hospitals for treatment often got lost in the system and neither received the specific treatments for flying related conditions, many of which were only just starting to be understood, nor were they correctly convalesced back to operational status. The Service of Supply also had a habit of treating recovered patients simply as basic recruits and rather than returning them to their original unit, sent them to replacement centres for redeployment. Some fully trained air crew were even returned to army units other than the air force, a situation that the USAAF, having made a huge investment in training these men, understandably considered intolerable. To alleviate some of these problems, Service of Supply began to allow USAAF flight surgeons to begin working alongside regular army medical staff in its hospitals, particularly those closest to American operational airfields, to oversee the care of air force personnel.

One of the first to operate in such a manner was the 2nd Evacuation Hospital, which opened in December 1942 at Diddington near Cambridge. From then on, the most serious AAF casualties started to be channelled through this hospital until those more local to other airfields were established. Despite this hospital becoming available, some of the more westerly USAAF groups preferred to use air evacuation as a means of reaching hospitals in Oxford, as it was quicker than using ambulances for long cross-country journeys.

Once station hospitals serving groups of airfields were established, serious casualties were directed to these. The first was constructed in the grounds of Lilford Hall near Molesworth, and the new facility became the 303rd Station Hospital. This may be where some of the confusion regarding terminology stems from, as this unit was established only a short distance from one of the earliest bomb groups to arrive in Britain – the 303rd BG, stationed at RAF Molesworth; the similar numbering of both units was simply a coincidence.

Further station hospitals were constructed in other areas of the country, serving clusters of airfields, particularly those in East Anglia. They were still, however, ostensibly army rather than air force hospitals, operated under the jurisdiction of the Service of

Supply. This arrangement eased the situation considerably and was employed for the duration of the Second World War, lessening the debate for USAAF specific hospitals. In addition to these arrangements, the USAAF was permitted to open and operate a number of rest homes. Although these were not convalescent homes in the traditional sense, their introduction gave combat airmen a place to relax and recuperate mid-combat tour. This considerably reduced the number of cases of men affected by combat stress, enabling them to return to active status more quickly. Known as 'Flak Houses' by those that used their services, the first one was established in late 1942 at Stanbridge Earls, near Romsey in Hampshire. They were operated for the USAAF by the ARC, and provided an environment, normally for a week at a time, totally outside of any military routine where thoughts of combat could, at least temporarily, be put behind them. Around twenty such facilities were eventually established in various parts of the British Isles, with 87,000 air crew in total passing through their doors.

Even though technically no hospital came under the specific control of the USAAF during the Second World War, due to the high numbers of air personnel stationed in Britain one could argue that many hospitals became air force by default, particularly after D-Day when vast numbers of regular US Army forces departed Britain's shores. For those unfortunate casualties too seriously wounded to be returned to active duty, they would, when able, be returned to the US. Initially transported by hospital ship, the USAAF later established regular 'medevac' flights to speed up journey times and lessen the discomfort to patients. These flights generally became the preserve of larger cargo aircraft such as the C-54 Skymaster, the military version of the Douglas DC-4. Brought into service in time for D-Day, the service provided a tremendous morale boost to all US service personnel, particularly the injured.

What the USAAF medical service was able to accomplish, completely within its control, was to expand its own research and development (R&D) programmes. To better serve the requirements of the European theatre a medical R&D department was established in High Wycombe close to the 8th AF HQ. This unit was tasked with the investigation and resolution of many of the physiological and psychological problems that were manifesting themselves as a result of this new intensive form of combat.

As well as the aforementioned combat stress, particular problems encountered by fliers were infections of the respiratory system and a specific condition that was identified as *aerotitis media* – an inflammation of the middle ear. As knowledge and experience increased, the organisation found itself in great demand to train army medics in the treatment of such conditions as well as many other aero-medical situations. Other important programmes developed by the department included instruction of air crews on the correct and safe use of oxygen equipment at high altitude and these were considered instrumental in reducing deaths from anoxia during missions.

For those crews who survived the onslaught of German fighters and flak while on missions but had to ditch their aircraft in the North Sea, it was through the development work carried out at High Wycombe that improved methods of surviving such events were discovered. Members of the medical R&D team, in association with the British company Wilkinson Sword, were responsible for the development of armoured flak suits and helmets to counter the increasing number of air crew deaths from German anti-aircraft ordnance. Many of these initiatives came directly from the findings of medical personnel at group level, while dealing with the day-to-day effects of aerial combat.

There were many problematic areas within air force supply and the supply of medical equipment was little different as it too came under the Service of Supply and the resultant shortages plagued medical staff, particularly during the first year of operations. The issue was partly expedited by procuring items locally, particularly consumables, from British sources; however, to due to material shortages some of this material provided was considered substandard. In a bitter twist of irony, the 8th was also provided with a certain amount of American manufactured equipment, supplied to Britain under lend-lease!

Eventually the 8th was able to circumvent the Service of Supply by establishing its own supply lines from the US, although this achieved little in the way of improved harmony between the two organisations. The first USAAF medical supply depot was established at Thrapston in Northamptonshire under the jurisdiction of SAD 1 at Honington. Ultimately the air depot network expanded the number of USAAF medical stores significantly.

There was much co-operation and interaction between British, American and other Allied medical personnel, as well as within the wider sphere of health and hygiene specialists such as dentists and veterinary staff. Much was made of opportunities to operate exchanges between each other's hospitals and research establishments to gain and disseminate knowledge on new techniques, procedures and discoveries. All of this medical knowledge was pooled for the greater good of the United Nations, not only for the treatment of those involved in the air war but ultimately for all combatants on both sides.

The Sick Quarters

Aside from the usual facilities found on all dispersed sites, such as latrines, blast shelters, picket posts etc, the main facilities comprised several other larger structures. The biggest of these was the main hospital building. This was usually constructed from either temporary brick huts or a grouping of Nissen huts, similar to those that used for dining halls, and comprising wards, treatment rooms and other support facilities. Examples of both construction types still exist, with a temporary brick hospital at Horham and a Nissen hut type at Ridgewell. Both sites contain museums dedicated to their former station's history.

Close to the hospital block was a smaller building constructed in the same manner as the hospital; this was the ambulance shed and mortuary. The building was normally of a size sufficient to park and maintain one ambulance at a time. The last group of buildings on a sick quarters site were accommodation buildings for medical personnel. These could be constructed from virtually any of the temporary hut types of the time, but were often Nissen-type huts.

The main buildings of the former station sick quarters at Horham, now being renovated and turned into a museum. In the foreground is an emergency static water tank. 30 June 2006. (Bob Clarke)

The rear portion of the ambulance garage contained a small mortuary for the storage of bodies prior to transfer for burial. The grim reality of war shows bier racking still in situ in the mortuary at Horham. Unfortunately there were many times when these facilities were utilised, particularly after the return of aircraft from some of the more savage missions over enemy territory. 30 June 2006. (Author)

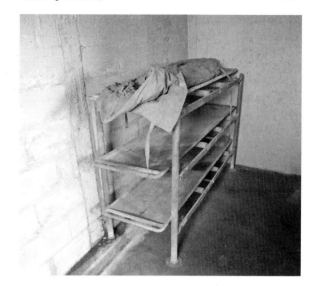

Staffing

As previously stated, medical cover, particularly for the early bomb groups, was often initially established by personnel from some support units. These personnel were often drawn from the Station Complement Squadron as it was they who were normally tasked with establishing the group's presence at a new station. Once the Group Headquarters and individual bomb squadrons started to arrive at their respective airfields, the sick quarters staff would be expanded with more medical personnel. The HQ medical section was headed by the group surgeon, who was the senior medical officer and would normally assume control of all group medical provision.

With the reorganisation due to the change from Service Squadrons to the Sub-Depot system, as well as the arrival of the new dedicated USAAF Medical Dispensary units, a restructure of individual station sick quarter cover was implemented. Many of those reassigned due to these changes found themselves transferred into the HQ medical section. Others were returned to the station complement and were utilised within their unit. Once Medical Dispensary personnel arrived, they were used to provide additional staffing levels and specialist skills in support of the group chief medical officer and his team.

The initial operating procedure for all personnel based at individual stations would be for those unable to work due to illness or injury to report to the station sick quarters. This often led to severe overcrowding at morning sick call. This was necessary not only to categorise those unfit to work, but to provide further information regarding station strength from this registration process. Once the medical cover at individual bomb groups was reorganised and supplemented with Medical Dispensary units, many of the previously pooled medical personnel were able to return to their parent units. Once this had occurred, clinics or dispensaries were established by individual units, in particular each squadron, at their HQ building, normally located on the technical site. The effect of this was not only to considerably reduce the crowding at the station sick quarters that occurred on many mornings, but also permitted the medical staff of individual units to provide the correct organisation of first echelon medical cover to their own unit personnel.

For bomb groups arriving in England later, the situation was fairly well established, with many of the early upheavals and reorganisations straightened out and the structure of a group remaining fairly stable for the rest of the war. Although organisationally very much part of the group, the station medical staff were able to operate as a semi-

The bad winter of 1944/1945 caused a minor epidemic of common colds among mechanics working in rain, freezing fog or snow. At Bassingbourn, a half gram sulfadiazine tablet was issued to each soldier coming through the dinner line. Left to right T/Sgt. Chris Christenson, of Creighton, Nebraska, S/Sgt. Charles Grinolds, of Mauston, Wisconsin, and Cpl. Ray Finley, from Pickens, South Carolina, all medical technicians; T/Sgt. Norman Wilquet, of Green Bay, Wisconsin, and Cpl. Harry Davis, from Champaign, Illinois, both mechanics. (USAAF)

independent organisation, as both their working environment and personnel living accommodation were grouped together on the one small site. Although still pooled, the staffing arrangements did permit a degree of autonomy over their area of specialist duties.

Tabled strength for a bomb group HQ provides three medical officers. One would be the station surgeon, normally a major, and one a dentist, usually a captain. The group was also tabled to include nineteen enlisted men ranging from such specialists as administrators, medical technicians, surgical technicians, pharmacologists, radiologists, sanitation specialists and general medical corpsmen. Every bomb squadron was to have one medical officer, usually a captain flight surgeon and three enlisted men, one an administrator and two medical corpsmen. Medical Dispensary (Aviation) units could, in their standard format, be quite large. Most bomb groups had either smaller detachments attached to them or, as was more often the case, another type, a Medical Dispensary (Aviation) RS, or 'reduced strength'. These smaller units had three officers and thirteen enlisted men allocated to them, including drivers, clerks, medical technicians, surgical technicians, X-ray technicians and cooks – the last speciality being vital, as the station sick quarters had its own kitchen to provide for the particular dietary requirements of its patients.

Some female nursing provision was, on occasion, made at individual base level but normally was more common in hospitals from the station type upwards. Nursing personnel were usually provided by the army nursing service or the ARC and even in some cases British nurses were provided, especially in the early stages of the 8th AF's establishment.

Facilities

The main building of the sick quarters functioned as a small hospital; surprisingly well equipped, it contained a number of elements that would be found in a much larger establishment. The larger part of the building would be taken up as wards. Separate wards were provided for officers and enlisted men and usually formed two sections of the hospital. A smaller side ward was also usually kept for the treatment of female personnel if required. One medical officer was on duty and in charge of the wards at all times.

Due to the previously stated Service of Supply ruling, personnel hospitalised here would normally have been suffering from illnesses or injuries that would keep them off duty for an anticipated four days. If conditions worsened then they would be transferred to a station or general hospital. Jack Gaffney's experiences at Bassingbourn are typical of the sort of illness that care was provided for:

We were first stationed at Kimbolton which had been a British fighter base and they sent 8 men from each squadron and group, forty men in all, to train to fight any German paratroopers if they hit our base. I was one of the lucky ones to go to it. While I was there the rest of the group was moved to Bassingbourn and after our training was over we rejoined our group there. About 2 days after I got back on the ground crew, I came down with pneumonia and walked to the base hospital, they checked me out and told me to go back and get my helmet and gas mask and come back. When I got back they put me on a gurney and put me in an ambulance in front of the medical building, the ambulance made a quick u-turn to the other side of the street and into the base hospital. When I was carried in the door, a Sgt. said 'sick or romance ward'. The medic said 'he is really sick'. They gave me some huge pills I called horse pills and in the middle of the night I woke up in a pool of water. In 2 days I was back on duty.

A ward in the station sick quarters of the 381st BG, Ridgewell – one of the ward buildings shown in the first photo of this chapter. The two men sat at the table are updating patient records. (USAAF)

Also incorporated within the main building was a small operating room, available for emergency surgery or minor surgical operations. Each sick quarters would also have an X-ray room close by, furnished with equipment brought in from the US, although again some groups would have been supplied with British equipment for this and many other specialist tasks. As is typical with all buildings designed for provision of medical care, a number of smaller treatment rooms existed within the hospital block. These would be where the majority of daily cases of illness and injury would be examined, assessed and the necessary treatment provided.

Morning sick call was handled by all the medical officers available for duty, which was vital at times of high workload. Fortunately many of those reporting for morning sick call would require little more than some form of medication or minor treatment to have them back to work. Sometimes treatment was given to local British civilians by base medical personnel. Bernie Fosdike recalled that on one of his visits to Leiston Airfield with his father to remove the 'night soil', a group medical officer noticed that he had a poorly bandaged finger and asked the reason. Bernie told him he had a whitlow or abscess near the nail of the offending finger and, like many people of the era, was hoping it would sort itself without his having to pay for medical attention. The officer said he couldn't stand by and see him suffer and immediately took Bernie to the station sick quarters to carry out the necessary treatment. He then returned the grateful Bernie back to his father.

Another duty undertaken at the sick quarters was the regular assessment of air crew fitness to fly. Due to the high incidence of respiratory and ear problems in air crew, many attended the sick quarters. This and the problems associated with combat stress or fatigue required that it was essential that crew members were regularly monitored and if necessary treated to keep them fit for active duty.

Two flight surgeons would normally attend all mission briefings and witness mission departures. It was also often the duty of medical staff to make sure that combat rations had already been distributed to all crews. After their return, medical officers would be in attendance at post-mission interrogation, particularly on the lookout for ill effects of high-altitude flying or combat stress.

Further facilities within the main hospital block included a main office where medical administrators consolidated medical reports and individuals records as well as the records of the medical situation at the airfield and maintenance of all medical equipment. The base medical team had among its responsibilities the overseeing of the continuing health of all personnel on camp and as such carried out investigations into any hygiene issues, especially those that had an impact on sanitation arrangements. The medical team at Ridgewell, for instance, introduced a series of surprise kitchen and ablutions blocks inspections after repeated outbreaks of diarrhoea and vomiting during August and September 1943, which affected station personnel. Poor standards of cleanliness in these areas at the time were considered to have been a contributing factor.

Also within the general administration area of the hospital was located the group surgeon's office. From here he would control operations and liaise with HQ on the continuing combat worthiness of base personnel. As well as medical services, the sick quarters would also usually contain a dental clinic. These were normally well equipped, containing all the usual 'instruments of torture'! Due to equipment shortages, some dental chairs had to be made locally before tabled equipment supplies from the US could catch up. The clinic would also normally contain a small dental X-ray area.

The station pharmacy would also normally be contained within the sick quarters, usually stocked with a considerable quantity of medication. Many USAAF pharmacists were drawn directly from the same civilian profession directly into the air force. A small medical laboratory would also often be located near to the pharmacy. Supply of all medical items to the sick quarters, as well as all first-aid equipment on the station, in vehicles and on aircraft, would be administered and controlled from the medical supplies store, which was located in another room in the hospital block.

This clinic is taking place at Ridgewell with members of the 381st BG adding to supplies,
19 August 1944. (USAAF)

Sick quarters were also used at regular intervals as blood donor clinics, operated by mobile
units travelling between stations. John Sloan describes a typical event with the 92nd BG at
Podington:

> On August 27 (1944), the US Army Bleeding Team No. 6 collected 51 500cc bottles of
> blood in three hours at the station. On August 28, 210 bottles were taken and on the
> following day enough additional blood was donated by members of the Group's ground
> personnel to bring the total collection to 325 bottles. This whole blood was used to aid US
> wounded in France and for distribution in Military Hospitals in England. The team was
> composed of one officer and eight EM.[1].

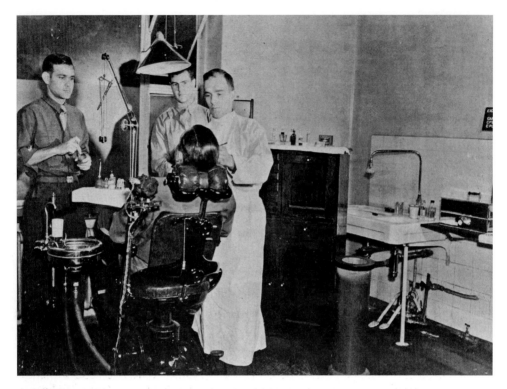

A dental clinic on an 8th AF base, showing dental equipment loaned from RAF supplies. (USAAF)

Situated a distance from the communal site, the sick quarters would normally contain its own kitchen, as it would be impractical to bring food to the unit. Some patients would also require specific diets, and this was easier to administer if meals were produced on the premises. Allied to this requirement for self sufficiency, the sick quarters site usually had its own standby generator, housed in another room in the hospital block and a vital necessity should mains power fail, particularly if emergency medical procedures were being undertaken at the time.

An Unfortunately Common Problem

Military personnel from time immemorial have sought the services of professional women for comfort, especially when away from home, under threat and lonely. Those posted during the Second World War to the ETO and Britain in particular were no different. Unfortunately, many of these liaisons were not without their risks.

Incidence of venereal disease (VD) within USAAF personnel had, by January 1943, become so severe as to prompt the posting of a VD control officer to the USAAF in Britain. Responsible to the chief surgeon in Britain, his job was to form a link between army authorities and civilian organisations and to arrive at structured plans for control and reduction of these incidences. In the days before HIV and Aids became a major sexual health issue, the worst two diseases were syphilis and gonorrhoea, with the latter by far the most common. From July 1942 to June 1945 there were nearly 35,500 recorded VD cases of all sorts, among all USAAF personnel of all races. Of these over 31,000 were cases of gonorrhoea.

The 92nd BG at Podington held, at times, the dubious record of being one of the 8th's high scoring groups where the contraction of VD was concerned. All personnel on enlistment were given information about VD regarding both its prevention and, if necessary, its treatment. The emphasis was on abstinence, and if that could not be achieved then the correct use of barrier control methods to help to avoid contraction.

The statistics emerging at the time suggested that the message given so far was not enough. The VD control officer implemented a wide-scale education programme involving many agencies from the US forces, particularly from medical services and the chaplaincy, and from American and British civilian organisations; after all it was a joint problem. The programme included poster and film campaigns as well as talks from all sorts of individuals from various organisations, both military and civilian. From 381st BG Medical Detachment records for 4 December 1943, the following report rather indelicately introduces some visitors who lectured on the potential dangers:

> Three rather decrepit, ancient meatballs from the E.V.S. Nursing Staff were here to interrogate our wayward personnel on the source of the 'Piccadilly Flak'. What an odd way for three nice old ladies to make a living![2]

'Piccadilly Flak' refers to the potential for contracting VD from ladies of the night, colloquially known as 'Piccadilly Commandos', who patrolled certain areas of the West End of London praying on servicemen and plying their trade under the cover of the darkness afforded by the blackout in shop doorways and other convenient locations.

In the US Army, treatment for VD was free, because it came under the remit for medical welfare, though it was not generally confidential, as under military rules contracting it was a punishable offence for deliberately putting oneself in a position of ill health. However, it was often the military police or cooks who bore the brunt of punishment if they contracted VD in any form: the military police were expected to have a greater regard for military rules and tended to be made examples of for any infringement, and cooks would be unable to work for longer periods than most as they were forbidden to handle food until all traces of any disease had gone.

All GIs were issued with prophylactic kits containing condoms and early treatment kits in case of infection. These were normally stored and distributed at the main gate while personnel were signing out camp on periods of leave. Further equipment in more extensive kits was available to medical staff at the sick quarters for use when personnel presented with infection.

Ambulance Service

One small office in the sick quarters would be used by the ambulance dispatcher. The dispatcher organised ambulances for routing to the airfield and then returning to hospitals if they contained more seriously injured personnel. It was the dispatcher's job to keep account of the whereabouts of station ambulances.

Normally several ambulances would be sent to the airfield around half an hour prior to the ETA of aircraft from a mission. Generally they would park close to the flight line in readiness, sometimes at the end of the runway, ready to chase any aircraft with injured passengers aboard and be on the spot when the aircraft came to a halt. Operating procedures normally permitted a dispatcher to keep at least one ambulance at the ready at sick quarters to immediately replace any that came in with casualties.

Numbers of ambulances assigned to groups are difficult to accurately ascertain, but according to some photographic evidence it could have been well into double figures. Certainly many of the component units of a group were tabled to have at least one

An injured crewman lies stretched out in front of the wreckage of a Consolidated B-24 which crashed prior to landing. The crewman has already been treated by flight surgeons and is being made comfortable by medical corpsmen just before being rushed to hospital in one of the base ambulances. (USAAF)

ambulance as part of their allotted equipment, although whether they actually received all of them would be open to doubt. This then was the reason why many groups were supplemented with British vehicles.

First–Line Triage

When ambulances were stationed to await the returning aircraft, in addition to their crews, at least two medical officers would be in attendance. Not only were they equipped with the standard on-board ambulance medical kit but also with a full surgical kit for use in emergencies. Ambulances normally evacuated the injured directly to the sick quarters unless the patient was in immediate need of blood or oxygen, as it was discovered that loss from shock could be minimised if oxygen and/or plasma could be administered immediately, sometimes, if necessary, actually before removal from the aircraft. It became standard operating procedure to bring a patient out of shock before transportation by ambulance.

The two main ambulance types used by the 8th AF in Britain were the British Austin K2Y and the American Dodge WC54. The Austin was the standard British heavy military ambulance with a body built by Mann Egerton. It could carry ten seated casualties or four stretcher cases. Just over 13,000 K2Y ambulances were built at Austin's Longbridge plant between 1939 and 1945. Weighing a little over 3 tons, it was powered by an Austin six cylinder 3,462cc petrol engine. The Austin was two-wheel drive, running through

The cost: A dead air-crewman, the navigator, is removed from a B-17 at an un-named station somewhere in England. Note the female nurses in attendance and the large flak hole in the side of the aircraft. (USAAF)

a gearbox that it was said required a little learning to use! It had a top speed of 50mph and carried a crew of two or three. Some groups initially had their ambulances crewed by British personnel.

The Dodge, by comparison, was a four-wheel-drive design, based on their standard 3/4t capacity truck chassis. The WC-54 was powered by the standard Dodge T-214, 232in³, six-cylinder petrol engine, through a four-speed gearbox. Leaf spring suspension offered more comfort to crew and passengers. It sported a steel panel body by Wayne Corp. of Indiana, with a closed cab and double rear doors. Two men were assigned to the vehicle, the driver and an ambulance orderly. Weighing a little over 2½ tons empty, it could carry seven seated casualties or four stretcher cases. The WC-54 became the most widely used type of ambulance throughout the Second World War and between 1942 and 1945 over 29,500 were produced on behalf of the US armed forces.

It must be remembered that to the medical personnel of the 8th AF came some of the grimmest reminders of the reality of war. It was they who had the most exposure to the horrors that aerial combat can afflict on the human body and would have regularly removed these broken bodies, hopefully for repair. They also had the unpleasant task of removing dead or clearing human remains from crash sites, and according to one veteran's account, were often only given a pair of rubber gloves and a basket with which to carry out the task. The all too frequent task of transporting those remains for burial would also have fallen to ambulance crews, initially to Brookwood in Surrey and later to Madingly near Cambridge.

11

The Final Act

The 8th AF flew its last operational missions on 25 April 1945 when 307 B-17s of the 1st Air Division bombed the Skoda armaments factory at Pilsen in Czechoslovakia. At the same time 282 B-24s of the 2nd Air Division bombed rail yards in the vicinity of Berchtesgarten, Hitler's mountain 'sanctuary' in southern Germany. Even at this late stage in the war, the 1st Air Division lost six fortresses to German anti-aircraft guns. The last of 696,450 tons of bombs dropped by the 8th AF were appropriately released from an aircraft of the 384th BG from Grafton Underwood. It was from that airfield thirty-two months previously that twelve B-17s had set out on the 8th AF's very first operation.

The next phase of 'missions' over northern Europe was to be of a very different nature.

Operation MANNA/CHOWHOUND

For their part in assisting in what turned out to be a premature belief in the end of their occupation, Germany had been restricting food supplies and systematically starving the Netherlands through the closing months of 1944. By early 1945 a desperate situation existed for more than 3 million Dutch people under German control. After pleas for assistance from Prince Bernhard of the Netherlands to the Allied leaders, a truce was brokered with German forces during the closing days of the Second World War. This paved the way to allowing mercy flights by the Allies to drop food to civilians in certain areas of the country.

Beginning on the morning of 29 April 1945, the RAF started its missions under the code name Operation MANNA. Continuing until 7 May, they delivered 6,680 tons of food, mostly dropped at low level from around 500ft. The USAAF began their involvement under the codename Operation CHOWHOUND on 1 May and flew 2,268 sorties, dropping a total of 4,000 tons of food until the end of their missions seven days later. Despite the majority of enemy guns remaining silent, there were still losses from accidents.

Nearly 400 B-17s of the 8th's 3rd Air Division participated in the American operation. Some of the ground personnel were permitted to go on the flights to assist with distributing food. One individual who took part in the air operation was Paul Kovitz, flying with aircraft from the 390th BG at Framlingham:

> Towards the end of the war we did some food drops over Holland and I got to go on one, it was really an experience! We were that low to the ground I remember seeing civilians on the ground and German troops sitting on the dykes with their guns. We dropped on marked out zones, and the people were waving at us. I don't know if they'd told the Germans the war was almost over but they didn't shoot at us so I guess so!

B-17s of the
390th BG drop
food over Holland
during Operation
CHOWHOUND, in
early May 1945.
(USAAF)

Paul continues:

> Years later I was working in Holland as a Pratt and Whitney rep, I told the people I was
> with I was on that food drop, well they hugged and kissed me, it was really something!

VE Day

The end finally came for Germany on 7 May 1945 with the signing of the surrender
document. The following day, the 8th, was declared Victory in Europe (VE) Day. The Allied
nations erupted into celebration. The lights could finally come on again after six dark years
in Britain and even more in other countries of Europe. This wasn't the end of matters:
Europe was in a state of turmoil with hundreds of thousands of displaced persons and
unimaginable amounts of damage to repair that would take decades to reconstruct. These
celebrations were obviously tempered with sadness at the huge loss of life, and no more so
than at the bases of the 8th AF.

On many of the USAAF airfields men were restricted to camp for the day; Rod Ryan
said that he and the other men of the 305th BG at Chelveston were confined to base. John
Appleby of the 487th BG at Lavenham had his theories why:

> Around 10.30 the Station Commander made the official announcement over the Tannoy
> of victory over Germany. We were released from duty for the day, but the edge was taken
> off our joy by the fact that we were all restricted to the field. Guards were doubled to
> make sure that no one escaped and all motor vehicles were grounded. This was probably
> a wise precaution, for we had a small but vociferous minority who tried to make life
> pleasant for our English hosts by getting drunk in their pubs on their beer and telling
> everyone within hearing distance just what was wrong with England and the Limeys.

'Germany Quits' shouts the headline in *The Stars and Stripes,* the daily newspaper of the US Armed forces in Europe. Personnel of the 303rd BG at Molesworth take in the momentous news. (USAAF)

> The English exercised incredible restraint in putting up with them, but I do not think on that particular day they would have been in any mood for listening to these characters telling them how we had won the war for them – again.[1]

The 95th BG at Horham was also similarly hobbled. Art Watson recalls the day:

> On the day that the Nazi's gave up and the war was over, there were a lot of celebrations on the base. Some got drunk and partied some sat down and wrote letters home, some went to the chapel to pray and some gathered with their buddies and discussed what they would do when they got home; go back to school, marry their girlfriends, go back to their old job etc.

For those who happened to be away from the camps on leave at the time, they were able to see and join in the celebrations with everyone else first hand. Rich Creutz:

> I was on a 7 day furlough to London on VE day. I saw the great happiness of the English people and some overreacted by starting fires, overturning taxis etc. you always have the good and the bad, but for me it was an awesome experience.

C.J. Leleux:

> On VE day I happened to be London on leave and helped celebrate this day with all the folks who were on the streets of London.

Lawrence Sholtze:

> I happened to be near Southampton visiting a friend of mine from my home town when VE day was declared. We sure celebrated that day and night – danced in the streets until morning!

Trolley Tours

No sooner had the war ended, than 8th AF Command permitted the operation of a number of flights allowing ground personnel to see first hand the results of the campaign. These flights, known as 'trolley' missions and nicknamed 'cooks tours' by personnel, were extremely popular, often with group intelligence staff travelling and acting as tour guides to point out the (remaining) landmarks. Arthur Ferwerda:

> Two days after the war ended in Europe (VE Day), we were told that we could fly over Germany. We mapped out a tour and flew about 500 feet above Germany. The devastation was really bad. I remember seeing German soldiers marching as far as the eye could see, separated from their units without food or water. Everyone got a chance to go, the cooks, the maintenance men, the MPs.

Rich Creutz:

> On our return to base [from the VE day celebrations], they took all the ground personnel on an 8 hour tour of Europe, from Belgium to France, at low altitude, so we could really see the damage our boys did. That was tremendous, I flew tail gunner and [what] a great view.

Repatriation

While the 'trolley' missions were operating, other groups were taking part in revival missions. These were another important series of flights to repatriate large numbers of former Allied prisoners of war (POWs) and some civilians. British and American air crews worked tirelessly to see the completion of these operations as quickly as possible. The situation required expediting with the utmost urgency due to the critical situation of malnutrition and disease affecting German camps, which was becoming ever more problematic with every passing day. For the American effort, each B-17 taking part was swiftly modified with wooden benches to enable it to carry up to forty passengers for repatriation.

Redeployment

For the personnel of many groups there now followed a period of waiting and anticipation of what was to come next. Confusion, rumour and counter-rumour seemed rife but for most the only desire was to return home. Most groups organised official parades to honour their fallen and provide an official end to their combat operations in Europe. A large flypast and presentation at the 8th Bomber Command Headquarters at High Wycombe was also organised, with various groups participating.

The war however, was still continuing in the Pacific and there was much concern that many would simply be transferred there to join the fight against the Japanese. This was, in the event, the case for some groups while others were to stay in Europe, but the structure of the 8th was about to significantly change. Air Force Command finally decided that three P-51 Mustang fighter groups and nine B-17 groups were to stay in Europe as part of the occupation forces in Germany or retained for other duties.

For the 8th AF, however, as an organisation it was to be redeployed to the Pacific. As more bombers rather than fighters were required in the Pacific, those bomb groups that were required started to return to the US for conversion to operate the Boeing B-29 Superfortress. All usable B-17s and B-24s were flown back to the United States, generally in the reverse of their original ferry flights. Before departing, all were checked and serviced to ensure that they were in peak condition for their long flights. They were also modified to carry another ten or so passengers, normally long-serving ground crews, in addition to the regular ten air crew. Paul Kovitz:

> We closed up operations and prepared the aircraft to take 22 people back to the US through Scotland, Iceland, Greenland, Labrador and the US, get new B-29s and go to the far-east in June 1945. We came back to Sioux Falls to retrain to go to Japan and continue fighting over there, then America dropped the bomb - thank God for Harry Truman! Boy what a mess Sioux Falls was the night they announced the Japanese surrender! – people drunk and partying everywhere!

Art Watson:

> I left on June 10 or 12th to fly back to USA. I was assigned to ship no. 32783 and while waiting for orders to return to the states we went out to the plane and worked on it to make sure that it was in prime condition. As it was we still lost an engine and had to land in Iceland. We were given another plane and continued on to America. I was assigned to go to Okinawa, but the Jap's surrendered before I was shipped and so I was sent to Fort Dix for discharge.

Although some return flights staged through Prestwick in Scotland, the vast majority passed through RAF Valley in North Wales, which due to its connection with homebound flights became known as 'Happy Valley'. The return flights again were not without tragedy: a 351st BG B-17 from Polebrook crashed into a Welsh mountain while making for RAF Valley, a 44th BG B-24 crashed near Gairloch in Scotland and a 446th BG B-24 disappeared over the Atlantic. All passengers and crew were unfortunately killed in all these incidents.

Once returned to the United States, personnel were normally given a period of leave before being sent to new units for conversion. Most of the aircraft they flew back in went immediately

A B-24 crew, on 'Dead End Kids' along with passengers drawn from the ground echelons, tuck into their 'K' rations during their homebound flight. (USAAF)

Homeward bound, ground echelons of the 8th Air Force board the *Queen Elizabeth*, docked at Greenock, Scotland. The official caption states: American personnel walking up the gang plank are not impeded by their equipment, for thoughts are running ahead of them to the home shores of America. This first load of 15,000 soldiers to be transported to the States marks the beginning of a plan for mass embarkations of American personnel during the coming months. (USAAF)

into storage prior to being scrapped. All the remaining ground personnel in Britain were transported to either the Clyde ports or Southampton to make their return journeys by sea.

The 8th AF officially relocated from 16 July 1945 to Okinawa, but the headquarters had barely had time to unpack and set up operations when B-29 Superfortresses of the USAAF dropped two atomic bombs on Hiroshima and Nagasaki on 6 and 9 August respectively. This finally ended the Second World War, causing the Japanese to surrender on 15 August. Those units who had returned to the US to train for the Pacific were now surplus to requirements and the majority were discharged from service by late autumn 1945. Rich Creutz:

I left Horham 20th July 1945 and went by train back to the Firth of Clyde and boarded the Queen Mary. We left on 21st July 1945 and arrived in the US on the 26th July. We boarded a train and I finally got home to Chicago on 2nd August after being away from home for 30 months. I received a 30 day furlough and during that time Japan surrendered. After the 30 days I had to report back to service at Sioux Falls South Dakota, I was then discharged on 25th November 1945.

Lawrence Scholze:

We were given the chance to go home and train on B-29s and go over to fight the Japanese or stay on in Europe for the army of occupation of Germany. I chose to stay. But then it wasn't very long and we dropped the A bomb on Japan so that ended it. I was real happy then. Then my Commanding Officer came to me and said (if I was to stay in Europe) I would have to sign away my chance of going home for at least three years. So I told him as long as Japan had surrendered just send me home, so that started my process for leaving England. I was sent back to Southampton to wait for a ship. That took a few weeks, then one day they said our boat was here so we prepared to load up and what do you know when we got to the dock, what do you believe – the Queen Mary was waiting for us. That made my day. 3½ days later after we left Southampton we landed in New York. So from there we went to New Jersey for a steak supper and then back on a troop train to Chicago. After arriving I had a 7 day furlough and headed home. I had to come back afterwards to get my army discharge papers. I was a free man again, I spent 3 years 7 months in the army, I enjoyed the experience very much although I know there were many soldiers that were not so fortunate.

For those staying in Europe, most would move to the continent to form part of the aforementioned occupation forces. The 305th BG at Chelveston, for instance, were given the task of the aerial photo mapping of Europe and North Africa. This they began at Chelveston in late June 1945, before being redeployed to St Trond in Belgium. Rod Ryan recalled that their last jobs at Chelveston were the clearing of all the surplus ordnance from the bomb dump, before moving out.

Other groups would continue to participate in the redeployment of US forces home in an operation entitled the 'Green Project'. Such was the task awaiting the 92nd BG, as Walter M. Stubbs recalls:

> On May the 8th Col. Wilson our CO, assembled the entire group around the group's boxing ring (an area of concrete laid at Podington for sporting activities) and announced that today the war in Europe was over. He also said that we should prepare to move but didn't say where. Since we were the oldest group in Europe we expected to be among the first to return home. It was not to be.

The Green Project was an operation set up to expedite the return of the majority of US ground forces to the US as swiftly as possible. The plan involved flying service personnel back to the US via the southern ferry route, from airfields in North Africa.

For their part in the operation, the 384th and part of the 92nd BGs moved to Istres in southern France, while the 303rd and 379th BGs relocated to Casablanca in North Africa. The services of the latter two groups were upon further evaluation not required and they too returned home shortly after. The former two groups were to ferry ground troops from Europe to North Africa for onward transportation by air back to the United States. While engaged in these operations a significant number of displaced civilians were also repatriated to their home countries in Europe.

The air elements flew to Istres from Podington and Grafton Underwood, but the ground personnel had to load up their trucks with all their equipment and make the long journey from Britain to the south of France and North Africa by road.

Base Clear Up

After the years of inhabiting RAF stations, US forces had accumulated vast amounts of equipment, all of which had to be cleared before officially handing them back to the RAF. All equipment allocated to bomb group units, as per their T/O&Es, would have to be inventoried, packed and loaded. Surplus equipment held in stores, such as new or usable spare parts, would be returned to the relevant air depots; for the most part this tended to be BAD1, Burtonwood. Quartermaster stores stock would also have to be returned via their systems of control.

There would also be an enormous amount of surplus equipment that just wasn't wanted any more as it had little or no military value. Things such as furniture, paperwork, racking, work stands, surplus or worn flying clothing and even scrap aircraft and parts. Much of the latter category had been stockpiled for potential use during the early periods of activity, when the spare situation was particularly difficult. A lot of this was simply disposed of by any means possible. Leroy Keeping remembers the situation at Framlingham:

> We cleared up the camp, there were 10 or 12 of us on base who married local girls, and they kept us back to last to stay with our wives while we sorted their travel to the States out. We stayed on to the end to clear up before handing the camp back to the RAF. Most stuff was either burnt or buried, most non burnable stuff like bed frames etc was taken to some nearby pits and dropped in and buried. We finally got shipped back to the States in November 1945.

The issue of equipment buried by the Americans when clearing out at the end of the war has been the cause of perpetuated rumours through the years. Huge stocks of unused equipment are said to have been disposed of; particularly high on the apocryphal tale list are stories of brand new Jeeps in crates. However, the evidence to date suggests differently; we know things were buried, we have the veteran's account for it, but it was generally rubbish. Military vehicles still had a value even in the civilian sector and as the huge post-war auctions of equipment bear testament, were eagerly purchased by a civilian market starved of new vehicles throughout the war. As Leroy Keeping states, that which was buried was fairly worthless to the military machine. All stations, for instance, had domestic rubbish tips and some, like the one at Debach, have in recent years yielded a large quantity of small personal and day-to-day items.

A large collection of metal aircraft components has been found recently at a dig at an old gravel pit site in Suffolk. Again most of these items appear to have been unserviceable at the time of disposal; oxygen cylinders recovered in particular appear to have been deliberately punctured. As by the end of the Second World War both B-17 and B-24 types were being considered obsolete and scrapped on their return, used spare parts would have had little value. This suggests that most of this particular 'hoard' was probably dumped because it was too much trouble to return through the correct channels for disposal. Bicycles too no longer had any value, and many were given away to local civilians, but even so, large numbers were gathered at airfields. Many of these were simply piled up and driven over with tracked vehicles to crush and flatten them prior to disposal.

After the war a not inconsiderable amount of books and periodicals had to be cleared once the libraries that had been established on each camp closed. Again many items were probably burnt, but John Borchert tells of the official disposal process that was being carried out:

> I moved into very comfortable quarters with division ordnance officer, Major Paul Wilcox. Among the tasks he had after V-E Day was the decommissioning of base libraries. He showed me a Quonset hut filled to the roof with piles of books which he was trying to figure out what to do with. One big part of the collection was high school and college texts. I began to spend my growing amount of spare time browsing through this stuff, pulling out books in the earth sciences that looked interesting.
>
> I came across a copy of Elements of Geography, by V. C. Finch and G. T. Trewartha, Professors of geography at the University of Wisconsin. I read the book carefully because it seemed to me to be a combination of geology, meteorology, and cartography, implicitly applied to the understanding of human use of the earth. It struck me as something that might give me an opportunity to combine an interest in college teaching, developed at DePauw, with my experience in both meteorology and geology and an unarticulated lifetime interest in human settlement patterns. Unlikely that anything would come of it, but the thought stuck in the back of my mind. I had no idea at that time where it would lead.

Once the clear-up had been completed, the last task for the remaining American personnel before finally moving out would be a short ceremony at the main gate. This would entail lowering the American Stars and Stripes for the last time and raising the British Union Jack and RAF pennant, and thus handing the station, officially, back to British control. This ceremony on many airfields would have been the last official parade as a number were either closed immediately or placed under 'care and maintenance' for a short while, before being disposed of.

War Brides

As is well known, large numbers of US servicemen married local women while stationed overseas during and after the Second World War. The total figure is estimated at approximately 65,000 – including 50,000 from Britain. This doesn't include the additional large number of women with babies born to American fathers who didn't, for one reason or another, get to the US after the war. As hostilities came to an end, the logistics of 'redeployment' of these 'GI brides', many with children, was another headache faced by American authorities, but it wasn't going to happen until the majority of service personnel had returned home. In co-operation with the US military and the US State Department, the ARC provided care for these women and their children and established assembly centres where they could be grouped prior to travelling to America. Here they tried to prepare the women for their new life. The military outfitted twenty ships to transport brides to the US and they were accompanied by ARC workers during the crossings, who also provided a number of services, some lasting for years, through local chapters at their final points of destination.

Of the veterans that appear within this publication, Leroy Keeping, Rod Ryan, Walter Stubbs and Paul Kovitz all married English girls while stationed in Britain. Quite a number of brides returned to their home countries within a short period of time as the marriages forged during war were unable to endure the peace. Paul Kovitz explains that the experiences of his new wife Hilda were typical of many war brides, although her reception and integration into American life was a lot more positive than many experienced:

When I left my wife I didn't know if I'd see her again, as we were going to Japan. I left her some money to try and get a flight over to the States but she couldn't get one. In the end she went to a bride's camp in Southampton and finally got on bride's boat which got over in February 1946. She said the sailing was pretty unpleasant, it was on a Liberty ship and it wasn't a smooth crossing. She didn't like the communal toilets and there were babies crying everywhere, but she survived! She became an American citizen and she has loved it since.

Before we got married I had to get a declaration signed that I could look after her and she wouldn't become a public charge. When she arrived I met her in New York and took her to meet my family and my mother took to her like she was her own daughter.

Post-War

Much has been written about the wartime experiences of veterans in this and many other publications. Although an extremely memorable period, this was but a small time frame in their lives. What happened to them after the war and how did they adjust to post-war life? Many returned to their old jobs while others took the opportunity provided by the US government to return to education and study for new qualifications. Many were inspired by what they had achieved during their military service, others by their exposure to lectures and educational programmes offered while overseas. Some stayed on and made a career in the military. Many married and had families, providing the 'baby boomer' generation of the 1960s. Altogether they did their part to rebuild a country and economy affected not only by war but more critically the prior depression, and returned industry back to civilian production.

Paul Kovitz

After his wife rejoined him in 1946 they had a family. Paul was discharged from the air force but almost immediately rejoined as he didn't think much of the work situation at the time. He stayed in the air force for another twenty-three years, and retired a Lieutenant Colonel. He then went to work for Pratt and Whitney as a field engineer on jet engines before retiring in 1976. During his time with Pratt and Whitney he came to Britain and lived for a while in Wales, as well as working in Holland during the 1970s. It was while there he had cause to get into discussion regarding the CHOWHOUND missions he had been on. He and his wife Hilda retired to Florida. Paul is active in the 390th BG Veterans' Association.

Leroy Keeping

Leroy's wife made it to America from England in April 1946. For nine years they farmed in Minnesota during which his time wife returned to England to visit her family. On her return she was very homesick and depressed. Leroy said this cost quite a bit in medical fees so he decided as he could make his home anywhere, it made more sense to return to England, and this they did. They had two daughters, one born in the US and one born in England. His wife died in 1983, but as his family all live in the area he continues to live in Framlingham. The restoration of the Framlingham control tower began in 1976 and Leroy became involved in 1981. He has been active in the group ever since.

Leroy Keeping at Framlingham, 1 July 2007, during the Operation Bolero military vehicle weekend, organised to commemorate the sixty-fifth anniversary of the arrival of the USAAF to Britain. He is standing in front of the author's GMC CCKW-353 tipper, marked up for Leroy's squadron and group. (Author)

Rod Ryan

Rod came out of the USAAF after returning to the States in 1946 but retained a volunteer reserve status. His wife then arrived in the US. He said he realised after a couple of years that if he rejoined the air force he could get posted back to England, which would be good, particularly for his wife. They came back to Britain, and he was posted first to RAF Croughton, which at the time was being rebuilt to a new role for the USAAF, and then to Alconbury. They went back to America for a while and he also served in Vietnam and Germany. Rod finally retired from the USAF in 1971 and settled in Northampton, England.

Lawrence Scholze

Lawrence was born and raised on a dairy farm in Humbird, Wisconsin. When he came home from the war he says he just went back to helping his parents run the farm.

Joseph Harlick

After his return from England Joe was awarded an Honourable Discharge from the air force at Fort Douglas, Utah on 13 September 1945. There followed a working life continuing his passion for photography. His first venture after leaving the air force was to build and operate a photographic studio in his home town of Hot Springs, Montana.

In September 1957 he was offered a job with the Boeing Company in Seattle. His first assignment was photographing the Pan American 707 on its delivery flight. He became supervisor of the Technical Photo Group, which covered all of Boeing's research and development. During his career Joe worked in many areas of technical industrial photography, developing many innovative processes. After twenty-six rewarding years with Boeing, he retired in July 1983.

The late Joe Harlick, explaining the intricacies of strike cameras at Petersen AF Base Museum, Colorado, during the 91st BG reunion in September 2006. (Bonnie Selje)

Joe's wartime photos have appeared in many books, in particular Marion Havelaar's work on the 91st BG, *The Ragged Irregulars of Bassingbourn*. Two of Joe's photographs are also displayed in the Smithsonian in Washington DC. Joe died in April 2009.

Richard W. Creutz

When he returned from service Richard went back to the same lighting and merchandising display company that he had worked for before the war. He worked for them for a total of fifty-six years, including his time in service. He worked his way through the ranks, as a sheet metal worker, a foreman, a plant superintendent, and ended up as a lighting design engineer. He said he did a lot of travelling in that job meeting with customers to plan their lighting needs. He didn't fully retire until the spring of 1997. He married in 1949 and he and his wife have three children and five grandchildren.

John R. Borchert

Following the surrender of Germany in May 1945, John joined the staff of a new bomber wing scheduled to return to America temporarily. They were to pick up a fleet of B-29 bombers and go on to a base in Okinawa for bombing and support of the invasion of Japan. He was the staff weather officer for the wing. Plans changed with the Japanese surrender in August, and in September John returned to America to join his wife Jane and his two-and-a-half-year-old daughter born while he was in England. There he was discharged from the army, and the family began life together.

Returning from his discharge at Camp McCoy in Wisconsin, he passed through Madison, home of the University of Wisconsin. His wife suggested that he stop at the university and talk with one of the authors of the book he had found and been inspired by in England. This he did and ended the day by taking a class. This was his epiphany and he found in that hour what he wished for his life. There followed a life of scientific study, teaching and travel. Ultimately John was appointed Regents' Professor Emeritus of geography at the University of Minnesota. John died in March 2001.

Summing up 'The Mission'

The rights, wrongs and effectiveness of the Allied bombing campaign have continued through the generations since the Second World War and no doubt will continue to do so as long as historians take an interest in such things. This is not the place to discuss the issue, but instead to highlight what the campaign did achieve.

It is safe to say that much vaunted weapons such as the Norden bombsight did not provide the widely anticipated knockout blow to German industry. Conversely, it can be stated with much conviction that the air campaign was decisive in the ultimate defeat of Germany – a viewpoint held by parties from all sides. It did open a battlefront when the Allies desperately needed one, taking the fight to the enemy. It also provided much needed support to Russia due to Germany's need to keep more air defence units back from the eastern front. This in fact was one of the air campaign's greatest successes. Operating as it did it restricted the Luftwaffe to a primarily defensive role. Tying down aircraft manufacturing mainly to fighter production, it starved the Luftwaffe of more advanced offensive bomber designs, in particular the jet programme, and limited the development of many air weapons that Germany was planning.

The 8th AF had nowhere near reached its anticipated strength by the end of the Second World War; up to sixty bomb groups had been planned with another two divisions in preparation. Even so during the latter stages of the war it could and regularly did orchestrate getting in excess of 3,000 bomber and fighter aircraft into the air on a single day. They all needed to be maintained to keep them flying. In contrast with the 200,000 plus air force personnel stationed in Britain, a much smaller proportion were air crew, the rest played a part in organising the vast operation.

Precise statistics for the support provided by ground personnel are difficult to quantify, but according to the records of the 444th Sub-Depot based at Molesworth, in support of the 303rd BG, they carried out over 1,500 major repairs to damaged aircraft. If this figure is doubled then somewhere near the total number of repairs carried out by Sub-Depot and squadron ground crews can be established. However, this is just combat damage and doesn't include any regular servicing or engine changes. Multiply this figure by forty groups and we have a greater understanding of the work undertaken out on the airfields day in and day out for three years.

The losses, particularly during the early months of the 8th's air campaign were almost crippling; at one point it was considered statistically impossible for air crew to complete the twenty-five mission tour requirement at the time. Although nowhere near the number of combat losses, there were also a significant number of ground personnel killed in various accidents on and around the airfields, as illustrated in a previous chapter, while going about their duties.

Through skills and resourcefulness learnt in the depths of depression, the youth of America rose to the challenges faced by war. The ground personnel of the 8th AF adapted to the privations faced when establishing their mighty air armada in Britain and saw the job through; they all knew they were in for the duration and had to get on with things as best they could.

The Legacy of the 8th Air Force

It is interesting to note that although the vast majority of the British temporary airfields that were allocated to the 8th and 9th AFs fell out of use and were disposed of fairly soon after the Second World War, most can still be detected on the landscape. All have suffered some form of demolition and although there are those that are still reasonably intact such as Attlebridge (despite being covered in turkey sheds), others like Grafton Underwood have been virtually erased from the landscape by removal of concrete, much of which was recycled for road construction during the 1970s and 1980s. The odd remaining building or hint of concrete road is all that is left. Viewed from the air, even long-gone runways can be traced fairly easily by crop marks or lines of trees planted as windbreaks along their length, the pattern of the Class A; three interconnecting runways are seemingly incredibly difficult to completely remove from the landscape.

It is those sites that have continued in military usage that have changed the most, and their original functions are sometimes less easy to detect, evolving as they have over the years into new roles. Most pre-war permanent stations continued in use as airfields for many years; many were then taken over by the army, such as Bassingbourn, although the original layout of these sites is still fairly obvious. Horsham St Faith is still used for flying, though it is now civilian, as Norwich City Airport. Molesworth and Chelveston have probably been the most altered during the intervening years. Both continued to be used by the USAF until more recent times, and experienced total redevelopment to new functions during their service lives. Molesworth still exists in its final transformation, though Chelveston has completely disappeared and has been returned to pasture.

Second World War military buildings in the British landscape are diminishing rapidly but many do still exist and some are even in better condition than ever before. Individual

Framlingham bomb sight store on the former headquarters site, now carefully converted to a bungalow. The step around the building below the roofline gives away its former identity. 1 July 2007. (Bob Clarke)

buildings have found new purposes, many for agricultural or other commercial purposes. Farmers were eager to regain land once airfields were closed and were glad of the additional storage many former hangars and sheds could provide. In fact it is entirely likely that many of the buildings on former dispersed sites survived for further use only because they had services, particularly water, connected to them. In some instances large areas of former airfields, particularly technical sites, have been converted to small industrial units or estates, such as at Rougham and Eye.

Some of the more interesting building conversions include the former operations blocks at Debach and Attlebridge, the former now commercial premises and the latter a house. Much has already been said about control towers, particularly now taking the role of museums, but those at Lavenham and Podington are now an office and a house respectively. One of the more interesting examples of reuse is the former Norden bombsight store at Framlingham, which is now a house.

Even though US air forces left Britain after the Second World War, it wasn't long, due to increased tensions with the USSR, before they returned. From the late 1940s right up to the present day there has been a continued USAF presence in Britain, and although now once again greatly reduced, it still forms an important part of NATO's obligations. The presence has also become an important part of the local culture and economy, particularly (as with the original connection) in East Anglia and the east Midlands. Maybe because of this long association with American air power, Britain has become in recent years more conscious of the sacrifices made both by our own RAF crews and those from the US air forces. Most airfields of the Second World War era now sport superb memorials to their former inhabitants and nowhere more so than at those formerly occupied by the USAAF.

As well as at the airfields, other memorials have appeared in recent years to commemorate events from times past. These memorials, whether at crash sites, on park benches, village signs or church windows, are all examples of the enduring camaraderie, respect and interest in events long ago. The most moving of all tributes to those lost in combat has to be the American cemetery at Madingly, Cambridge, where many of those killed still lie or have their names recorded on the wall of the missing.

As well as the increasing number of museums established at the former airfields, Britain's premier

May 2005, veterans of the 95th BG and their families assemble before a USAF colour party from RAF Lakenheath for a service of remembrance at the former NCOs Red Feather Club at Horham. Now restored as a memorial and museum by members of the local community, the club buildings have played host to several events for returning veterans. (Kevin Taylor)

attraction of the type is located within the Imperial War Museum complex at Duxford, itself a former 8th AF fighter station. The American Air Museum houses an outstanding collection of former USAAF and USAF types as well as memorabilia, explaining Britain's connection with US air power. Duxford is also home to Britain's only remaining flying example of a Flying Fortress, B-17 Preservation's *Sally B*.

Recent years have seen a huge increase in interest in all aspects of the Second World War and, in particular, the collecting of equipment and items from the war. Some have taken this further by restoring vehicles of the period, both military and civilian, and those with even deeper pockets tirelessly work at putting vintage aircraft into the air again. The re-enactor movement is another area that has also burgeoned in recent times and numerous events are organised up and down the country each year, many paying homage to former USAAF activities.

The links between British and American citizens, forged during wartime, have endured through the years, often being passed down through the generations. Many of the former USAAF groups, be they bomber, fighter or transport, have very active veterans' associations. Even though now the numbers of veterans are rapidly diminishing, the baton has been taken up by the younger generations. Starting in the 1970s and 1980s, veterans' associations started organising return visits to Britain and many continue to this day, although fewer actual veterans are now able to make the long journey. When they or their families do arrive they can be assured of a warm welcome.

Conington village sign. The village was the location of many communal and domestic sites attached to Glatton airfield. The sign immortalises a B-17 from the station's former inhabitants, the 457th BG. (Author)

SWEATIN' OUT THE MISSION

The wind howls around the desolate watchtower,
the windowpanes rattle as its icy breath sweeps around.
Imprints of the past fade away as the winter sun rises.
Remembering, reminiscing, they shrink in to the background, as the elements pile their wrath
on the building.
Looking back, the watchtower would be a hive of activity,
but those days are gone.
Those days when the heavy bombers would roll out
and take to the skies like birds being freed.
Some on their first mission, some on their last, some never to return.
Their ground crews eagerly waiting, some realising theirs would never return and that they
would be forever, sweatin' out the mission.

By Jess Holland

References

Introduction

1. Bomber Offensive by Sir Arthur Harris, Marshall of the RAF.
2. Roosevelt's second 'Fireside chat', broadcast 7 May 1943.
3. Lend-Lease Act statement, Public Law 77-11, 11 March 1941.

Chapter 1

1. T/O&E, 1-117, July 1944, Heavy Bombardment Squadron.
2. www.ibiblio.org/hyperwar/AAF/I/AAF-I-17.html – 13/11/2007.

Chapter 2

1. PRO AIR 14/1057 319970.
2. Ref. Bomber Command Administrative order No.1, United States Bomber Forces in the UK, 2 February 1942,
   PRO Air 14/999 319970.
3. *The Army Air Forces in World War II*, Vol.6, 'Men and Planes'.
4. *The Hub - Fighter Leader*, as told to Roger A. Freeman.

Chapter 3

1. www.381st.org/histories/medical_06-1944.html – 31/08/2005.
2. Ref. X464/209/8 - Bedford and Luton Archives.
3. From *The Route as Briefed*, John S. Sloan.

Chapter 4

1. T/O&E 1-112, June 1944, Headquarters Heavy Bombardment Group.
2. www.303rdbg.com/unusual-2.html – 10/05/2010.
3. www.381st.org/histories/medical_03-1944.html – 31/08/2005.
4. *War through the hole in a Donut*, Angela Petesch.
5. www.fdrlibrary.marist.edu/psf/box32/a304pp01.html - 22/02/2009.
6. The George C. Marshall Interviews No.17, p.154, 20 February 1957, for Forest C. Pogue. Larry L. Bland (Lexington Virginia 1991).

Chapter 5

1. *The Forgotten Man – The Mechanic – The Kenneth A. Lemmons Story*, Cindy Goodman & Jan Riddling.
2. The Official Guide to the Army Air Forces, June 1944.

3. War Department Technical Manual, TM 1-415 - Airplane Inspection Guide (17 August 1943).
4. Aircraft Inspection and Maintenance Guide for B-17 Series, 15 May 1944.
5. 390th BG Veterans Association newsletter, notes from *The War Stories Luncheon*, 390th BG Reunion, Spokane, 1994, Major Albert Engler.
6. www.303rdbg.com/ground-accidents.html – 4/1/2008.

Chapter 6

1. www.381st.org/histories/448th_november43.html – 31/08/2005.
2. www.91stbombgroup.com/91st_tales/harlick2.html – 10/05/2010.
3. From *The Route as Briefed*, John S. Sloan.
4. www.381st.org/history/wardiaries/1207thQM.aspx – 31/08/2005.
5. From *Suffolk Summer*, John T. Appleby.

Chapter 7

1. *The Mighty Men of the 381st – Heroes All*, James Good Brown.

Chapter 8

1. The Quartermaster Review January – February 1944 by Major General Robert M.G. Littlejohn. www.qmfound.com_ww11.html – 17/05/2009.
2. *The Route as Briefed*, John S. Sloan.
3. http://www.redcross.org/museum/registry/profile.asp?id=620 – 10/05/2010.
4. *The Mighty Men of the 381st – Heroes All*, James Good Brown.
5. Lt Gen. Brehon B. Somervell CG, Army Service Forces. AAFES official history – Private papers of Lt Gen. Brehon Burke Somervell.
6. *Air Force Chaplains*, Vol.1, 'The Service of Chaplains Army Air Units 1917–1946', Daniel B. Jorgensen.

Chapter 9

1. http://www.381st.org/histories/medical_12-1943.html – 31/08/2005.
2. *An Old Co-pilot Remembers*, Ken Blakebrough.
3. www.453rd.com/stories/u.k_memories.pdf – 06/04/2010.
4. *The Route as Briefed*, John S. Sloan.
5. http://www.381st.org/histories/448th_april45.html – 31/08/2005.

Chapter 10

1. *The Route as Briefed*, John S. Sloan.
2. http://www.381st.org/histories/medical_12-1943.html – 31/08/2005.

Chapter 11

1. *Suffolk Summer*, John T. Appleby.

Glossary

AAC	Army Air Corps
AES	Army Exchange Service
AAFES	Army & Air Force Exchange Service
AF	Air Force
AM	Air ministry
AMDGW	Air Ministry Directorate General of Works
AML	Air Ministry Laboratory
AMWD	Air Ministry Works Directorate
ARC	American Red Cross
ASC	Air Service Command
ASDIC	British underwater sound detection system (Allied Submarine Detection Investigation Committee)
ASG	Air Service Group
AWOL	Absent Without Leave
BAD	Base Air Depot
BCF	British Concrete Federation
BEF	British Expeditionary Force
BG	(Bombardment) Bomb Group
BS	(Bombardment) Bomb Squadron
'Buncher'	Navigation beacon, often used for mission formation
CCC	Civilian Conservation Corps
CCRC	Combat Crew Replacement Centre
Class A	Standard British WW2 airfield layout
CO	Commanding Officer
CQ	Charge of Quarters
EAB	Engineer Aviation Battalion
EAFFP	Engineer Aviation Fire Fighting Platoon
EFFP	Engineer Fire Fighting Platoon
ETA	Estimated Time of Arrival
ETO	European Theatre of Operations
ETOUSA	European Theatre of Operations United States of America
FCO	Flying Control Officer
FIDO	Fog Investigation and Dispersal Operations
GEE	RAF radio navigation system
GI	General Issue, commonly used as a reference to American soldiers
GHQ	General Headquarters
GPO	General Post Office, former state controllers of British postal and telephone system
H2X	American development of British H2S radar navigation system, also known as 'mickey'
HILVL	High Intensity Low Visibility Lighting
HQ	Headquarters
HFDF	High Frequency Direction Finding

HVAC	Heating Ventilation and Air Conditioning
IFF	Identification Friend or Foe
Luftwaffe	German Air Force
Lt	Lieutenant
'mickey'	See H2X
MAD	Mobile Air Depot
M&E	Mechanical and Electrical
MAP	British Ministry of Aircraft Production
MOS	Military Occupational Specialist
MP	Military Police
M/Sgt	Master Sergeant
MT	Motor Transport
NAZI	shortened form of the German National Socialist Party
NCO	Non-Commissioned Officer
NFE	Night Flying Equipment
NFS	National Fire Service
Norden	A mechanical analogue computing bombsight
OBOE	RAF blind bombing targeting system
PBX	Private Branch Exchange – station phone exchange
POL	Petrol, Oil, Lubricants
PT	Physical training
PX	Post Exchange
'Pundit'	Morse code station identifier
QMC	Quartermaster Corps
QM Co.	Quartermaster Company
RAF	Royal Air force
R&D	Research and Development
RTO	Railway Traffic Office
SAD	Strategic Air Depot
SBA	Standard Beam Approach
Sgt.	Sergeant
Sonar	Underwater navigation system, from sound navigation and radar
SOS	Service of Supply (US Army)
'Splasher'	Navigational beacon often used for mission assembly
Tannoy	Public address system on wartime airfields
T/Sgt	Technical Sergeant
'Tokyo' tanks	Additional wing mounted fuel tanks fitted to B-17s
T/O&E	War Department Tables of Organisation and Equipment
USAAF	United States Army Air Force
USAF	United States Air Force
USFI	United States Armed Forces Institute
USO	United Services Organisation
VIIIAFSC	8th Air Force Service Command
VHF	Very High Frequency
V Weapons	German retaliatory weapons, derived from *vergeltungswaffen*.
WAAF	Women's Auxiliary Air Force, women's branch of the RAF
WAC	Women's Army Corps, women's branch of US Army/AAF
W/T	Wireless Telegraphy
QEC	Quick Engine Change

Veterans

ARTHUR G. WATSON
Staff Sergeant Art Watson, Bombsight Technician, 335th BS, 95th BG, Horham

WHIT HILL
Crew ChiefWhit Hill, Sheet Metal, 323rd BS, 91st BG, Bassingbourn

JACK GAFFNEY
Sergeant Jack Gaffney, Crew Chief, 401st BS, 91st BG, Bassingbourn

JOSEPH HARLICK
Sergeant Joe Harlick, Photo Lab Technician, 324th BS, 91st BG, Bassingbourn

PAUL KOVITZ
2nd Lt Paul Kovitz, Engineering Officer, 569th BS, 390th BG, Framlingham

ROD RYAN
Rod Ryan, 1632nd Ordnance S&M Co., 305th BG, Chelveston

LEROY KEEPING
Staff Sergeant, Leroy Keeping, Power Turret Specialist, 570th BS, 390th BG, Framlingham

RICHARD W. CREUTZ
Corporal Richard Creutz, Airplane Sheet Metal Specialist, 457th Sub-Depot, 95th BG, Horham

LAWRENCE J. SCHOLZE
Master Sergeant, Lawrence J. Scholze, Mechanic, 335th BS 95th BG, Horham

C. ARTHUR FERWERDA
Arthur Ferwerda, Crew Chief, 409th BS, 93rd BG, Hardwick

WALTER M. STUBBS
Technical Sergeant Walter Stubbs, Crew Chief, 407th BS, 92nd BG, Bovingdon, Alconbury and Podington

C. J. LELEUX
C.J. Leleux, Mechanic, 715th BS, 448th BG, Seething

RUDI STEEL
Erwin R. (Rudi) Steele, Sheet Metal/Mechanic, 322nd BS, 91st BG, Bassingbourn

JOHN BORCHERT
2nd Lt John Borchert, 18th Weather Squadron, Detachment 111, 306th BG, Thurleigh; Detachment 104, 93rd BG, Hardwick; Detachment 118, 392nd BG, Wendling; & 2nd Air Division HQ

KENNETH LEMMONS
Master Sergeant Ken Lemmons, Flight Chief, 351st BS, 100th BG, Thorpe Abbotts

ALBERT E ENGLER
Major Al Engler, Group Engineering Officer, 390th BG, Framlingham

HENRY G. JOHANSEN,
Henry Johansen, Machinist, 444th Sub-Depot, 303rd BG, Molesworth

CARLTON M. SMITH
Carlton M. Smith, Photo Interpreter, HQ, 303rd BG, Molesworth

ROBERT GOULD
Robert Gould was a civilian electrical engineer during the Second World War. He was foreman of the construction department working for Edmondson's Electricity Corporation

Bibliography

Airfields of the 8th Then and Now, Roger A. Freeman, After the Battle

Air Force Chaplains Volume 1, The Service of Chaplains to Army Air Units 1917 – 1946, Daniel B. Jorgensen, Office, Chief of Air Force Chaplains

Airfield Focus special – Chelveston, John N. Smith, GMS Enterprises

Airfield Focus No.63 – Podington, John N. Smith, GMS Enterprises

Army Air Forces Medical Services in World War II, James S. Nanney, Air Force History and Museums Program

At His Side – The American Red Cross Overseas in WW2, George Korson, Coward – McCann, Inc New York

381st Bomb Group, Ron MacKay, Squadron/signal publications

92nd Bomb Group (H) Fames Favoured Few, Turner Publishing Company

Bomber Offensive, Sir Arthur Harris, Marshall of the RAF, Collins

Britain's Military Airfields 1939-45, David J. Smith, Patrick Stephens Ltd

British Airfield Buildings of the Second World War, Graham Buchan Innes, Midland Publishing Ltd

British Military Airfield Architecture, Paul Francis, Patrick Stephens Ltd BSM Division, Department of Armament, USAAF

Combat Profile: B-17G Flying Fortress in World War 2, Roger A. Freeman, Ian Allen

Eighth Air Force Bomber Stories, Ian Mclachlan & Russell Zorn, Patrick Stephens Ltd

Fields of Little America, Martin W. Bowman, GMS Enterprises

'Flak' Houses then and now – The story of American Rest Homes in England during WW2, Keith Thomas, After the Battle

Fortresses of the Big Triangle First, Cliff T. Bishop, East Anglia Books

From Somewhere in England, D.A. Lande, Airlife Publishing Ltd

Glen Miller in Britain Then and Now, Chris Way, After the Battle

Love Sex & War Changing Values 1939-45, John Costello, Guild Publishing

Piercing the Fog, John F. Kreis, Air Force History & Museums Program

Medical Support Army Air Forces in World War II, Mae Mills Link & Hubert A. Coleman, Office of Surgeon General USAF

Production Line to Front Line 2, Boeing B-17 Flying fortress, Michael O'Leary, Osprey Aviation

Psychiatric Experiences of the Eighth Air Force, The Air Surgeon Army Air Forces, Josiah Macey Jr Foundation

Savernake at War, Roger Day, self-published by Roger Day

Suffolk Summer, John T. Apleby, East Anglian Magazine Ltd

The American Red Cross, A History, Foster Rhea Dulles, Greenwood Press

The Archaeology of Airfields, Bob Clarke, The History Press

The Army Air Forces in World War II, Vol. VI Men and Planes, W.F. Craven & J.L. Cate

The Best and Worst of Times, The United States Army Chaplaincy 1920-1945, Robert L. Gushwa, University Press of the Pacific

The 1000 Day Battle, James Hoseason, Gillingham Publications

The Forgotten Man – The Mechanic, The Kenneth A. Lemmons Story, Cindy Goodman and Jan Ridling, CinJan Productions

The Friendly Invasion, Roger A. Freeman, East Anglian Tourist Board
The Hub Fighter Leader, The Story of Hub Zemke, America's great WW2 Fighter commander as told to Roger A. Freeman, Airlife Publishing
The Legendary Norden Bombsight, Albert L. Pardini, Schiffer Military History
The Lockheed P-38 Lightning, Warren M. Bodie, Widewing Publications
The Man Who Flew the Memphis Belle, Col. Robert Morgan USAFR Ret., New American Library
The Royal Airforce Builds for War, HMSO
The Mighty Eighth, Roger A. Freeman, Cassell & Co.
The Mighty Eighth War Manual, Roger A. Freeman, Arms and Armour
The Mighty Men of the 381st: Heroes All, James Good Brown, Publishers Press
The Norden Bombsight, Maintenance and Calibration Manual
The Officers Guide, The Military Service Publishing Company
The Official Guide to the Army Air Forces, The Army Air Forces Aid Society 1944
The Route as Briefed, John S. Sloan, Argus Press, Cleveland Ohio
The Story of the 390th Bombardment Group (H), The 390th Memorial Museum Foundation Inc., Turner Publishing Company
The US Eighth Air Force in Camera 1942 – 1944, Martin W. Bowman, Sutton Publishing
USAAF Handbook 1939-1945, Martin W. Bowman, Sutton Publishing
TM 1-415, War Department Technical Manual, Airplane Inspection Guide
War through the hole of a Donut, Angela Petesch, Hunter Halverson Press

Other Sources:

Airfield site plans, various, Air Ministry published by Motorbooks or from RAF archives.
B-17F Airplane – Pilots Flight Operating Instructions. 25 December 1942, USAAF
    Technical Order 01-20EF-1
    Tables of Organisation and Equipment (T/O&Es)
    T/O&E 1-112 Headquarters Bombardment Group, V Heavy, Heavy or Medium
    T/O&E 1-117 Bombardment Squadron, Heavy
    T/O&E 8-450 Medical Dispensary, Aviation
    T/O&E 8-450 (RS) Medical Dispensary (Reduced Strength)
    T/O&E 9-417 Ordnance Supply & Maintenance Company, Aviation
USAAF Pilots Information File – AAF Form No.24, 4-1-43

Index

Bomb Groups
34th BG, 47
44th BG, 139, 202
91st BG, 23, 40, 42, 99, 108, 112, 116, 126, 129, 136, 141, 152, 155, 208
92nd BG, 50, 51, 56, 59, 92, 102, 104, 150, 159, 171, 179, 193, 195, 204
93rd BG, 64, 145
95th BG, 14, 22, 23, 39, 96, 136, 151, 200, 212
100th BG, 120, 172
303rd BG, 43, 64, 93, 140, 153, 164, 176, 186, 200, 204, 210
305th BG, 49, 199, 204
306th BG, 65, 96, 133
379th BG, 65, 66, 89, 130, 134, 155, 204
381st BG, 54, 67, 69, 101, 103, 107, 108, 114, 121, 155, 156, 163-166, 174, 185, 191, 193, 195
384th BG, 198, 204
385th BG, 46, 47
386th BG, 73
389th BG, 161
390th BG, 15, 23, 42, 47, 53, 67, 68, 76, 77, 79, 85, 92, 105, 106, 113, 118, 119, 139, 150, 153-155, 183, 198, 199, 207
392nd BG, 65, 90
398th BG, 180
401st BG, 41, 63, 74, 137, 150, 154, 160, 164
457th BG, 175, 213,
486th BG, 95, 151,
487th BG, 120, 199
493rd BG, 40, 87, 128, 167

Fighter Groups
56th FG, 38
357th FG, 55

Air Forces
9th AF, 16, 25, 34, 37, 73, 147, 163, 176, 210
12th AF, 37
15th AF, 37

Air Divisions
1st Air Division, 35, 37, 38, 198,
2nd Air Division, 37, 38, 65, 198
3rd Air Division, 37, 38, 107, 198

Others
18th Weather Squadron, 19, 65, 132, 134, 177

Abbots Ripton, 37
ABC-1 Conference, 20
AEC, 87, 110
Aeroclub, 150, 151
Air Ministry, 27, 28, 30, 40, 43, 50, 54, 56-58, 71, 98, 105, 111, 118, 122, 125, 128, 146, 148, 168, 171-173, 175
Air Service Command, 18, 36, 37
Air Service Group, 18, 19, 38, 51, 97
Airspeed Oxford, 127
Alconbury, 37, 93, 171, 208
AMDGW, 27
American Red Cross (ARC), 9, 20, 67, 151, 181, 144, 145, 150-153, 180-182, 190, 206
AML Bomb Trainer, 98, 118, 119
AMWD, 54, 58
ARCADIA Conference, 10, 15, 21
Army Exchange Service, 157
Arnold William R., 162
Arnold, General H.A., 11, 12, 22, 35, 162, 184
ASDIC, 69
Attlebridge, 122, 210, 211
Austin, 110, 137, 196
Autocar, 110
B-17 (Flying Fortress), 12, 17, 23, 24, 37-39, 46, 47, 52, 74, 76, 77, 80, 81, 84-90, 93, 96, 99, 106-109, 112, 116, 120, 128, 131, 133, 139, 141, 175, 197-199, 201, 202, 205, 212, 213
B-24 (Liberator), 12, 17, 37, 38, 47, 64, 80-82, 84, 85, 87, 88-90, 93, 95, 106, 108, 133, 183, 196, 198, 202, 205
BAD1, 37, 204
BAD2, 37
BAD3, 37
Baldwin, Prime Minister S., 7
Barnham, 50
Base Air Depot, 37, 101
Bassingbourn, 31, 39, 40, 42, 43, 49, 60, 76, 77, 84, 95, 99, 105, 108, 109, 112, 113, 116, 122-124, 126, 129, 136, 141, 146, 152, 155, 170, 190, 191, 209, 210
Battle HQ, 46
BCF, 173
Bedford, 50, 148, 182
Berchtesgarten, 198
Biederman, 109
Boeing (Corporation), 11, 12, 17, 106, 202, 208
Boiler, 56, 57, 62, 76, 144, 146, 170, 177
BOLERO Operation, 22, 23, 207
Bomb Dump, 31, 32, 48-52, 88, 93, 140, 204
Bomber Command 8th AF, 15, 21, 24, 35, 65, 132, 201
Bomber Command RAF, 7, 8, 21, 30, 34, 169
Bombsight, 13, 23, 60, 61, 69-73, 91, 113, 119, 142, 209, 211
Briefing, 44, 55, 60 -67, 82, 91, 93, 127, 131, 133, 134, 139, 142, 177, 192
Brinkman P., 95
Bristol, 185

Brookwood, 197
Brown, Chaplain J G., 142, 156, 164
Buncher, 129
Burtonwood, 33, 37, 105, 204
Bushey Park, 21
C-47, 106
C-54 Skymaster, 187
Cambridge, 50, 109, 182, 186, 197, 211
Camp Holabird, 137, 138, 158
Camp Pontchartrain, 135
Carnaby, 107
Carpenter, Chaplain C., 163
CCC, 9, 23, 162
CCRC, 118, 127
Chamberlain, Prime Minister N., 69, 70
Chaney, Major General J., 20
Chanute Field, 15, 16
Chaplaincy, 9, 11, 161-163, 195
Charge Quarters, 176, 177
Charlton, Air Commodore L., 7
Cheltenham, 45
Chelveston, 34, 46, 49, 52, 199, 204, 210
Chemical Company, 19, 47, 48, 51-53, 101
Chevrolet, 52, 109, 138
CHOWHOUND, Operation, 198, 199, 207
Chrysler, 109
Church Army, 87, 157
Churchill Hospital, 185
Churchill, Prime Minister W.S., 9, 10, 21, 22
Class A (Airfield), 27-29, 34, 37, 39, 55, 90, 128,
    144, 184, 210
Cletrac, 109
Clubmobile, 67, 87, 158
Consolidated (Aircraft), 12, 17, 196
Cranwell, 135
Crew Chief, 75-81, 84, 87-93, 95, 96, 106, 142
Crossley, 137, 140
Darky, 127
David Brown, 110
Debach, 40, 71, 72, 87, 122, 128, 167, 205, 211
Deenthorpe, 41, 63, 74, 137, 150, 154, 160, 164,
    182
Denver, 117
Diddington, 186
Dispersals, 28, 30, 41, 42, 51, 75, 76, 79, 83, 130
Dispersed (Airfield), 27-29, 32, 32, 41, 43, 46, 56,
    57, 68, 97, 114, 134, 146, 168, 172, 184, 188,
    211
Dodge, 109-111, 138, 140, 185, 196, 197
Dodgeson, Chaplain A.S., 163
Doolittle, Lt. General J.H., 38
Douglas (Aircraft), 11, 187
Douglas DC4, 187
Drem, 128
Duxford, 26, 212
EAFFP, 135, 138, 139,
Eaker, General I.C., 12, 21, 22, 24, 35, 38, 62, 125
EFFP, 135, 137
Eglin AFB, 138
ETO, 21, 79, 96, 115, 118, 147, 150, 151, 158, 159,
    194
Expansion Era, 26-28, 48, 122, 124
Federal, 78, 90, 109, 110
FIDO, 127, 128
Finance, 20, 60, 68, 104, 159, 160, 167
Fire Fighting, 14, 19, 20, 42, 54, 101, 135-139
Flak House, 187
Flying Control Officer, 125, 130

Ford, 109, 137
Fordson, 55, 137
Form No. 1A, 80-82, 90-92, 142
Form No. 41B, 80, 81
Fort Benjamin Harrison, 162
Fort Dix, 202
Fosdike B., 56, 192
Framlingham, 30, 39, 42-44, 47, 53, 67, 68, 71, 74,
    76, 77, 84, 86, 92, 98, 105, 106, 113, 116, 118,
    119, 122, 139, 143, 148, 150, 151, 153, 154,
    181, 183, 198, 205, 207, 211
Free Gunnery Trainer, 98, 118, 119
Frenchay Hospital, 185
G Suit, 184
Gable, C., 69
Gaffney J., 95, 140, 155, 191
GEE, 63
General Motors, 109
General Post Office (GPO), 55, 130
Gibson, Commisioner, 180
Glatton, 54, 171, 175, 213
GMC, 109-111, 138, 207
Grafton Underwood, 34, 50, 198, 204, 210
Grant, Major General D.N.W., 184
Great Ashfield, 31, 46, 47, 60, 168, 171
Great Dunmow, 73
Guardhouse, 42-44, 138, 163
H2X, 63, 129
Halesworth, 38
Halton, 184
Hardstand, 28-31, 46, 73-77, 83-85, 88, 89, 91-93,
    100, 105, 112, 120, 130, 140-142
Hardwick, 64, 65, 75, 82, 84, 87, 145, 179
Harris, Marshall of the RAF Sir A., 8
Hartford, 135
Headquarters, 15, 18, 21, 24, 30, 31, 33, 35, 37,
    42, 45, 46, 60, 61, 63, 65, 66, 68, 97, 114, 122,
    132, 133, 138, 171, 177, 189, 190, 201, 203,
    211
Hendon, 21
Heston, 127
Hethel, 122, 161
HFDF, 129
High Wycombe, 21, 24, 187, 201
Hitcham, 37
Honington, 37, 188
Horham, 39, 44, 59, 68, 71, 84, 98, 99, 151, 155,
    173-175, 188, 189, 200, 203, 212
Horsham St Faith, 27, 123, 124, 170, 210
IFF, 126
Jam Handy trainer, 119
John Deere. 109
Judge Advocate General, 45
Keesler Field, 116
Kettering, 182
Ketteringham Hall, 133
Kimbolton, 34, 39, 40, 65, 66, 89, 105, 122, 130,
    134, 191
Langford Lodge, 21, 33, 37
Langley Field, 15
Lavenham, 120, 122, 182, 199, 211
Leiston, 55, 56, 192
Lend Lease, 10, 15, 17, 57, 69, 103, 105, 111, 135,
    179, 188,
Liberty Run, 45, 103, 153, 179, 182
Lilford Hall, 186
Line Shack, 75, 77
Link trainer, 98, 118-120

Little Staughton, 34
Liverpool, 23, 39, 50
Lords Bridge, 50
Madingly, 197, 211
MAGNET Force, 21
MANNA, Operation, 198
Manston, 107
Marshall, Chief of Staff G.C., 71
Material Command, 18
Medmenham, 111
Memphis Belle, 69, 95
Mendlesham, 47
Metfield, 54, 93
Mickey, 63, 129
Military Police, 20, 43-47, 195
Ministry of Aircraft Production, 109
Ministry of Fuel and Power, 57
Mitchell, Brig. General W.E., 12
Mobile Air Depot, 107
Molesworth, 34, 43, 64, 93, 101, 106, 140, 153,
    168, 171, 176, 186, 200
Morris Motors, 109
NAAFI, 87, 149, 150, 157, 158
Napalm, 19, 48, 50, 53, 53
Neaton (Griston), 37
Nissen, 42, 50, 59-61, 74, 98, 112, 129, 138, 145,
    151, 158, 161, 169, 171-173, 175, 176, 185,
    188
Norden, 13, 61, 69-73, 91, 113, 119, 209, 211
Northampton, 182, 188, 208
Northern Ireland, 20, 21, 23, 33, 45, 158, 180
Norwich, 27, 76, 124, 133, 179, 182, 210
Nose Art, 94-96
Nuthampstead, 32, 41, 50, 180
Oboe, 63
Odstock Hospital, 185
Oliver Tractor, 109
Operations Block, 60, 61, 62, 65, 71, 211
Orlit, 173, 185
OVERLORD Operation, 16, 159
Oxford, 109, 125, 185, 186
P-51 Mustang, 37, 202
PBX, 62
Photography, 68, 111-113, 208
Pillbox, 46
Pilsen, 198
Podington, 31, 34, 50, 51, 56, 58, 71, 92, 102, 104,
    113, 122, 148, 150, 159, 171, 193, 195, 204,
    211
Polebrook, 34, 69, 202
Portal, Air Chief Marshall C, 22
Postal Unit, 20, 167
Prestwick, 202
Princess Elizabeth, 96
Pundit, 127
Putt Putt, 87, 92
PX, 113, 143, 157-160, 166
Pyote, 163
Pyrene Co., 137
Pyrotechnic, 50, 123
Quartermaster, 19, 57, 114, 115, 147, 148, 158,
    159, 165, 166, 204
Quonset, 100, 171, 205
Railway Traffic Office (RTO), 115
Rattlesden, 122
Reciprocal Aid, 17, 110, 111, 115, 166
Red Line, 83
Reo, 109

Reynolds, Chaplain M.W., 162, 163
Ridgewell, 31, 45, 53, 54, 59-61, 67, 69, 93, 98,
    101, 103, 108, 114, 121, 123, 142, 144, 156,
    161, 169, 174, 182, 185, 188, 191-193
RMS *Queen Mary*, 22, 151, 203, 204
RMS *Queen Elizabeth*, 22, 23, 203
Romney Hut, 98, 171
Romsey, 187
Rossevelt, President F.D., 8-10, 13, 20, 69
Salisbury, 185
Sandra, 127
Selective Service, 13
Service Squadrons, 19, 97, 189
Sharnbrook, 50
Shepton Mallet, 45
Shipdham, 139
Slawson, Chaplain M.O., 164, 165
Snettterton Heath, 71, 168
Somervell, Lt General B.B., 158
Sonar, 69
Southampton, 201, 203, 204, 206
Spaatz, General C., 12, 16, 21, 22
Special Observer Group, 20, 21
Special Services, 61, 116, 143, 153, 155, 160
Splasher, 129
Stanbridge Earls, 187
Standard Beam Approach, 127
Station Complement Squadron, 19, 58, 98, 110,
    125, 138, 143, 146, 148, 166, 167, 177, 189
Strarcer A., 95
Strategic Air Depot, 37, 107
Studebaker, 109
Sub-Depot, 19, 23, 36, 38, 39, 57, 62, 78, 79, 83,
    84, 86, 95-110, 114, 121, 151, 177, 183, 189,
    210, 218, 219
Sudbury, 67, 95, 151
Sutton-on-Hull, 135
T/O&E, 17, 18, 58, 61, 77, 114, 146, 204
Tannoy, 60, 130, 199
Thorpe Abbots, 31, 75, 120, 122, 172, 182
Thrapston, 188
Thurleigh, 58, 65, 96, 133
Tokyo Tanks, 86, 90
Training Command, 18, 116, 162
Troston, 37
US Navy, 11-13, 20, 95
USEAB, 25, 30, 40
Valley, 202
Vargas A., 95
VHF, 129
VIIIAFSC, 19, 38
WAAF, 62, 143, 144, 168, 169
WAC, 62, 168, 180
Watchfield, 119, 125, 127
Wattisham, 37
Watton, 7
Welles S., 70
Wellington Bomber (Vickers), 26
Wendling, 65, 71, 90, 177
Wharton, 33, 37
White, 110
Wilkinson Sword, 187
Wincanton, 113
Woodbridge, 93, 106, 107, 128
Wray, Lt. Colonel S., 40
Wroughton, 184
Wyler W, 69
Zemke, Colonel H., 3